DATE DUE			

GAYLORD M-2   PRINTED IN U.S.A.

LOUIS XI

LOUIS XI
(From the painting in the Château of Saint-Roch attributed to Colin of Amiens)

LOUIS XI

BY

PIERRE CHAMPION

Translated and Adapted

by

WINIFRED STEPHENS WHALE

With eight Plates in Half-tone

BOOKS FOR LIBRARIES PRESS
FREEPORT, NEW YORK

First Published 1929
Reprinted 1970

944.027
C 35L
69407
March, 1970

STANDARD BOOK NUMBER:
8369-5226-X

LIBRARY OF CONGRESS CATALOG CARD NUMBER:
73-109617

PRINTED IN THE UNITED STATES OF AMERICA

PREFACE TO THE SECOND FRENCH EDITION

THE first impression of this book met with so enthusiastic a welcome, both from critics and the general reader, that we feel ourselves under an obligation to prepare a second edition.

Yet we do this with some reluctance. For an author who takes his work seriously is always more affected by criticism than by praise. Time is his best collaborator.

Our books are all provisional; they express but a single phase of our knowledge and our life ; they are a mere halt in our thinking.

We should like to take this opportunity of thanking those historians who have corresponded with us about our book and who have made certain critical observations which a work of so general a character could not fail to provoke, and which we take in good part : MM. Antoine Thomas, Membre de l'Institut, Charles Petit-Dutaillis,. Henri Stein, Richard de Newhall, Alfred Douet and others.

As we have said elsewhere, our intention was to give no more than an outline of the extremely complicated diplomacy of the reign. The forthcoming important work by M. Joseph Calmette in collaboration with M. G. Périnelle on the relations between France and England during the reign of Louis XI, which we announced in our earlier preface, has not yet appeared. It will no doubt contain the last word on the subject.

We offer our apologies to Miss Cora L. Scofield, to whose fine book, "The Life and Reign of Edward IV" (London, 1923, 2 vols.), we ought to have referred.

It was in no spirit of narrow nationalism that we treated the English invasion of France.

In our picture of the King at work we gave a mere sketch of Louis XI's relations with the towns. That subject has been exhaustively treated by M. Henri See, in his excellent book, " Louis XI et les Villes " (Paris, 1891), which we have used and cited.

We must repeat that the object of this work is not to give a complete and detailed account of the reign, but rather to present the portrait of a King whom romantic legends have grotesquely caricatured. This manner of dealing with our subject has, to our surprise, met with the approval not only of general readers but of historians and specialists.

We find that few of our readers quarrel with us for having tried to write a lively book, and for having extracted out of dry and ponderous documents all that is of vital interest. But there are some who are not so well pleased : certain scholars would have liked us to bring out into the light all the contents of those dark drawers into which we stuff our notes and papers. But this age of ours is a hurrying age ; and perhaps the writer's aspiration to sketch the physiognomy of a king and more especially of a man of the past may not be wholly inexcusable.

An attempt to represent a series of events in their relation to the life of a historical personage has something in it of the novel. The form that inevitably results is that of the novel. It is not our fault if the life of Louis XI assumes this form : rather is it the fault of history, which frequently outstrips our boldest imaginings, thus becoming identical with the novel.

It is true that this book is written with passion, because the writer has been passionately interested in it. But his one object has been to find out truth and to express it in the simplest terms.

TABLE OF CONTENTS

PAGE

INTRODUCTION 1

PART I.—THE DAUPHIN LOUIS
1423–1461

CHAP.

I. CHILDHOOD 43

II. A CHILDREN'S MARRIAGE 48

III. LOUIS MAKES A GOOD BEGINNING . . . 54

IV. AT THE SIEGE OF MONTEREAU AND IN PARIS
"LA GRAND' VILLE" 59

V. LOUIS' COMMAND IN LANGUEDOC . . . 64

VI. THE PRAGUERIE 69

VII. LOUIS IN COMMAND AGAINST THE ENGLISH . 77

VIII. LOUIS AT DIEPPE 82

IX. PEACE WITH ENGLAND 87

X. WITH THE FREEBOOTERS 92

XI. ON TOWARDS THE EMPIRE 96

XII. NEGOTIATIONS AT NANCY AND CHÂLONS . . 100

XIII. THE DEATH OF THE DAUPHINESS . . . 106

XIV. TEN YEARS IN DAUPHINÉ, 1446-1456 . . 113

XV. ALLIANCE WITH SAVOY, FLIGHT TO GENAPPE . 120

XVI. AT THE DUKE OF BURGUNDY'S 127

XVII. THE DEATH OF KING CHARLES VII, 1461 . 135

TABLE OF CONTENTS

PART II.—KING LOUIS
1461–1483

CHAP.   PAGE

XVIII. The Coronation at Reims . . . 143

XIX. The King and the Duke of Burgundy at Paris 149

XX. Home and Foreign Affairs, 1461-1463 . 153

XXI. The King at Work, 1461-1465 . . 163

XXII. La Ligue du Bien Public, 1465 . . 177

XXIII. The King at Péronne, 1468 . . . 189

XXIV. From Péronne to Beauvais, 1468-1472 . 201

XXV. The English Invasion, 1474-1475 . . 210

XXVI. The End of Charles the Bold, 1476-1477 . 225

XXVII. A Portrait of King Louis . . . 230

XXVIII. The Households of the King and Queen . 246

XXIX. Louis at Orléans and at Tours . . 255

XXX. The Destruction of Arras, 1477 . . 263

XXXI. The Conquest of Burgundy, 1477 . . 269

XXXII. Mary of Burgundy and the House of Austria, 1477-1481 273

XXXIII. Louis' Declining Years, 1479-1482 . . 280

XXXIV. Father and Son. 290

XXXV. The King's Last Days at Plessis-lez-Tours, August 1483 295

Index 307

LIST OF ILLUSTRATIONS

Louis XI, from the Painting in the Château of
  Saint-Roch, attributed to Colin of Amiens . *Frontispiece*

To face page

Marie of Anjou, Queen of France, Mother of Louis XI . 44

Charles VII of France, Father of Louis XI . . . 76

The Dauphin Louis 118

Philip the Good, Duke of Burgundy, and Charles the
  Bold, Duke of Burgundy, Son of Philip . . . 136

Philippe de Commynes, Lord of Argenton . . . 208

Charlotte of Savoy, Second Wife of Louis XI . . 250

The Château of Plessis-lez-Tours 296

LOUIS XI

INTRODUCTION

THIS story of the life and reign of Louis XI is entirely derived from original sources : contemporary French and Burgundian chronicles, public and private accounts, diplomatic notes, the King's own letters and ordinances promulgated in his name. Such an undertaking, involving the examination of masses of documents, not all recently discovered, but so abundant as to afford as ample opportunity for error as for arriving at the truth, will seem to scholars extremely ambitious, more especially as an attempt will be made to give some idea of the spirit of France in King Louis' day and some description of his collaborators as well as of other actors and supers of the reign.

The first part of the book is a kind of preface : it presents Louis as Dauphin and tells of his 'prentice years.

Louis was one of those who knew how to learn from experience. He had to amend the error of his ways. He could hardly have been a worse son.

To understand him as King we must study him as Dauphin. Character is generally most strongly marked in youth. And Louis, in his adolescence, displayed all that restless energy, that impatience for kingship, that longing to see men and things, that passion for organisation which he was to evince later.

The first part of the book will describe France in the closing years of Charles VII's reign : France freed from foreign domination and a prey to feudal faction. We shall follow the Dauphin in his wanderings up and down his father's kingdom, and in his various provincial governorships. We shall see him organising his Dauphiné as he

I

will organise his kingdom later. We shall go with him to the Duke of Burgundy. And there, at the court of that great rival of the French crown, who had harboured Louis when he was in exile, we shall see him always keenly observant, even in the midst of the pleasures of youth.

The first eight-and-thirty years of Louis' life—from his birth in 1423 until his father's death in 1461—may be passed over rapidly because they have been adequately dealt with by several conscientious historians. The second part of the book is much more extensive and complicated; for here, we may confess at once, though with all modesty, we enter on a comparatively untrodden field. Little help has been derived from earlier histories of Louis XI. The Academician Duclos, in the eighteenth century, was judicious but cursory. A more detailed history by Urbain Legeay, Professor of Literature at Grenoble, which appeared in 1874, is interesting as revealing an intelligent use of the King's ordinances and also as representing a re-action against that romantic conception of the King, which had totally disfigured him. A work by an English writer, Christopher Hare, which appeared in 1907, and which is based on such of the King's letters as had been published by that time, gives a clear and sympathetic description of the reign. But the best picture of Louis XI is that of M. Petit-Dutaillis in Lavisse's " History of France."

Most of the original documents we have consulted are in la Bibliothèque Nationale and les Archives Nationales at Paris, but others are to be found among the municipal records of such towns as Lille, Dijon, Tours, Tournai, Arras, and Amiens. The Dijon records are particularly important as reflecting public opinion on the death of Charles the Bold ; and especially interesting also are those of Tours, a town which Louis might almost be said to have created and of which he might almost be described as having been mayor

In unravelling the intricate web of international relations, we have tried to be impartial. With regard to those between France and Catalonia we are deeply indebted to M. Joseph Calmette's book "Louis XI, Jean II et la Révolution Catalane" (Toulouse, 1903). This author has also in preparation a great work on Louis XI's relations with England. But a book like ours, which is essentially personal, must be mainly based upon correspondence. Louis XI wrote and caused to be written an enormous number of letters. Few historical documents are more alive and more thrilling than the two thousand letters of the King that have been preserved. Here we have the hand of a master, of a shrewd and crafty statesman, of an indefatigable worker, of a great schemer. Louis XI wrote as he spoke : there is no doubt that he personally dictated most of his letters. Here we see him as he was : genial yet severe, simple and familiar, trying to understand everything and to make everything understood. Louis XI was a politician on the grand scale ; he was also an administrator. He reveals his personal tastes in his letters, and above all his passion for dominance. His is a clear and rapid French, as clear and rapid as his signature, inscribed with a bold and sure hand, that *Loys* which, once seen, is never forgotten.

Another source from which we have drawn freely is the collection of the King's ordinances. To such documents in any ordinary case one might look in vain for any personal note. But the King's individuality is so strong and so marked that it may even be traced in preambles, to which his secretaries had given their final form. Consequently we may place these ordinances side by side with the letters as revealing not merely the King's excellent administration but also the principles of a policy essentially practical though not in the least Machiavellian.

The contemporary chroniclers, from whom material for a history of Louis' reign may be derived, are so partisan that we are obliged to arrange them in two opposite camps : French and Burgundian. Only one of them, Philippe de Commynes, was broad-minded enough to rise above party ; and he dominates all the others.

Commynes was of Flemish origin. Like his father, the Mayor of Ghent, he served the Duke of Burgundy, who was his godfather. He fought against King Louis at the Battle of Montlhéry. There the Mayor's son delivered the Duke's son, the Count of Charolais, out of the hands of the people of Ghent. When at Péronne, he found the King of France in the power of a young and irascible master and helped him to escape from his violence. Was it Louis' money or his intelligence that appealed to Commynes? Possibly both; the Fleming was shrewd, moderate, but not malevolent. We shall find him, in 1472, going over to the King, forsaking his lord, who was ravaging Upper Normandy, his lord, who was brutal as well as stupid and old-fashioned, his lord, who belonged to an older and more feudal age. For eleven years Commynes was to be the friend, the observer, the loyal and astute servant of King Louis. He was to make his fortune in the King's service. Following the example of his royal master, he was to amass fat lands, without inquiring too carefully into their history. But Commynes, the soft-spoken, was also the candid friend, no mere partisan, but a devotee of reason and intelligence. Thus, in 1477, he dissuaded the King from laying violent hands on Burgundy, when the desired result might be obtained by a marriage. Relations were sometimes strained between King Louis and Commynes. But reconciliation always followed misunderstanding. And when the King fell ill he could not do without his friend; Commynes slept close at hand. Louis liked to hunt over his friend's estates. He employed him in his negotiations with Italy and Burgundy. Commynes always kept his master under close observation, indulging in philosophic and religious reflections, loving him and understanding him. Commynes remained with him to the end. Why should the King's faults be concealed? When he came to draw his master's portrait, he made it lifelike and convincing. Commynes will live in his recollections of the King.

Commynes' object in writing his " Mémoires " is not

4

so much to relate his own adventures as to represent the remarkable man whom he had the honour to serve. In his judgment of Louis he anticipated the judgment of history. He put his heart into his work, but even more his intelligence. He wrote for his friend Cato, but he addressed posterity. Montaigne loved his *langage doux et agréable, d'une naïve simplicité, la narration pure et en laquelle la bonne foy de l'autheur reluit évidemment, exempte de vanité parlant de soy, et d'affection et d'envie parlant d'autruy*.[1] Who could help liking Commynes ? We might almost say that we have written this book as much for love of Commynes as for love of truth.

In comparison with this, other French sources are very meagre. A Parisian notary of the Châtelet law court, one Jean de Roye, secretary to the Duke of Bourbon and porter at his Paris house, is thought to have been the author of a diary of Louis' reign known as " La Chronique Scandaleuse." The title, invented by an editor of 1611, is singularly inappropriate, seeing that the diary, published for the first time in the reign of Louis XII (1498-1515) is neither scandalous nor slanderous, but, on the contrary, chiefly valuable because of its accuracy, its sincerity, and its reproduction of anecdotes current in Parisian circles at the time.

In much the same vein is the " Journal de Jean Maupoint," bachelor in theology, which, however, goes no further than November 1469.

More worthy of the title of " Chronique Scandaleuse " is the famous Latin history of Thomas Basin, Bishop of Lisieux (long cited under the name of Amelgard). Basin was a venomous stump orator, who tried to imitate Suetonius, and who is largely responsible for the legend of Louis XI. In spite of the accuracy of its detail, this history of the reign is little more than a pamphlet. Though part of it was written during the King's lifetime, it is

---

[1] His " sweet and pleasant language, naïvely simple, pure narrative revealing the author's glad nature, free from vanity when he writes of himself and from affection and envy when he writes of others."

animated by that spirit of reaction in favour of feudalism
which pervaded France immediately after his death, a
spirit which contrasted the wisdom of the father with the
cruel dominance of the son. The author personally
revised his work in 1487, enabling us thereby to observe
his mind distilling the venom of his hatred into his various
corrections.

Thomas Basin was a Norman, born in 1412, of a
Caudebec family. Like any Norman worthy of the name,
he was destined for the bar. During the English conquest
he had taken refuge in Rouen, where the Basins lived until
their return to Caudebec in 1420. Thomas Basin's life
was, as he says, a veritable pilgrimage through a land of
invaders. As a young and brilliant Master of Arts, he
lived at Paris. He studied at Louvain. He saw London,
Ferrara, Hungary, Florence, before being nominated canon
of the cathedral of Rouen. He associated with Poggio
and his disciples. He raved over the beautiful Latin of
Cicero and Sallust, which he dreamed of imitating. He
taught canon law at Caen. He lived at Bayeux, where
he was nominated canon and later the bishop's vicar-
general. Then he took up politics, spoke on the side of
the Duke of York, and obtained the See of Lisieux. So
here we have him count and bishop ; he who in his youth
had fled from English persecutors is the man of the
English ; he sits in the seat of Pierre Cauchon.[1]

Nevertheless, Basin was the first of Norman prelates to
surrender to the French army. He conducted it to the
cathedral and there took the oath of allegiance to King
Charles VII. He declared in favour of Joan of Arc's
rehabilitation. The audacity of this ambitious young
bishop may have appealed to the Dauphin Louis. He,
like Basin, was dreaming of consolidating the kingdom.
He was casting greedy eyes on Normandy, where he wanted
the Estates to pass some resolution which would facilitate

[1] 1371c-1442. Bishop of Lisieux. He conducted the trial of Jeanne
d'Arc. See " Procès de Jeanne d'Arc," by Pierre Champion, Vol. II,
note 1.

his nomination as Lieutenant-General. With this object, and in order to test public opinion, Louis sent out secret emissaries, instructed to represent the value of Normandy as an annex to the kingdom and the importance of placing it in the hands of some trustworthy person. Was not the Dauphin precisely that person ? This was the gist of a memorandum Louis addressed to the Bishop of Lisieux, whom he appealed to as an intelligent man, capable of understanding and divining him. Louis offered him a handsome salary and held out the prospect of a magnificent future : Thomas Basin, as a true Norman, refused. This in itself was a bold action. But Basin was foolish enough not to keep it to himself. Did he fondly imagine that he could make Charles VII pay for his confidence ? At any rate Basin sent the King his son's letters. Henceforth war to the knife between Basin and Louis was inevitable. Through Basin the Dauphin had to flee from his father's kingdom. Henceforth the Bishop was to be King Charles's man and the champion of the liberties of the Gallican Church.

However, when Charles VII was dead, and Dauphin Louis was about to be crowned King, Basin went to Reims, prepared to suffer his punishment without complaint, disposed to lift up his voice on behalf of his country. Louis apparently received him as a friend and invited him to the coronation. Basin's opinions were his own : Louis' father had impoverished the kingdom ; Louis was to be its saviour, its reorganiser. On the day after the coronation Thomas Basin was given the opportunity of preaching in the monastery of Saint-Thierry on the sufferings of the people and the hopes that all good folk placed in the newly-crowned King. This was not a bad idea. And Louis, who did not usually care for sermons, was delighted. He lavished compliments on the preacher who had so thoroughly understood him. Let his counsellor indicate the remedies for the evils he denounced. Basin went off to Paris, where he wrote a memorandum on this rather vast subject. Though the memorandum is no longer extant, we may guess what remedies it proposed : the reduction of the army, no doubt, and also of pensions. Louis seemed to agree with Monsieur de Lisieux. He continued, however, to keep up his army and to buy consciences.

Basin, who had been Charles VII's man, remained the defender of the Pragmatic Sanction,[1] that is, of a national church, with elected bishops. Louis, to please the Pope, had annulled this arrangement, but he returned to it three years later, and then appealed for support to the Bishop of Lisieux. Basin, in a French document, argued that the King had merely pledged his word to Pius II personally, and that after the Pope's death, he was no longer called upon to keep it. This collaboration between the King and the Bishop was not destined to last long. For when La Ligue du Bien Public was formed against the King and Louis saw the Bishop surrendering his town to Breton rebels, he conceived an undying hatred for him. Basin was ruined. Banished from the kingdom, then recalled, suffering the confiscation of his goods, finally fleeing to Rome, Basin devoted the remainder of his life to the composition of his " Apology and History of the Reigns of Charles VII and Louis XI." In what spirit may well be imagined.

In this book nothing pleases him. The King is a tyrant, who can neither govern nor convince men ; a monster of vice, so depraved that there is not one grain of good in his whole personality. As Dauphin he was a criminal, as King he was even worse. Physically, he was without distinction, his appearance insignificant, his legs long and thin. Anyone who did not know him would take him for a buffoon or a drunkard. The pamphleteer even insinuates that Louis was a leper. He spoke with a lisp. There was nothing royal about him, no feeling for dignity. He dressed like a poor man ; his shirts were of

---

[1] An agreement made at Bourges in 1438 between King Charles VII, the emissaries of Pope Eugenius IV and of the Council of Bâle, considerably limiting the papal authority in France.

coarse linen. On his entrance into Abbeville, no one
dreamed that he was the King. He used to hide in back
streets. He was a chatterbox and a bore. Both his
words and his actions were extravagant. He replied
almost before he was spoken to, and without listening.
His irony was nothing but rudeness. He expressed himself badly. People laughed at him behind his back. He
was a grotesque paralytic. His roguery was infinite.
Totally without scruples and utterly unbalanced, he had
no courage worthy of the name; he did not know how
to make use of his army. What a hunter he was! One
who set his dogs to chase rats in his room while he was ill,
just as Domitian killed flies. Coldly licentious, Louis was
never in love. In his cruelty, he was mad for he actually
plotted to assassinate Charles the Bold. He had his brother
poisoned. He reduced his subjects to misery. For the
innocent he reserved drowning and torture. He threw his
victims into prison without any form of trial. He drove
monks and nuns from their dioceses and compelled them
to declare their revenues. He exacted enormous sums
from his people for the purpose of religious foundations
which were to procure forgiveness for his sins. Louis
drank like an obscene buffoon. From Marius to Nero no
tyrant can be compared to him. He surrounded himself
with menials and with men who were given over to vice.
During his last illness he despatched two vessels to fetch
him a medicament from beyond Cape Verd.

The anonymous pamphlet, which Basin entitled "The
History of Louis XI," was first published by Jacques
Meyer, a historian devoted to the House of Austria, in
his "Annales de Flandre." The author was regarded as
the free lance and lover of liberty that he represented
himself as being; but in reality, when not merely
animated by his personal animosities and disappointments,
he had nothing to advocate but the sheer anarchy of
feudalism. The details of his history may be accurate;
but the conclusions he draws from those details are
generally tendentious. This vigorous pamphleteer and

eloquent doctrinaire died Bishop of Utrecht on December 3rd, 1491.

From this highly suspicious source most of the histories of King Louis have been derived.

BURGUNDIAN CHRONICLERS

Louis XI, though a student of history, never caused any history of his own reign to be written. The House of Burgundy, on the other hand, made a point of having a careful chronicle compiled by paid historiographers, who were styled "indicators" (*indiciaires*). Consequently it is from Louis' enemies that we derive most of our information concerning him. Burgundian documents, both abundant and famous, were for long almost the only sources historians consulted.

Treated with great consideration, if not well paid, these loyal servants of the House of Burgundy—Chastellain, Olivier de la Marche, Molinet, Jean Lemaire de Belges—all write of Louis in a partisan spirit, though not with Thomas Basin's perpetual disparagement—personal rancour being much more bitter than party prejudice. Of that verbose, grandiloquent orator Chastellain, the Great George, whose meaning was sometimes so obscure as to become utterly unfathomable, only fragments remain to us. But, in spite of his deplorable style, Chastellain was a good fellow.

He was born in 1405, in the county of Alost. Brought up by *la main de Bourgogne*, he lived in France for ten years, 1435 to 1445, in constant touch with the court. In Chastellain's estimation France ranked first among Christian nations. He liked King Charles VII, and continued to do so all through his long duel with Philip the Good. *Le gros homme flamand*, as he was called, was, however, a member of the Duke's household, and the tutor of his son Charolais. A lover of pomp, pageantry and all manner of court functions, he has drawn some masterly portraits. He observed his lord's household carefully. He deplored the violence of his passions. The historian's curiosity was aroused when he saw Louis coming to Genappe. On his accession to the throne of France, Chastellain declared his loyalty and devotion to Burgundy's royal guest. And it was not until he discovered the King to be incapable of gratitude that Chastellain changed his attitude towards him. The Gallant George could not find it in his heart to continue the friend of a sovereign so base as to turn against a house that had entertained him. A true knight, however, Chastellain never over-stepped the bounds of moderation. He died in 1475.

The work of the Great George, though fragmentary and representing only a very small part of his original chronicle, is extremely valuable. After Commynes' " Mémoires " it is the source we have consulted most, especially Books IV (1454-1458) and VI (1461-1470), and the fragments of Book VII. Of course, one must not take Chastellain literally any more than Livy. He embroidered lavishly on the conversations he heard. But the man deserves our admiration and respect. He tried to be impartial, although he never completely realised how fundamental was the antagonism between the Houses of France and Burgundy. He could read the hearts of princes, and for a study of the Dukes of Burgundy and the secret intrigues of their house, there exists no better guide.

Olivier de la Marche, a contemporary of Chastellain, was a Burgundian of Marche-sur-Saône. He also was a fine character, an excellent functionary, interested in his office. Not content with telling stories of ambassadors and knights, he describes life in princes' houses from the throne-room to the kitchens, the meals and the table-manners of the times, and also a meeting of the Chapter of the Golden Fleece. To read him is like wandering through the magnificent kitchen and the stately hall of the Duke's palace at Dijon.

Olivier de la Marche was the son of the Duke's equerry. His mother was Burgundian by birth and descent. Olivier was page to Philip the Good, and remained loyal to his family. A regular knight-errant he was, for ever on the road, interested in jousts and tourneys, banquets and hunting, moralities and mystery plays. At forty-five he began to write his " Mémoires," as an amusement, and in order, so he puts it, to " embalm " his remembrance of the " fine, noble and majestic things " he had seen. Olivier, master of the pantry to Philip the Good's son, Charolais, and a famous inventor of sweet dishes, endeavoured to bring about a reconciliation between the Duke and his master. He saw the Dauphin Louis at Genappe. He struck him as a prince who was fond of dogs and birds, and given to great liberality. Olivier was present at Louis' coronation and at his entrance into Paris. About 1464, he began to change his opinion. He expressed his indignation at the attempt to capture his master—attributed to the Bastard De Rubempré. In the Battle of Montlhéry he fought boldly on the side of Burgundy and was dubbed a knight. After being charged with many secret missions, he took part in the famous siege of Neuss and was taken prisoner on the battlefield of Nancy. On the death of Charles the Bold, he became master of the pantry to his successor Maximilian. He advised the Archduke to revive the Order of the Golden Fleece. He accompanied him in his northern campaign against the King of France. Our Burgundian had turned Fleming. While King Louis lay dying, Olivier was educating Maximilian's son, Philip the Handsome, he was completing his " Mémoires," writing poetry and describing all the glories of the Dukes of Burgundy for the benefit of his pupil.

An excellent fellow this Olivier! He had fought against the King, but he will not slander him. " He is a prince," were the concluding words of his portrait of Louis at Genappe. But he records the King's death without one word of comment. Olivier notes Louis' double-dealing with the House which is so near his heart. He refers to the King's suspicious nature. " He attached himself lightly to people and dismissed them lightly from his service ; but he was liberal and free-handed, and he paid generously those whom he employed."

Our third Burgundian source is Jean Molinet.[1] Olivier describes him as " a venerable man and canon." But Jean Molinet was no eyewitness like Chastellain and Olivier de la Marche. He lived at Valenciennes. He was the man in the street, a wonderful artist in words, whose prose has all the virtues and the defects of the romanticists. He never knew the King. But he hated him with the hatred of a good Burgundian, and also of a poor priest, a man of the people, who had seen Louis' cruel warfare in Picardy, for whom Louis was above all things the destroyer of crops. In brief, Molinet was the champion of the people's wrongs, the turgid poet of *La Chanson de Guinegate*, and something of a wind-bag.

At the time of the Battle of Montlhéry, Molinet was thirty. Employed as a scribe in the Cardinal's College, he lived at Paris on the Sainte-Geneviève Hill. But we must not expect to find any account of the battle in the poems of this impoverished Bohemian. Of its sequel, however, and of daily life and carousing in the French and Burgundian armies, as they encamped over against one another in the vineyards round Paris towards the end of that summer, we do find a striking memento in Molinet's queer poem, *le Dit des Quatre Vins*. The garlanded French wine-grower, striving to gather in the grapes of Auxonne, is King Louis XI ; the wine-grower who wants to disgorge the wine of the Somme is that good Count of Charolais, already the patron of the poor but gay Molinet, who was vegetating at Paris. Molinet becomes a much better informed witness and a real chronicler when he tells of the siege of Neuss on the Rhine, in 1474. This he actually saw. With his own eyes he had beheld Charles the Bold leading the assault. The verses in which he describes these famous episodes are in a fine and picturesque style. Henceforth our poet will be decidedly anti-French.

[1] See Pierre Champion, " Histoire Poétique du Quinzième Siècle." II, p. 392.

At the siege of Liége, he curses the King of France, "the universal spider" as he calls him. During Louis XI's cruel campaign in Artois, in July 1477, when he sent a thousand reapers to Quesnoy to destroy the crops, Jean Molinet, a true son of the soil, accuses the French of causing the Burgundians to suffer a veritable "passion," and of destroying the gifts sent by God in His mercy. In his *Temple de Mars* he describes the destruction of the Abbey of Saint-Waast. In his *Ressource du Petit Peuple* he evokes the terrible demon of war and the wailings of the people. In his *Naufrage de la Pucelle*, written for Marie de Bourgogne, he tells of the ruin of the Burgundian House. Later, he mourns over Marie's death; and in another poem, *La Robe de l'Archiduc* (a quarter of which robe France had appropriated) he sings the triumphs of her husband, Maximilian. In everything he writes about Louis XI Molinet is prejudiced. Consequently he exaggerates the importance of the indecisive battle of Guinegate (1479) and represents the French as nothing but boasters, brigands, tyrants, Turks, Mamelukes and Tartars. These are Molinet's opinions until the accession of Charles VIII and his Italian expedition, which he regards as the prelude to a crusade.

Molinet never knew Louis XI, so he was not in a position to appreciate the man who was to ruin the House he served. The "very Christian" King of France appeared to him as the worst of tyrants, forgetting all the examples of his noble predecessors, ruining the House of Burgundy, a house which was the pillar of justice. All that can be said in his favour is that he died a good Catholic.

Another of our Burgundian historians is Jean, Bastard of Wavrin, Seigneur de Forestel, Chamberlain to the Duke of Burgundy. After many years of travel and fighting he devoted himself to writing chronicles. He had been in England in 1467, in the train of Antoine, Bastard of Burgundy. At Calais, in 1469, he had met Warwick, who had presented him with a fine nag. In 1471, when he was well advanced in age, probably about seventy-three, he had seen Edward restored to the English throne. He had thought of dedicating a seventh book of his " Anchiennes Croniques " to the English King. The only fragment extant of his work is extremely informing. It tells of the last phase of the Wars of the Roses, of the Duke of Burgundy's war against the people of Liége in 1468, of the wedding of Charles the Bold and Margaret of York in 1471 ; and it repeats the story, taken from an English text, of the reinstating of Edward IV on the throne of England. Jean de Wavrin bears witness to Louis' courage. He refers to his choleric disposition and to his faithlessness.

The other Burgundian authorities are less important. Jean de Haynin must be consulted on certain military and diplomatic points (he was present at the Battle of Montlhéry). The chief interest of the " Chronicle " of Jacques Duclercq, who spent most of his life at Arras, lies in its description of manners. Though his history contains certain diplomatic documents, he himself was an eyewitness only of the happenings in Picardy and in his own city. And Arras, we must remember, was destroyed by the King's command.

The Legend and History of Louis XI in the Works of Annalists and Novelists

We have already seen that there was nothing in Louis XI likely to make a popular appeal. A man who lives simply, who is a good administrator, who taxes his kingdom more heavily than his predecessors, first in order to keep up an army, which he uses but seldom, and second, in order to buy consciences and provinces, is not likely to be popular. To attract the public eye one must be either a brilliant personality or the victim of some great misfortune. The so-called victims of Louis' cruelty, the Constable Saint-Pol and Jean Balue, have attracted much more attention than Louis himself. No one stops to ask whether the Constable was really a traitor or whether that literary, unscrupulous and somewhat inscrutable prelate, Jean Balue, had actually played a double game, which might have reconstituted the League of Public Weal, and which did nearly deprive Louis of his throne. Things that stick in the average mind are Saint-Pol's and Nemours' tragic deaths, embroidered with all manner of apocryphal details, as, for example, in the case of Nemours, with the presence of his children drinking his blood.

Two of the examples of Louis' cruelty most frequently cited are Nemours' imprisonment in the Bastille, and Jean Balue's long confinement, said to have been in an iron cage which apparently neither hindered him from devoting ten hours a day to legal and theological studies nor from granting benefices. But it was not King Louis who invented iron cages : they were in general use in his day ; they were placed in castle halls, in order by their conspicuousness to prevent the escape of prisoners. Even now captives in the prisons of Morocco are treated in much the same way instead of being sentenced to the more modern torture of solitary confinement.

The accounts of Louis' household show that far from being extraordinarily cruel, he could be indulgent, charitable and considerate of the possessions of the poor, especially during the hunting season. We find the King compensating a poor woman for a sheep which his harriers had killed, giving alms to the destitute and dowries to poor girls to enable them to marry. His dog, Muguet, carries off a goose from a poor woman near Blois ; and the King gives her a crown. The royal guard, taking a short cut to the main road, tramples down the corn of a poor man near Le Mans ; and the man is compensated. The King's dogs have killed a cat near Montlouis, between Tours and Amboise ; and the King grants compensation to the poor woman to whom the cat belonged.

Basin is the author of the legend that Louis arrogated to himself hunting rights over the whole of France !

16

That such a decree has never been found goes without saying.

The romantic imagination represents the Castle of Loches as a grim dungeon. But it was once a royal residence. The guides of to-day delight to propagate the legend canonised by the Revolutionary Tribunal when, on the 14th of July, it decreed the destruction of the cages in which political prisoners had been confined, more especially after the time of Louis XI. And what of the ordeal by water, which under the old régime was merely a method of legal inquiry, what of the terrible irons, pillories and chains with bells attached? All these instruments of cruelty weigh heavily on the memory of King Louis. And when one contrasts them with the King's piety, with his generous endowments of churches and offerings to patron saints, one soon arrives at that conception of the refined and cruel hypocrite which romanticists like Sir Walter Scott, Casimir Delavigne and Victor Hugo have imposed upon posterity.

We are not so foolish as to think that a book like this will ever destroy old legends. They appeal far too strongly to the imagination and to democratic prejudice.

We have seen how personal rancour and disappointed ambition produced the portrait of a tyrant drawn by that faithful adherent of feudalism, Thomas Basin. We have seen party spirit and devotion to their own ruling house influencing the judgment of Burgundian historians. So much for the King's contemporaries.

It must not be forgotten that an immense reaction in favour of feudalism set in after Louis XI's death. Evidences of this reaction are to be found in the records of the States General of 1484, and in the trials of Louis' ministers, Olivier le Daim and Jean de Doyat, of which the least one can say is that they were a disgrace. The great feudal lords, in the name of liberty (in reality of anarchy) endeavoured to react against the unifying and centralising policy of the late King. The following is the

picture of the King's administration, drawn by the judge,
Du Forez :—

"You know that lately, in the days of King Louis,
the State was dishonoured, the elections were dis-
gracefully manipulated, hands were laid on church
property, unsuitable persons received bishoprics
and benefices. . . . The nobles were no better
treated. . . . There is no need to remind you of the
informers, the calumniators admitted to the court,
nor of the favour shown to greedy profiteers and tax-
gatherers. The greatest favour was shown to the
most unscrupulous. Virtue and innocence were not
merely left unrewarded but were often made to suffer
punishments which should have been inflicted on the
guilty. Have you not often seen the innocent
arrested and even executed without a trial, while their
property has been given to their accusers ? As for
his extravagance and his wasteful expenditure, is it
not common knowledge ? He took and he gave
without a thought. As for the people, all I can say
is that during the lifetime of this cruel King, they
were ground down and crushed by the enormous
burden of taxation. . . . Only think that during
Louis' reign the people paid five times as much as
during the reign of King Charles. . . ."

Another contemporary of King Louis, Jean Masselin,
went so far as to denounce the huge sums spent by the
most frugal of Kings on his table and his wardrobe, to say
nothing of the costly methods of his administration. The
people of France could not tolerate mercenaries. A paid
army is always characteristic of a tyrant. "The strength
and salvation of a country lies not in paid troops, but in
wise counsels and in the people's love for their native land."
Conditions in Normandy, Picardy and Languedoc on King
Louis' death are described as terrible. At the meeting of
the States General in 1484, the Church demanded a return
to the old state of things, the nobles clamoured for their

hunting rights, the people protested against the sacks of gold carried to Rome on mules' backs, paid as tribute to England, used to foment strife at Barcelona and filtering out of the kingdom by way of the Lyons Fair.[1] Meanwhile, says the compiler of this document, the poor were dying of hunger. He who was once called "free" (frank — *françois*) was now more miserable than a slave, ground down by taxes and imposts. Louis was even accused of having alienated the royal domain by gifts to his favourites. All these accusations are mere pretexts invented to justify a new régime.

No story was too extravagant to be told against Louis : he is said to have lain in his own tomb at Cléry in order that accurate measurements might be taken, to have drunk the blood of infants as medicine during his last illness. But one of the narrators of these fantastic tales, Robert Caguin, cannot forbear expressing a regret that Louis did not live a few years longer, until his heir had gained a little more experience in war and the art of governing.

Among those who found it to their interest to denounce Louis' tyranny was his kinsman, the Duke of Orléans who, married against his will and for political reasons to the King's poor little deformed daughter, was now trying to obtain a divorce.

The associates of Louis' brother, Charles of France, with whom he had been on the worst of terms, hoped to turn to their own advantage the rumour that the King had attempted to commit the crime of fratricide.

It was Claude de Seyssel, Ambassador of Louis XII (1498-1515), later Bishop of Marseilles, who popularised the opinion that Louis XI had tried to poison his brother. This story is without the slightest foundation ; we know that Charles died of a decline. But it was embroidered upon by Jean Bouchet in his " Annales d'Aquitaine," and of course worked up by Brantôme (1540-1616), whose books " Vies des Hommes Illustres," " Vies des Femmes

---

[1] This Fair, so popular and flourishing to-day, was, like the Fairs of many other French towns, first instituted by King Louis.

Illustres " and " Vies des Femmes Galantes " are treasure-houses of legend.

" Les Louenges " of the good King Louis XII, the Father of his people, a work by Claude de Seyssel (Paris, Antoine Vérard, 1508), is nothing but a long diatribe against the eleventh Louis and a dithyramb in honour of the twelfth. All that de Seyssel says of the child-hood of Louis' son, Charles VIII, is invalidated by contemporary documents. If Louis confined Charles in the Château of Amboise, and placed him in the care of his most faithful servant, it was not from any fear of his son, but because of his anxiety lest the heir to the throne should be kidnapped by his father's enemies. Louis took the greatest care of the Dauphin and of his health, worried about his colds, and when the child had caught a chill hunting with his father, ordered that he should be kept from such pursuits for a while, not, as has been alleged, in order to retard his development, but in the interests of his health. The King had been a very bad son and a rebel. If he had not passionately desired, he had at least waited impatiently for, his father's death. But when his own end drew near, he summoned his child, hailed him King, and in an admirable last will and testament gave him sound political advice. When Louis, on the point of death, needed his nurse no longer, he sent her to Amboise to look after his son.

From beginning to end, Claude de Seyssel's work is legendary and prejudiced. He was delighted to see the parliamentarians of 1484 undoing the King's achievements. To Seyssel we are indebted for the tradition, embroidered by Sir Walter Scott and Théodore de Banville, of corpses hanging from the forest trees.

" And when he commanded in the heat of his passion, he always had Tristan l'Hermite, his Provost of Merchants, at hand to execute the royal command so pitilessly and promptly as to leave no opportunity for appeal or reprieve. Consequently, wherever the King happened to be corpses might always be seen hanging from the branches of trees, and all the neighbouring prisons and houses of detention filled with captives, whose heart-rending cries might be heard day and night, to say nothing of those who were thrown into the river."

This Tristan, who figures in romance as the cruel and stolid executioner, the most terrible instrument of Louis' cruelty, the companion of his last days at Plessis—and who in reality died about 1477—was a comparatively obscure person, more like a justice of the peace than a provost, but at any rate intelligent and educated and a brave soldier who had faithfully served Louis and his father.

So much for Claude de Seyssel—and he was almost the King's contemporary.

It was at Louis' command that Pierre Choisnet, astrologer and physician, compiled for the Dauphin " Le Livre des Trois Éages," an extremely important extract from " Les Chroniques de France," which no doubt the King himself revised. He wished his son to know the history of his predecessors, of their kingdom and of those troubles which threatened it ; the hatred and envy of the English, internal divisions and family quarrels.

It was also for the Dauphin's education that Pierre Choisnet was commanded to compile the admirable " Rozier des Guerres," a book of maxims for a sovereign, first printed in 1522, which became a classic. " Le Rozier des Guerres " may be ranked with the King's letters, his instructions to ambassadors and the preambles to his laws as reflecting more clearly than any other document the mind of the King, his earnest desire for peace and for the public good, and his conviction that experience is the best method of instruction.

Louis' personality was extremely complex. There is no denying the fact that he was a cynic, and that some of his utterances are revolting. But this is no reason for

21

ignoring those fundamental and guiding principles, which, in his case, as in those of most French kings, were in accordance with morality and the true interest of the people.

Historians of the great classic age of the seventeenth century, remote from the Orléans-Valois quarrels, presented the King in a more favourable light. Pierre Mathieu, who wrote a History of Louis XI in 1640, is much less bitter than Seyssel, though he takes the opportunity of praising the charming manners of his patron, Henry IV. Tristan l'Hermite de Soliers, brother of the dramatist, was the first historian of Louis XI to make a collection of original documents concerning him. His "Cabinet du Roi Louis XI," which appeared in 1661, is mainly a collection of his letters. Tristan lays stress on the monarch's good qualities as well as on his cruelty.

But le Sieur de Mézéray, the historiographer of France, whose work appeared in 1685, was far in advance of all his predecessors. In marginal notes he cites authorities— Commynes and "La Chronique Scandaleuse." But he believes in the poisoning of Charles of France, and suggests that Louis may have died of remorse.

In 1689, Varillas wrote a History of Louis XI for the instruction of Louis XIV. This work, which was widely read, praises Louis, and represents him as having made only three mistakes in his whole life, while Louis XIV, to whom the book is dedicated, made only one. A gross exaggeration in both cases.

With the eighteenth century we enter the golden age of scholarship. To a Jesuit, le Père Daniel, we are indebted for a famous "Histoire de France," accurate in all essentials, citing authorities and giving references. Le Père Daniel was the first to represent Louis as changeable. He showed that his real design was to make himself absolute master of his kingdom ; and he explained the reasons for the King's unpopularity.

Henri Sauval was not only an erudite historian, but the most original and whimsical of men. His description of

Louis in his "Galanteries des Rois de France" is disconcerting. It provided Victor Hugo with the material for his elaborate romance, for example, with those accounts of the Provost's court, of which Hugo made such excellent use.

An Oratorian, the Abbé Le Grand, made an admirable collection of documents concerning the King's reign, and wrote an extremely well-informed and impartial history, which unfortunately has never been printed. But it was used by the Academician, Duclos, whose History of Louis XI is useful even to-day on account of the original documents it reproduces. In fact, Duclos' work is the earliest history of the reign worthy of the name. Except for certain documents which Lenglet du Fresnoy inserted in his edition of Commynes in 1747, Duclos' history remained the last word on the subject for many a year. Though it makes Louis too much of a clever schemer, the portrait of the King presented in its closing pages shows great insight into his character.

Finally, to a woman, Mlle de Lussan, we are indebted for a long and painstaking "Histoire du Règne de Louis XI," in which the author has consulted printed sources only. Her book appeared in 1755, and was dedicated to le Prince de Condé.

The figure of King Louis strongly attracted writers of both the seventeenth and eighteenth centuries. Bossuet, for example, in 1658, introduced him into his eulogy of St Francis of Paola, delivered at l'Eglise des Minimes on la Place Royale. Fénelon made him the subject of four of his *Dialogues des Morts*, representing him in converse with Cardinal Bessarion, Balue, Philippe de Commynes and Charles the Bold.

Voltaire in his "Essai sur les Mœurs" anticipates the romanticist conception of King Louis.

Voltaire was the first to realise clearly that Louis XI's reign marks the close of the feudal system in France. But in Voltaire's opinion the King made an ill use of his power ; his father had governed well. Louis was a barbarian who shared his people's belief that a false oath sworn on a piece of wood (the true cross of Saint Laud) is inevitably punished by the death of the perjurer before the year is out. Voltaire's Louis was always false, and compelled Duke Charles of Burgundy to be false also. Deceiving all his neighbours, he forced them in turn to resort to double-dealing. The suspicion that he poisoned his brother is well founded. By buying off the English he fell into the undignified position of their tributary. Instead of appointing ministers Louis sought collaborators and found them in the gutter. Few tyrants have had more of their subjects executed. The dungeons, iron cages and pillories, which are the monuments to his memory, fill one with horror. Philippe de Commynes was nothing but a famous traitor, whose " Mémoires " are written with all the restraint of a courtier, and who is afraid to tell the truth even after the King's death. There was not a single great man in the whole of his reign. Louis degraded the nation and destroyed all virtue. Obedience was all he demanded ; and his people enjoyed the peace of convicts at the galleys. He was hard and crafty ; he fasted and made pilgrimages, covered with relics, wearing in his cap a leaden image of Our Lady, of which he is said to have asked forgiveness for his murders at the moment when he was committing them. He it was who introduced the Italian custom of ringing bells at noon and saying an Ave Maria. Bigoted and superstitious, when lying at the point of death he sent to Calabria for a holy man, believing that he could change the decree of the Eternal. To reanimate his own blood, he drank the blood of children. He was the first French sovereign to style himself " the very Christian King." But side by side with all these vices he possessed certain good qualities : courage, liberality ; he knew men and understood business ; he desired justice and would allow no one to be unjust save himself. Louis XI repopulated Paris. He was the first to humiliate the great. He protected the first printers and established a postal system. He increased the resources of his kingdom by his industry. His reign marks the transition of France from anarchy to tyranny. The impudent charlatanism of the doctors equalled the King's own imbecility. " This portrait," Voltaire concludes, " is not only that of King Louis but of nearly the whole of Europe. The more one knows of the history of that time the more one despises it. If the main concern of princes and their subjects were to learn from the misdoings of barbarous governments one could not employ one's time better than by reading history."

A few lines from " L'Encyclopédie " will suffice to show how extraordinary was the view of history taken by Diderot.

> " The French people were absolute slaves until the time of Philippe Auguste. The nobles were tyrants until Louis XI, who was a tyrant himself, and whose one object was to increase the power of the sovereign."

In the year II of Liberty, Brizard, a citizen of the Théâtre Français section of Paris, published through Garney, of La Rue Serpente, his " Discours Historique sur le Caractère et la Politique de Louis XI." The work is dedicated to his fellow citizens, whom he addresses thus : " Frenchmen, I offer you this picture of despotism. Read and judge whether you ought to love Liberty. At the very name of Louis XI, the heart shudders, humanity groans, sadness and pain possess one's whole being." Then follows a long disquisition by the author, who says he has read the papers of the Abbé Le Grand and the history of Duclos, whom he represents as a plagiary and a nincompoop.

Louis XI and the Romanticists.

It is high time we came to the novelist whose work dominates the whole legend of King Louis. Sir Walter Scott heads the procession of those writers of fiction who deal with the King. His " Quentin Durward," published in England in 1823, was translated into French in the same year ; and in France its success was as great as that of " Ivanhoe " had been in England.

What reader can ever forget the young Scottish traveller, who had come to France to join the King's guard ? How proud and loyal he was, though rather dazed by his encounter with the stranger wearing a leaden image of the Virgin in his cap ! How unforgettable is one's impression of that imposing castle of Plessis-lez-Tours with its drawbridges and moats, its traps and snares and its oak tree, with the corpses of criminals dangling from its branches. Ever present in the mind's eye are the scenes of the enrolling of the Scotch guard, and the boar-hunting, the scenes in which the sentinel and the astrologer figure, the journey to Flanders, the siege of Liége, and that innocent love story of Durward and Isabelle de Croye. A poor plot, digressing suddenly when Sir Walter, in his solitude at Abbotsford, falls under the spell of Philippe de Commynes, of " La Chronique Scandaleuse," of Gaguin and of Brantôme. When we visit the novelist's house in Scotland and linger in his library, among his Gothic furniture, we can understand how these mediaeval surroundings among which he lived and dreamed inspired the imagination of Sir Walter Scott.

We must never forget that Sir Walter's portrait of King Louis was drawn under the influence of Goethe's Mephistopheles. Goethe had recently published *Faust ;* and Scott was a great admirer of his work, an admiration which Goethe reciprocated. Scott endeavoured to make Louis a devil, the incarnation of that spirit of criticism and of negation which Mephistopheles represents. One of the sources of his portrait of the King was Machiavelli.

" This monarch was of a character so frankly egotistical, so incapable of any thought which did not bear upon his ambition, his greed, or his desire for personal power, that he seems almost an incarnation of the devil let loose and given full power to do his best to corrupt our ideas of honour in their purest source. One must admit also that Louis, superlatively endowed with that cynical spirit which ridicules anything a man does to benefit his fellows, was extremely well qualified to play the part of a cold and mocking demon. From this point of view, the character of Mephistopheles, the tempter in that wonderful drama of *Faust*, seems to me a much happier conception than Byron's demon and even than Milton's Satan. . . . In this capacity, Mephistopheles, like Louis XI, possesses a gift of acuteness and sarcasm which is constantly employed to blame and disparage any action which does not tend to promote the direct and personal advantage of the doer. . . . The Prince's cruelty, perjury and suspiciousness, far from being alleviated, are rendered much more objectionable by the gross and despicable superstition to which he is a prey. His ostentatious devotion to the saints arises from that contemptible feeling experienced by some miserable employé who tries to attenuate the malversations of which he knows he is guilty."

But Louis understood the interests of France and never betrayed them. Among the nations of Europe, his example provoked mistrust and dislike rather than any desire to emulate him.

All this Fénelon and Voltaire had already suggested. But it was owing to the success of " Quentin Durward " that Louis became a familiar figure to the generation of 1823. Pigault-Lebrun clearly shows this in his sombre and puerile " Histoire de Louis XI " (1827) ; so also does M. de Barante in his " Histoire des Ducs de Bourgogne," a fine book with striking illustrations, which appeared about the same time. It was in that year, 1827, that Casimir Delavigne's play, *Louis XI à Péronne*, was staged at the Théâtre Français with great success. " We are promised," announces the producer, " a tragedy by the most brilliant of our poets, Casimir Delavigne, in which all the terrors which preceded Louis XI's end are said to be most powerfully described." Three years later Charles Liskenne, in another " Histoire de Louis XI," described Louis as " the only King whose cruelty was comparable to that of the two or three monsters produced by the Roman civil wars " ; but, he adds, " Louis rendered France great service by freeing her from a multitude of petty tyrants."

Victor Hugo's " Notre Dame de Paris "[1] appeals to us chiefly through its historical background. We admire Hugo as the wonderful poet of the stones of Notre Dame and of the Paris that may be seen from the heights of its towers. But there is no doubt that in the beginning Hugo regarded himself as a historian rather than as a novelist. It was not until later that he inserted those topical and archæological digressions which to-day constitute the chief interest of the novel, and by means of which he hoped " to inspire his countrymen with a passion for the architecture of la patrie." Hugo had read Jacques du Breul's " Théâtre des Antiquitez de Paris " (1612). He had also read " L'Histoire et Recherches des Antiquités de la Ville de Paris," first published in 1724, and had made excellent use of the copies of accounts, the dissertations and reveries here preserved. His hero Gringoire is but a name, and has nothing in common with the author of farces and moralities, who was Louis' XII's contemporary. Hugo was also indebted to " La Chronique Scandaleuse." He brings Coitier, Tristan l'Hermite and Louis XI on to the stage in much the same way as Sir Walter Scott. The Bastille is the retreat in which M. Louis de France tells his beads. There the King of France has his accounts read to him and shows the Flemish ambassadors the iron cage, which Hugo erroneously terms one of the King's *Fillettes*, though that epithet, according to Commynes, should only be applied

[1] Begun on the 25th of July 1830; completed on the 15th of January 1831.

28

to a chain with a ball attached. Louis examines the cage
of his accomplice Jean Balue, while M. de Verdun weeps
in the darkness. Maitre Olivier, the " Figaro terrible,"
gets numerous benefices out of the King. But Notre
Dame, the King's mistress, besieged by rogues, is really
rather too ludicrous an incident. The cinema public is
now in danger of growing too familiar with such violent
and fantastic scenes. And yet the mock antiquity of
le Boulevard du Crime may be preferable to the dull
solemnity of le Théâtre Français, seen for the first time
in this connection when, on the 11th of February 1832,
Casimir Delavigne's platitudinous *Louis XI*, so long
considered a masterpiece, but deserving nothing but
oblivion, was played for the first time.

At the opposite extreme are the " Contes Drolatiques "
of Balzac (1837) which describe with admirable gusto *les
Joyeusetez du Roy Loys le unzieme*. Here we have pure
Tourainian tradition, healthy and robust. For at Tours
there was nothing sad about the memory of Plessis. At
Tours, Louis was remembered as a hearty fellow loving
his jokes and just as pleased to shoot linnets and coneys as
more royal game. So the scribblers who described him as
furtive, show that they did not know him, for he was a good
friend, an excellent sportsman, and " such a laugher as
never was." This was the tradition at Tours, where
the wine is good, the food succulent and the people
gay : Louis was one of them. The reports of the
Milanese ambassadors would seem to confirm all this,
at any rate as far as Louis' youth and middle age were
concerned.

But Alexandre Dumas in his " Charles le Téméraire "
(1860), as in many of his other works, approaches much
nearer to the spirit of history. The charm and the
intelligence of that monster of impecuniosity were irre-
sistible. And to think that he was compelled to write for
so much a line !

Théodore de Banville's *Gringoire*, which was played
for the first time on the 23rd of June 1866, and which is

still acted at la Comédie Française, is a brilliant little one-act piece, appropriately dedicated to Victor Hugo by his faithful disciple. Gringoire, as we have said, was not a contemporary of Louis XI. It was really Villon whom Banville intended to put on the stage. And the play is little more than a story of hangings described in brilliant rhymed verse : the plot is absolutely conventional, the chief characters being Olivier le Daim, the starving poet Villon, Loyse, daughter of Simon Fournier, and the King, who pardons Villon and finds him a wife, instead of having him hanged.

But the nineteenth century was not merely the age of romanticists, not merely a period of poetic intuition and individual creativeness inspired by the Revolution, and of French assimilation of the spirit of foreign literatures. The genius of a Hugo, no matter how entrancing, must not deceive us. The nineteenth century was above all things the century of science and of history, the age of Pasteur and Augustin Thierry.

Though one hardly realises it, another discovery in addition to that of science had been made—the discovery of the most vast and the most mysterious field of human knowledge. The discovery of America and of other unknown lands is insignificant in comparison with that of the immense field of past history which the nineteenth century revealed to us.

The view of modern man is no longer confined to the present and the future. It is becoming possible for him to compare it with what he knows or imagines of that past time, which he can now evoke as if by magic.

Among the pioneers in this new field of study should be specially mentioned Honoré Capefigue, who, in his " Histoire de France au Moyen Age " (1838), has, in our opinion, given the truest representation of Louis XI. Capefigue has not been sufficiently noticed. His intention was to write a constitutional history. Though not a scholar of the first order, he had a well-balanced mind and an eye to perceive what was important in historical documents. He writes :—

> " For a thorough understanding of the reign of Louis XI, there must be a much more profound study of the facts and documents of his reign than has yet been made. The spirit which animated his legislation and consequently his own character must be studied in the two thousand five hundred charters signed by his own hand, in the rolls of his men-at-arms, in communal accounts, in his private letters to officials with whom he was intimate, and to his secret agents, and in his numerous treaties. In one respect ' Quentin Durward ' has been derogatory to serious history in that it presents us with a highly coloured picture of Louis in the midst of his Scottish guards. Then comes historical fact. And how cold it is in contrast with so romantic and imaginative a picture ! "

Michelet, who by his date belongs to the Romantic period, is, strange to say, essentially a modern. The pages he has devoted to Louis XI and his struggle with Charles the Bold are among the finest ever written by this passionate lover of France. They bear not a trace of that revolutionary declamation which began with Voltaire and culminated in the writers of 1830. Michelet is the man of documents ; they are his daily bread. Yet never do they stereotype the young and nimble mind of a visionary whose work is a veritable resurrection of the past, a synthesis of all his vast knowledge of the European world, a blending of the past with the present. In his portrait of the King there is no theatrical tinsel. Michelet intuitively rejects the legend of Louis XI, the torturer of himself and of others, who spends his life between his executioner and his doctor. For Michelet, Louis XI is the sage of the fifteenth century, the passionate innovator— in a word, the revolutionary. Michelet goes straight to the heart of his subject : the anti-feudal action of the King, the feudal reaction which held him in check for twelve years, and the end of that reaction in the ruin of the hostile House of Burgundy. He writes :—

> " It was the good fortune of France that really conquered, the unquestionable legality of France. Her solidity and concentration, the result of a long process of unification, seemed natural and inevitable when contrasted with the purely artificial State of Burgundy, a haphazard assemblage of provinces, possessing no unity either of race or of ideas."

The perfect flower of this noble genius, so lucid and so French, is to be found in the portraits of Jeanne d'Arc and Louis XI. Michelet had not then made his incursions into politics. His was an impatient soul, rushing into things instead of waiting for those slow results of laborious study at which some of us have now arrived. But it is work like this that will constitute the greatest glory of the last century. The task has been patiently performed by a whole army of researchers, our masters, who worked in l'Ecole des Chartres and elsewhere, an admirable procession of students, whose names are unknown to the outside public, historians and archivists of all nations, for scholarship and love of truth know no frontiers. This task has been one of minute detail, it is true, yet it has tended to vast results, to nothing less than a knowledge of mankind, to the solution of eternal problems, to an outline of the history of humanity which ought to reconcile warring multitudes, if ever they can be induced to be wise.

Among these master workmen, with respect to the reign of Louis XI, prominent place must be given to Jules Quicherat. Though he is little known outside the world of specialists, his fame ought to be spread abroad. Others whose laborious work deserves acknowledgment are Vaesen, editor of the King's correspondence ; Bernard de Mandrot, editor of Commynes and of the Milanese Ambassador's despatches, who has also explored the archives of the Swiss cantons ; P. M. Perret, Messieurs J. Calmette, G. Périnelle, Charles Samaran, H. Stein, A. Gandilhon, all accomplished scholars, whose works are epoch-making, as well as many other archivists and researchers who have studied local documents and private papers.

Not in the King alone has all this scholarly work centred : it has focussed on the personalities of the King's brother, Charles of France, and on those of his officials. By means of invaluable monographs it has added to our knowledge of the master by showing the parts played by his servants, the great nobles, Bourré, La Trémoille, Doyat and Du Bouchage. To this band of researchers we are indebted for all that is best in these volumes ; and it would be difficult to exaggerate our gratitude.

This mass of half a century of research has naturally raised countless new questions. Though the legend of the cruel King may have persisted through it all, the latest published documents have provoked many contradictory comments.

What are we to do ? Shall we in our turn take up all these questions and discuss at length the value of these documents, go through the immense masses of the King's diplomatic papers, describe the institutions of his day, his relations with the Church and State, and return to the comparison between father and son already made in a spirit, which to us seems prejudiced, by the States General of 1484 ? Shall we attempt to decide which of the two was the fox ? Was it the father, according to Voltaire and Anatole France ? Was Louis guilty of double-dealing in his relations with the House of Burgundy ? Was he the astute, far-sighted monarch of his well-informed and conscientious apologists, the Abbé Le Grand, Duclos and Legeay, or was he merely the clever schemer of our learned *confrère*, M. J. Calmette, in his book on Louis' relations with Catalonia ?

We cannot—who could ?—give a reply to all these questions. We are not in a position to form an impartial opinion. To perceive all the consequences of his deeds is not in the power of any man. King Louis was a ruler who often lived very wisely from day to day, learning by experience and profiting by his extraordinary good luck. When death came, his work was practically complete. Very often and very suddenly he changed all his guns. If a historian, writing to-day, in the silence of his study with all the documents spread out before him, should attempt to judge Louis in the light of subsequent events, he cannot possibly be just. It was impossible for Louis to foresee that a certain attitude towards Catalonia would result in the union of Aragon and Castile and in the foundation of the Empire of Charles V. Consequently one must hesitate before denouncing Louis' Burgundian policy because it provoked the hostility of the House of Austria, and thereby caused the wars which laid waste France and Europe down to the middle of the seventeenth century. These are mere historical hypotheses only remotely connected with actual fact. And a serious consideration of them would, in our opinion, involve history in a tangle of apologetics and political declamation which would darken historical truth.

In Louis we shall discern various personalities : first, a feverish youth, pining to govern, then the young King undoing his father's work, dominated at first by a spirit of hatred and reaction, dismissing and even arresting his counsellors, destroying the Pragmatic Sanction, the foundations of a Gallican Church. Louis' was not a straightforward nature. He liked crooked ways. He employed secret agents to stir up strife, to foment division between his enemies and their vassals, between communes and their lords. He divided in order to reign. He created a new weapon, his own particular method of diplomacy. But he was not always so cautious as he has been represented to have been. For example : he threw himself into the wolf's mouth at Péronne. He allowed himself to be taken by surprise by that formidable Ligue du Bien Public. But his unflagging energy delivered him from all his mistakes, even the worst of them. A new faith sustained him. He believed in order, national unity and the public weal. He sought support from the people, from the citizens, and the towns. Though he began by being his vassals' suzerain, he aimed at being absolute master of his domain. Louis ruled as a legist whose central idea was monarchy. The history of his reign is not a history of battles, although he was courageous. He was determined to repress that feudalism which found its most complete expression in the House of Burgundy. Consequently the Duchy of Burgundy as a fief was fated to disappear. It was Louis who destroyed it. He also ruined his Constable, Saint-Pol, his Marshal, Rouault, his vassal, Nemours, by legal procedure.

But Louis XI was not merely destructive. He was determined to be obeyed, to impose his will on the people. Nothing that went on in his kingdom escaped his knowledge, and he kept his vigilant eye on external affairs also. His posts and couriers were on every road. He bought lands and persons. He had a passion for organisation and legislation. No French King since Charlemagne had made so many laws. He developed business, mining, manufactures. The spring of administration he discovered to reside in the mayoral function, which he reconstituted everywhere. Communes were allowed to elect their mayors; aldermen were ennobled; magistrates were appointed. A portion of the taxes imposed by the King was allocated to keeping the gates and ramparts in repair. The townsfolk met on the public square, convoked by their municipal officers. The latter were empowered to collect rates and to impose duties on wine and salt. The towns were cleansed, chimneys swept and two dangers at least minimised—fire and epidemics. Every town had its merchant guilds, with their banners embroidered with pictures of saints and their strict rules, ensuring a high standard of production. In large centres like Paris these corporations were organised into groups which took the oaths of allegiance. In this way the King ruled supreme over the arts and crafts of his kingdom. For men-at-arms the same discipline, inexorable and far-reaching. Louis

35

put an end to brigandage. He insisted on fixed canton-
ments, reviews, payment for everything taken from the
people. He made strict game laws for the nobility. The
right to shoot and hunt was a royal privilege, since it went
with the possession of property. Not that Louis spent
his time in sport ; he had other things to do, and had
to be content with breeding dogs and coursing. But
Louis did not allow others, either nobles or peasants, to
hunt—a deprivation for the nobles, but a blessing for the
peasants. By permitting the purchase of offices of law
and by constituting other offices tenable for life, Louis
created a middle class, consisting of royal officials, who
gradually took the place of the nobility and grew rich,
buying lands and castles, which they fortified with the
sanction of the King.

We shall endeavour in this book to show the King at
work, exercising that monarchical function which was not
of his choosing. Our ambition will be to follow his
evolution, to show him learning from experience to
examine the ideas that guided him, the use he made of the
institutions and resources of his day ; to see how he both
destroyed and created, and to expose the spring of his
reaction against the religions and feudal powers of his time.
We shall endeavour to show the man playing his part in
that daily drama which any life may disclose if looked at
aright. We have not the slightest intention of making
any apology for the King. The facts will speak for themselves : they are surprising and singular enough. In the
words of an old Latin annalist, we have written to narrate
and not to prove. We shall strive against excessive
sympathy for a personage who has long stirred our imagination and occupied our hours of study. History must ever
be a search after facts, after truth, which ought on no
account to be solicited. Our review in preceding pages
of annalists and historians, philosophers and poets, who
have written about King Louis, ought to serve as a warning
against the snare of extravagant passion and uncurbed
imagination.

For us King Louis is a man, a man exercising his royal office. He possesses all the physical and spiritual weaknesses of the average human being. His very countenance was the inscrutable face of the peasant, the peasant with an insatiable hunger for land. We shall be only too glad if we can mitigate the horror of a figure which frightens little children and some adults who have never grown up. For here is no monster ; here are no iron cages, no sinister Plessis-lez-Tours, no odious hypocrite on his knees before Virgin and saints endeavouring to cast a veil over his crimes, both for his own sake and that of others. Our Louis is merely a man of his day, a peasant, crafty and land-loving, who augmented his domain, adding to it Anjou, Maine and Burgundy, a Frenchman who—though by means often dishonourable—prevented the English from ever returning to France.

One of the conclusions at which we have arrived is the futility of opposing father and son, as was done in 1484 and later. Louis often went in a contrary direction to his father. But the force of circumstances and of the monarchical institution frequently compelled him to continue his father's line of action. However widely they differed in temperament, the one inclined to be indolent, the other extraordinarily active, impulsive and restless, they both represented the trend of the royal House of France. Were we to summarise in a few words the spirit and achievement of Charles VII's reign, we should say that Charles reconquered the royal domain, that he organised it on a legal basis, that in a great measure he initiated the anti-feudal movement, and that by the great trial of the Duc d'Alençon[1] he brought to bay the whole French nobility and established the supremacy of the Paris Parlement. Charles VII was essentially a statesman, as may be seen from the three great measures which dominate the whole of his legislation : (1) the Pragmatic Sanction,

[1] Jean, Duc d'Alençon, condemned to death in 1456, for having had dealings with the English. The sentence was commuted to imprisonment for life. He was liberated by Louis on his accession.

confirming the liberties of the Gallican Church and regulating ecclesiastical elections; (2) the decree establishing a standing army, and assuring the crown of a regular revenue by fixing *la taille* ;[1] (3) an ordinance prescribing the codification of the various provincial customs.

With the first measure alone did Louis interfere ; he destroyed the Pragmatic Sanction, but only to re-establish it some years later. No French king ever assumed such an independent attitude towards the Pope as Louis, whom Voltaire represented as a bigot. In all other respects Louis continued his father's policy. He elaborated his father's organisation and discipline of the army, as well as his system of municipal organisation. From the *taille* and other taxes he derived much larger sums than his father who had invented them, and consequently brought down on his head an avalanche of curses from those who recorded and from those who paid them. Louis, like his father, divided up the authority of Parlements. The two reigns were equally litigious, equally suspicious of the House of Burgundy. One must remember that, when Charles VII died, war between the King of France and the great Duke of the West was on the point of breaking out. Charles had had to contend with rebellious nobles in La Praguerie, so had Louis in La Ligue du Bien Public.

But in Louis we have a prince whose passion was to see everything, organise everything, unify everything, do everything himself and do it swiftly, whereas Charles was cautious and inclined to await events. Louis attacked the privileges of the Church and the nobility. His royal inheritance was a veritable religion for him. Louis was energetic and courageous, carrying on his work in the midst of cruelty and artifice which equalled his own. His faith was that of a simple man of the people, whose garb

---

[1] One of the most ancient of French taxes, varying from age to age, called *taille* because the collectors carved the amounts due and those they received on a piece of wood divided into two parts (French *taille*, English *tally*).

he often wore. Louis, who had inherited all manner of physical weaknesses, towards the end of his life appealed to religious healers ; but Charles was no less pious. In many of his religious foundations, Cléry and Saint Aignan for example, Louis, following in the footsteps of his father, carried on the tradition of the House of Anjou—a blend of religious faith, instincts and practical politics—which had been the tradition followed by all his predecessors since Saint Charlemagne. Religious foundations were regarded in much the same light as the institution of a fair or a market. One went on a pilgrimage to a shrine and one did business. Our mystic was a practical man with a mind as keen as that of the Touraine air that he breathed. When he prayed to the Virgin it was not for himself alone. He always brought in his family, his wife, his son, and especially France. Can we find anything degenerate in all this ?

King Louis was a modern ; the only man in France who knew and admired Francesco Sforza. He did not believe in war ; but he recognised the wisdom of being prepared for it in order to maintain his dominance. There was, however, nothing like a good treaty for binding countries and provinces together, nothing like a good mayor for holding a town to its allegiance, nothing like a religious foundation for appealing to the ordinary believer, especially in a province which belonged to someone else. Louis believed in the written word, especially in the legal document. He threatened the perjurer with the vengeance of heaven. He made trade interests his own. Though pleased to welcome strangers, he was a protectionist. He was as modern as an Italian of that time. He believed in experimental science. He had a dog cut open in order to observe the effects of poison. He ordered the post-mortem examination of a man. He was Mayor of France, as he was of Tours and Angers. He believed that rights and duties are the same for everyone. All classes—artisans, nobles, citizens, even monks—took their turn in keeping watch on his ramparts. All paid taxes, with the exception of himself and his family. He was in advance of his time, so of course he was misunderstood. He frequently aroused the opposition of craftsmen because he insisted on controlling them. By his sanitary and hygienic measures, his institution of posts and fairs, and his working of the mines, he was essentially modern. A busybody, perhaps, but in the best sense of the word.

Auguste Brachet's representation of the King as having no faith in doctors, yet constantly appealing to them in the serious illnesses of his later years, which resulted from overwork, is pure romance. Brachet was but a mediocre historian. If Louis wished to prolong his life it was because he feared that his work would perish with him.

All that we know about his last illness is that it was some kind of cerebral attack; for we have no authority for stating that he was an epileptic. He had frequently suffered from pain in the head and from other infirmities of an arthritic nature. That he had three strokes, accompanied by aphasia, we know; but that is all.

Of greater importance is the fact that Louis, on his death-bed, ordered the ampulla containing the sacred oil to be brought from Reims. Louis died in mystic communion with the soul of France, in the sanctity of his holy office.

The strange figure of King Louis, like that of Richelieu, appeals not so much to our sympathy as to our admiration; an admiration which must be felt by all who have, without prejudice or bias, studied the documents of the reign. Justice is due even to politicians. We owe it to Louis for all he did for France. Taking upon himself a life of constant anxiety and hard work, he was one of the greatest kings of our country.

PART I

CHAPTER I

Birth at Bourges.—Baptism in the Cathedral of St Etienne.—Godparents.—Rejoicing in the Loyal Towns.—Nurses.—Poverty of
the Court.—Education.

ON Saturday, July 3rd 1423, between three and four
o'clock in the afternoon, Queen Marie of Anjou bore a son
to the Prince, who was at that time styled " Roi de
Bourges." The residence of the royal couple was at
Bourges in the imposing Bishop's Palace, still standing
in the shadow of the cathedral. It had just been
enlarged by the Archbishop Guillaume de Boisratier.

King Charles's heart overflowed with joy. To his
nobles, prelates and good towns he announced that Our
Lord in His mercy had delivered his beloved consort of
a very fine son. Mother and child were doing well.

King Charles's suffering people thanked God for this
token of divine grace and mercy. And straightway royal
messengers were sent to convey the good news to the
King's ancient allies, the sovereigns of Castile and Scotland,
to other foreign princes, and to the Pope.

The decoration of the birth-chamber according to
custom presented difficulties : the fine tapestry *de haute
lice*, with which it ought to have been hung, was in the
hands of the Duke of Bedford at Paris ; and for it had to
be substituted the tapestry of Duke Charles of Orléans,
who ever since the Battle of Agincourt had been a
prisoner in England. The hangings and canopies of cloth
of gold, embroidered with the arms of the Duke, were
brought from Orléans and mended. So Louis came into
the world in a merely temporary residence, and in a bed
the very curtains of which were borrowed.

The infant was made a Christian in the cathedral of

St Etienne, by Guillaume de Champeaux, King's Counsellor, Duke and Bishop of Laon and embezzler, who sprinkled the child with baptismal water, and pronounced the regenerating words with lying lips. For first godfather the Prince had that wild young Duke of Alençon, the handsome, eloquent, and loyal Jean. For second, the Bishop of Clermont, Martin Gouge, Chancellor of France ; for godmother Catherine de l'Isle Bouchard, Comtesse de Tonnerre. Should he be called Charles after his father, or Jean, as the Duc d'Alençon wished ? But the mother, Marie d'Anjou, would have her son named Louis after her father. And the gallant Duke gave way : the name was to be Louis, in memory of St Louis, the glorious example and patron of the house of Capet.

Bonfires blazed in all the good and loyal towns. At Poitiers the Parlement took a holiday. The people cried " Noël " even in the most remote of the King's lands, even in far distant Tournai. Pope Martin V deigned to write affectionate letters to the King and Queen. " After having tried thee, the Lord hath sanctified thee," he wrote to Marie d'Anjou ; " the peoples, for whom thou hast given birth to a future king, have rejoiced in thy joy, and we, we felicitate thee in God, Whom we praise and bless for having given a new son to us and to the Church."

But at the very moment when the Queen was being churched at Bourges, Paris, occupied by the English, was being illuminated in honour of the massacre, at Cravant, of the Armagnacs, who were supporters of the King of France. An English and Burgundian army marched round the fortress of Bourges and threatened to besiege the capital. Louis at his very birth might well have been captured by the enemy.

King Charles was twenty-one, knock-kneed, insignificant, shy, devout and frivolous by turns, rather doubtful of his legitimacy, but putting his whole faith in God.

The Queen also was gentle, pious and submissive, in spite of her descent from the wild Kings of Aragon and the adventurous princes of Anjou.

MARIE D'ANJOU REINE DE FRANCE·

morte en 1463.

MOTHER OF LOUIS XI

No wonder Louis grew up a frail plant in the garden of France. A good citizeness of Bourges suckled the King's first-born. His nurses were women of the people, Clémence Sillonne and Jeanne Pouponne. From their lips he learned the folk-songs of his country and that dear French tongue which he was to speak and write so well.

The little Prince soon had his own household, for the Queen's was constantly on the move. He had his own steward, who paid his butchers and bakers.

The Dauphin saw little of his parents ; for the King was always away on some military expedition, and the Queen generally accompanied him. His godmother, Catherine de l'Isle Bouchard, who, as Mme. de la Trémoille was to have so many adventures, looked after him. The city of Bourges was no safe place for the heir to the French crown. Civil war was threatening the province of Berri. So Louis was removed to the château of Loches, which was more like a prison than a château.

Later we find him at Vivonne, later still at Chinon, where the Queen had established her court. It was in the very heart of France that Louis spent his early childhood. He must have been at Loches in June 1429, when a young Breton knight, Guy de Laval, coming to fight against the English, under the command of Jeanne d'Arc, wrote to his most worshipful lady and mother : " I arrived at Loches on Saturday, and after vespers in the collegiate church I went to the castle to see Monseigneur the Dauphin, who is a very handsome and graceful seigneur. He must be about seven years old."

In his early boyhood, Louis lived a rustic life, playing with peasant children and boys of the town.

In those days the court was poverty-stricken. The King, at a loss where to borrow money, was reduced to selling his jewels and having his old doublets patched. His tailors refused to give him credit for a pair of gaiters. A sheep's tail and a few chickens set forth the royal table. The Queen was grateful to the town of Tours for a gift of linen, of which she stood in sore need.

But now Jeanne has appeared. Orléans has been delivered. The King has been crowned in his cathedral at Reims like a " true king, and one to whom the realm rightfully belonged."

Louis must have seen the Maid when she was at Loches. And soon afterwards a German clerk of Spire, by the mouth of a Sybil of France, prophesied a much more brilliant destiny for Charles's first-born than had been promised him by those who had cast his horoscope. " In twenty years the Dauphin (*i.e.*, Charles VII) will sleep with his fathers ; his eldest son, now a child of six years old, will succeed him ; he will reign with greater honour, glory, and power than any King of France since Charlemagne."

But many were the troubled years Louis was to live through and countless the difficulties he was to overcome before the fulfilment of this prophecy.

Meanwhile he resided mainly at Amboise, of which he was always to have pleasant memories, and often at Tours, which had almost become the capital of France. The inhabitants of this faithful town welcomed Louis with joy, and presented him with some linen and massive silver goblets engraved with his arms.

For tutor Louis had his father's confessor, a friend of the famous Jean Gerson, one Jean Majoris, Master of Arts, Licentiate in Law and Theology. Majoris was an excellent Latinist, a good logician, an ardent defender of the rights of the crown and of his Church.

It was the learned Chancellor of the University, Jean Gerson, who superintended the Dauphin's education and directed his tutor. The latter was adjured to consider God and His justice above all things and before the pecuniary reward of his labour. He was to read French books to his pupil, and to avoid imposing too onerous tasks upon him. He was also to avoid punishments as far as possible, being content with reprimands. Let him teach the Dauphin the names of the saints, their lives and their legends. The child must learn to know that there is a future life, in which all will be equal—poor and rich, kings and nobles. For his son's education Charles VII bought beautifully written and richly illuminated manuscripts, seeing that the magnificent library of Charles V at the Louvre was in the hands of the Duke of Bedford. After his alphabet Jean Majoris taught his pupil to recite the seven penitential psalms and to follow the services in his breviary. Then Master Jean d'Arcouville was appointed assistant tutor. Louis learned his *Catonet, i.e.,* his grammar book; and no doubt he was made to read that famous work "The Instruction of Princes," by Ægidius of Rome, who was inspired by the "Politics" of Aristotle. But the little Louis was most interested in the Lives of the Saints and in the history of France as related in the Chronicles of Saint Denis. History has ever been the breviary of kings; and of this breviary Louis was a passionate reader.

Thus Louis, at the age of ten, could be described by that good bishop, Jouvenel des Ursins—the bishop who summoned Louis' father to throw off his sloth—as a child *saige et bien morigéné* (good and well brought up), which amounts to saying that Louis was a studious little boy. We shall find him reading Latin with a facility unusual in kings, speaking French with the clarity of his nurses, annotating despatches from ambassadors in his large and decisive handwriting, and answering them himself without any intermediary.

But it would not do for a future king to be merely literary, so Guillaume d'Avaugour, Sheriff of Touraine, taught the Dauphin to draw the bow and to wield the sword and lance.

CHAPTER II

A CHILDREN'S MARRIAGE [1]

A French Embassy to Scotland.—Protracted Negotiations.—Jeanne d'Arc's Intervention.—England's Game.—Signing of the Marriage Treaty.— The Child Princess sails from Dumbarton.—Her Arrival at La Rochelle.—Introduction to the French Court and to her Boy Bridegroom.—The Marriage Ceremony at Tours.—Wedding Festivities.—Households of the Dauphin and Dauphiness.

THOUGH, in 1436, the Dauphin Louis was but thirteen, he was already a pious and serious little man, self-willed and impatient. His father decided it was time to marry him. His choice of the daughter of the King of Scotland as a bride for his son would enable him to pay an old debt of friendship to that country.

The affair had been arranged eight years earlier when Master Alain Chartier, the poet, had gone over to Scotland to implore the help of King James I. The two countries were both enemies of England. France was then at the end of her resources. Master Alain, the King's orator, had employed all his eloquence to solicit the aid of a body of those poor but valiant adventurers who had so often distinguished themselves in the French wars. A treaty had been signed with all the necessary formalities. It was sanctioned by a promise of marriage between James's eldest daughter, Margaret, and Charles's eldest son. The various conditions had been agreed upon; and the little princess, with a queen's dowry, was to cross to France. The rumour of these negotiations for the restoration of French fortunes flew rapidly from Tournai to Venice. It was, however, no Scottish princess who was to save France, but a maid of France, Jeanne d'Arc, a peasantess

[1] See Pierre Champion. " La Dauphine Mélancolique." Paris, 1927.

unskilled in the arts of war.   Since his coronation
Charles had forgotten his treaty with King James.   The
marriage was never mentioned.   The King of France had
no desire to carry out that clause in the treaty which provided for the surrender of Saintonge to Scotland.   Neither
was James in any hurry to expose his little daughter to the
perils of a sea voyage.   As for the good folk of France,
they did not crave the coming of the Scottish soldiers,
who were said to be drunkards and sheep-stealers.   But
the English—who knew King James, seeing that they had
brought him up and kept him a prisoner for many a year—
began a game which might well become dangerous for
King Charles.   They asked for the hand of the Scottish
princess for their young King.   It was doubtless this move
of the English, made in 1436, that decided the counsellors
of the French King to send new ambassadors to remind
King James of his treaty and his promise, at least as far
as the marriage was concerned.   In October, the Council
resolved to despatch to Scotland to fetch the Princess two
doughty diplomats : Messire Regnault Girard and Hugh
Kennedy, a Scotsman in the French service who had been
a comrade-in-arms of Jeanne d'Arc.

After a perilous voyage of fifty-six days over the North
Sea in the stormy month of November, they sighted
Ireland, landed in Scotland, and, on the 14th of January,
made their entry into Edinburgh.   The negotiations
dragged on until midsummer.   The King of France had
to be referred to and his replies awaited.   Charles would
not consent to keep in France the two thousand Scotsmen
who were to accompany the Princess.   But he promised
to care for her as his own daughter until the marriage.
The French squadron which was to be her escort arrived
in September.   And the French ambassadors did their
best to avoid further delay and to persuade James to
despatch his daughter to La Rochelle forthwith.   But
James still hesitated.   He urged the late arrival of the
ships and the Queen's fear of so dangerous a voyage at
that time of year.   Had Regnault Girard forgotten the

qualms of his own sea-sickness ? But the French ambassadors grew more and more insistent ; and finally James had to bring himself to let his daughter go. Margaret was taken to Dumbarton, whence the fleet set sail. The child was twelve. Her parents told her to be good in return for the honour done her by the King of France and the Dauphin ! King Charles's gifts were presented : for James a mule, an animal then unknown in Scotland ; for his Queen, barrels of fruit, rare in that inclement country. The tears shed at parting with the child were mingled with laughter at the unusual character of these presents.

The little Princess sailed in the huge vessel of Pierre Chepye, a high-masted whaler ; and Regnault Girard commanded the ship which escorted it. Other vessels carried the one thousand two hundred Scotsmen. The wind was favourable, and the fleet reached La Palisse on the 15th of April. The Scottish bride had had a narrow escape. For the English fleet had been lying in wait for her off Ouessant, but, unable to resist the attraction of wine-laden Flemish vessels, had gone off in their pursuit.

On her landing in France, the Princess lodged in the Priory of Nieul, where she was shortly waited upon by Monseigneur the Archbishop of Reims, the Chancellor, Monseigneur de Graville, and the Steward of the King's household. On the 5th of May, she entered the town of La Rochelle, which was decorated in her honour. A fine procession, worthy of a Queen of France—steeds gaily caparisoned, costly litters and horses with nodding plumes, —wended its way down the narrow streets, hung with gorgeously embroidered draperies. And then there were long files of monks and priests, the mayor and the municipal officers who came out to meet the Dauphiness elect. At a banquet that evening they presented the little girl with a service of silver plate. The chronicler assures us that she was highly pleased with the gift, the first she had received in France.

At Niort, Margaret was joined by the two ladies,

Madame de La Roche-Guyon and Madame de Gamaches, sent by the Queen to meet her. She rested for a while at Poitiers before her reception by the Parlement, the University and the Church. The Chancellor had borne the news of the Princess's arrival to the King; and his Council had decided that the wedding should take place on the morrow of St John the Baptist's Day, at Tours, where preparations for the ceremony were being hurried forward. Margaret made her entry into Tours on the 24th of June, riding a richly caparisoned nag, followed by Madame de La Roche and some of the ladies from Scotland on horseback, while others drove in chariots. The court was at the Château of Saint-Gatien. The Queen of France, the Queen of Sicily, Mme Radegonde, the King's daughter, and many others were assembled in the great hall. Monseigneur de Vendôme and a Count of Scotland introduced Margaret. The Queen of Sicily and the little Radegonde advanced to meet her and led her to the Queen, who was seated on a high, richly ornamented seat. Then the kind and sweet Marie of Anjou rose and went towards the child, took her by the hand and kissed her. The Dauphin meanwhile was in a lower room, surrounded by knights and squires. But now he came up into the hall. As soon as Margaret saw him she went towards him. The children put their arms round each other's necks and kissed. Then they played together in the great tapestried hall until supper was ready.

Outside, in the crowded streets, musicians were playing, and the organ in the Church of St Martin was accompanying the children's choirs, who were to be rewarded with bread, wine and cherries.

The next day was the eve of the wedding. The King arrived in time for the nuptial benediction, accompanied by a great retinue. He went to Madame's room, where she was being dressed. Her looks seemed to please him, for the face of this Scottish lassie gleamed like a star. Clad in her long regal mantle of velvet and cloth of gold, with a little diadem encircling her head, she walked up the nave of the chapel royal in the great fortress of Tours. And soon afterwards Louis appeared. He also wore regal dress. In stature he was insignificant, but he had a fine forehead, covered by a thick wisp of hair, a long, arched nose, piercing eyes with bristling brows, and a resolute chin. He was proud of his blue velvet costume embroidered with leaves of gold. His sword, said to have belonged to Robert Bruce, had been sent to him by the King of Scotland as a wedding gift. On its white leather hilt were figures of Our Lady and the Archangel St Michael.

The Queen of France held herself stiffly erect in her robe of bluish green embroidered with jewels. King Charles, booted and spurred, was in his grey travelling clothes, for he had not had time to change. The bride's gown and the ornaments she had brought from her country were greatly admired.

Monseigneur Regnault de Chartres, Archbishop of Reims, he who had already carried on so many negotiations between France and Scotland, pronounced the benediction. The wedding was a grand festival, though there was no jousting and though nothing particular happened. The wedding party sat down to the banquet. The Archbishop, the King, the Dauphiness, and the Queen presided at the high table. Next came the table of the Dauphin, who entertained the nobles from Scotland. It was a fine feast and plenteous. Of trumpeters, clarionettists, minstrels, players on the lute and psaltery, there was no lack. And many were the heralds and pursuivants.

The good people of Touraine and of the town took part in the games. There was morris dancing, and Master Robert le Diable danced so vigorously that he split one of his breeches. Tours and Chinon offered gifts of silver dishes, the clergy of silver goblets. There could not, of course, be any question of consummating the marriage, on account of the children's age, though the King had obtained from the Archbishop letters of dispensation ratified by the Parlement.

52

The main question was the departure of the numerous lords and ladies from Scotland, to whom the King made a few presents. They were under the impression of being summarily dismissed; and they went away disillusioned. Margaret was allowed to retain only a few of her compatriots. Her household was to consist of French retainers, who were charged to teach her the French language. Margaret was to keep in close touch with the sweet and pious Marie d'Anjou, who welcomed her as her own daughter.

Meanwhile, the Dauphin was given a household of his own. His governor was Bernard d'Armagnac, Comte de la Marche, who was charged to keep Louis under constant supervision. The Count's father had been assassinated by the Burgundians in 1418, during the Paris riots. His son was an austere man, a model of chivalry, wisdom, and devotion. When he entered a church, he would fall on his knees before the crucifix, with eyes downcast and hands outstretched to heaven, saying his prayers like any man of the people. In his own home, during meals, the Bible and other books full of sound doctrine and moral reflections were read aloud as in the refectory of a Cistercian monastery. Louis tolerated all this—but somewhat impatiently. As he no longer needed a tutor, Jean Majoris became his confessor. He had an Augustinian friar, Pierre Harenthal, for his chaplain, and for his physician, one Guillaume Leothier. His master of the horse was Joachim Rouault, knight, a good soldier, whose father, the King's chamberlain, had been killed at the Battle of Verneuil. His treasurer, Simon Verjus, received the modest sum of 10,500 livres tournois for the expenses of the household. His assistant, Jean Bochetel, who was styled controller of the household, was to be Louis' chief secretary.

So the children lived apart and rarely met. For Louis, who was old for his age, was already engaged in all manner of warlike tasks, while Margaret stayed with the good and pious Marie d'Anjou, learning French and reading her book of hours.

CHAPTER III

LOUIS MAKES A GOOD BEGINNING

Louis accompanies his father to Lyons, Dauphiné and Languedoc.—He learns statecraft in the Provincial Estates.—He pursues Rodrigo de Villandrando and his Brigands.—An attempt to set the son against his father.—Louis' first Command against the English.—His capture of Château-Landon.—Consummation of his Marriage.

KING CHARLES was in a good temper. The Treaty of Arras (1435) had realised some of the greatest hopes of his diplomats and pacifist counsellors, who on this occasion had certainly advised him well. Another political marriage had followed the Dauphin's : Charles had affianced his daughter Yolande to the little Amadeus of Savoy, Prince of Piedmont. The day after the ceremony the King and his son left Tours for a progress through the loyal provinces. After spending the summer of 1436 on the banks of the Loire, they started for Auvergne in October ; and before the following April they had visited Clermont, Lyons, Vienne, Béziers and Nîmes.

Hitherto the only parts of France Louis had known had been the peaceful landscapes of Berri and Touraine. Now his keen, eager, eyes saw other regions, and he came into contact with people who differed fundamentally from the crafty but amiable Berrichons and Tourainians among whom he had been brought up. The Dauphin Louis now discovered France. It was a more informing experience than any book learning. In Auvergne he was present at a meeting of the Provincial Estates presided over by his father. On New Year's Day he was at Lyons, the second city in the realm, on the border of France and the Empire, the city of holy martyrs, in whose churches reposed the bones of many a saint. One of them contained the column to which Jesus was bound on the eve of the Passion.

Louis' new year's gift from his father was four ells of cloth of gold, enough to fashion a robe of state, and probably the product of that Lyonnese cloth manufacture, in which Louis was to take so great an interest. It was at Charles's suggestion that Louis sent to Tours a fine full-length mirror, adorned with pearls, as a gift to his wife.

In Dauphiné Louis was introduced to that wild and rugged country which his history books told him would soon form part of his personal domain. He made the acquaintance of its proud nobility, its powerful bishops and its rough mountaineers. At the gates of Vienne he was presented with a cup of gold, equal in weight and in beauty to that given to his father. Here again he attended, at Romans, a meeting of the Provincial Estates, which voted a voluntary contribution of 10,000 florins.

It was about this time that Louis signed his first letter. It was one authorising the drawing of a sum of money. At the request of Jean Majoris, Louis had bought for him by his physician Leothier a silver gilt chalice, two vases, a silver paten, a missal, three altar cloths, an alb, an amice, a chasuble of cloth of gold—in short, the entire equipment for a movable chapel—to enable my Lord the Dauphin to hear Mass at any stage of his journeyings. At the same time, his master of the horse, Joachim Rouault, purchased an equally complete equipment for a travelling prince and warrior—saddle horses, trappings, swords and robes. And Louis made gifts to his companions on the lavish and royal scale we shall find him always adopting. A sense of service rendered was one of his most marked characteristics.

Then Louis, like a young colt, followed his father through the rich country of Languedoc. The King looked to this province for a goodly supply of gold coins. At Béziers an assembly of churchmen voted a hundred gold crowns for the necessities of Monsieur le Dauphin. On the 27th of February, the King and his son entered Montpellier, the centre of the trade of Southern Europe with the ports of the Levant. At Montpellier the royal travellers stayed two months. Here again Louis had the opportunity of attending a meeting of the Provincial Estates, over which his father presided.

One of the crying misfortunes of the day was the scourge of free-lances and brigands, who, under the leadership of the illusive chief, Rodrigo de Villandrando, were laying waste the country, pillaging and holding to ransom the loyal subjects of the rich southern provinces. At Pézénas the militia were called up to proceed against these plunderers.

But in April, King Charles heard that the brigands, who were expected in the south, had suddenly appeared in the centre. The sweet Queen Marie and the young Dauphiness, at the request of the townsfolk of Tours, had entered into communication with the robber chief, entreating him to spare the country of Touraine. Rodrigo was a gentleman. For the sake of Madame la Dauphine and to please Monseigneur le Dauphin, whose " loyal and grateful servant " he announced himself to be, the brigand consented not to hold the people of Touraine to ransom. Can this rough soldier already be plotting in favour of the Duc de Bourbon and trying to set Louis against his father ? The terms of Rodrigo's reply look rather like it. At any rate, Charles lost no time in marching against him. At the head of a formidable army—five hundred knights and squires and four thousand bowmen—he crossed through Bourbonnais going towards Saint-Flour. And Louis, following on his heels, could see the ravages committed by the bands of the robber chief, whose marauders pillaged the King's convoys and flogged the men-at-arms sent on in advance to pitch their royal master's camp. On the 14th of May, the King reached Saint-Flour unexpectedly. It was one of the chief towns of the kingdom, good and loyal and an excellent point for dominating central France, Languedoc and Guyenne. But neither Charles nor Louis was expected there, and the streets had to be hastily furbished up. The old families were called on to produce a few antique bowls to be presented to the royal guests. And the consuls contrived to appear in state, wearing their robes of black and red cloth. With them were the herald Courtebotte, the trumpeters in the town livery, green and blue, the aldermen and the town guilds with their banners, preceded by two flags of plain linen embroidered with the arms of the King and the Dauphin. And all the children of Saint-Flour drew up in procession, bearing a banneret, on which Jean de Saignes, artist and grocer, had painted the arms of France. The King and the Dauphin rode beneath cloth of gold ; white draperies hung from the windows. Now was the time for presents : twelve old cups for the King, six for the Dauphin, six for Charles of Anjou— nothing for anyone else. Only one torch was lit. There was no end to the war contributions required from the Estates ; and Auvergne could not help appearing stingy.

The King and the Dauphin never succeeded in coming face to face with Rodrigo and his brigands, who had devastated the country all along their line of march. Charles pursued them as far as Roanne. But the adventurer, putting the Rhône between himself and the King, had crossed over into the Empire.

During the summer of 1437, King Charles, who had returned to Bourges with a large force, resolved to lead an expedition against the small English garrisons on the Upper Loire. He bought two bay horses for his own riding. He decided to take the Dauphin and let him win his spurs. Not a few—and among them nobles of the blood, knights, squires and even people of the good towns and the countryside—had been thinking that the King had been forgetting his main business, viz. : to make war in person on his ancient enemies, the English.

So now the Duc d'Alençon's squire exclaimed joyfully : " Thanks to Our Lord's mercy, he has undertaken to make more merciless war on the English than has ever been waged in time past." The Dauphin, too, now a robust youth, was eager to show his courage against the ancient enemies of France. In company with his governor, le Comte de la Marche, he received a command.

They came to Gien-sur-Loire, the headquarters of bowmen and men-at-arms. Then throughout the whole countryside they resorted to methods which Louis would not forget in after years : they made what was known as *le gast*, which meant setting fire to the crops, felling the trees and destroying the vines in order to starve out the enemy. The Comte de la Marche, with between three and four thousand men, besieged Charny and carried it. But that pious soldier allowed all who would to escape, with their horses and harness. And such as returned to the King's allegiance received papers of indemnity for the evil they had wrought.

The King prayed and commanded processions in all his loyal towns. On the 5th of July, he attacked Château-Landon. It was a regular eagles' nest, towering over the Loing and commanding the ford leading to Montereau. The Dauphin soon arrived, " well and largely accompanied." His father's apparent inaction irked him. He wanted to capture the town without delay. So three days after his son's arrival, the King commanded the assault : the soldiers, fired by the Dauphin's youthful ardour, captured the castle with but a slight loss. Then, like a true prince, " he gave them all good cheer, knights and squires." But Louis was far from following the example of his merciful governor. All the English were hanged, and the French traitors beheaded. Those who tried to make him listen to reason wasted their time. For Louis was as passionate as he was impulsive : he could not brook opposition. And when he controlled himself it was rather because of his own caution than at the advice of others.

After God had granted him this successful initiation into the art of war, he went off to join his father at Gien, leaving the Comte de la Marche to take the fortress of Nemours, where he showed his accustomed mercy. At Gien, Louis found his little bride, Margaret of Scotland. And, having arrived at man's estate, he took her to wife.

CHAPTER IV

Charles and Louis outvie one another in energy.—The taking of Montereau.—Their entry into the Capital.—The Parisians, already almost starving, endure yet greater hardships as the result of the Royal Visit.

PARIS had long remained as completely without news of King Charles as if he had been in Rome or Jerusalem. But now, fired possibly by the example of his big and vigorous son, the King left Gien, and parting from Monseigneur le Dauphin and his company at Bray-sur-Seine, advanced on Montereau at the head of his army.

Then was seen a most unusual sight—King Charles disguised in common clothes, visiting his captains, inspecting the positions of cannons and bombards, and altering those that were not to his liking. When certain of his generals remonstrated against his exposing himself to danger, he replied that it was right for him to take his share of the work. Before long, breaches were made in the walls of the town. Then the King ordered the assault; and before any knight or squire of his company, he himself leapt into the moat, where the water came above his waist, and, sword in hand, climbed the ladder. The enemy took refuge in the château, which was ill-provisioned. The artillery was turned upon it and reduced it to ruins in a fortnight. But Charles refused to listen to those who spoke of negotiation. He was determined to take the place by storm.

The Dauphin joined his father. This time he did not indulge in cruelty; and through his intervention the English were allowed to retreat safe and sound and to carry off their goods. Were they not "foreigners who had been ordered to conquer our land, and who had not come of their own accord " ?

As for the French-speaking prisoners, they might well be hanged. Louis knew how to distinguish ordinary prisoners of war from traitors. He was learning by experience.

The capture of Montereau was the signal for general rejoicing, not in the army only, but even in the city of Paris. Winter was coming on. Food was only to be found in fortresses. Life in the open country was becoming impossible. The King and the Dauphin dismissed part of their army and decided to go to Paris.

The city had recently got rid of its English garrison. Led by the courageous Michel de Lallier, shouting and throwing stones, pots, and logs, the citizens had driven out the foreigner.

Now came the time for frank expression of opinion and also for a change of front. Thus the University of Paris, which had for so long been Burgundian and even English, invited the Dauphin and his father to enter the capital. They went down the Seine valley towards Paris ; and on the 11th of November, St Martin's Day, arrived at St Denis. This royal city lay almost in ruins. But the alabaster statues of the Kings of France were still standing on their marble tombs and still gilded. How august they must have appeared to the young Louis, who was well versed in the history of his ancestors. The most recent mausoleum was that of the mad Charles VI and his German Queen, Isabel of Bavaria. Louis may have reflected that when a King of France marries a foreigner he will be well advised to keep her out of politics. At any rate, that was the course Louis was to follow when he came to the throne.

Their preparations for the King's state reception may have afforded some consolation to the Parisians. In perfect silence they had watched the three hundred English from Montereau defiling through the city— murderers and thieves all of them ; the Parisians would have liked to see them hanged. Yet for no French victory had the people of Paris ever lit a single bonfire. Now they made up for lost time. No one, except the old men, remembered King Charles. All they knew of the Dauphin Louis was his brilliant marriage. Nevertheless from the Gate of Saint-Denis to Notre-Dame, the houses were hung with tapestry and decorated with branches. Platforms were erected for the performance of mystery plays. Fountains poured forth water, wine and milk.

After the vanguard and a body of eight hundred archers, rode Louis, a little behind the King, on a courser nobly caparisoned. He was in a suit of light armour, his head covered with a helmet of wrought gold. Behind followed pages in various colours.

At the first St Denis Gate a halt was called : the good Provost of the Merchants, Michel de Lallier, and the Aldermen came out to pay their respects to the King. They held a canopy over his head like that held over the Host on Corpus Christi Day. At the Convent of Les Filles-Dieu (a penitentiary and a hospital for poor women), was a fountain pouring from its four mouths water, milk, red and white wine. At la Porte aux Peintres Louis witnessed a performance of the Mystery of the Incarnation, at la Porte Saint Martin-des-Champs, of the Nativity, in which the angels sang sweetly : "Peace on earth and good-will towards men." In front of the Saint-Denis culvert, Louis paused to admire a fountain on which there was a vase, and in front of it a fleur-de-lys whence issued wine and water and hippocras. The fountain was carved with figures of dolphins in honour of Louis. At La Trinité, the Brotherhood of the Passion played "the Last Judgment." Monseigneur Saint Michel was seen weighing souls in his scales. At the end of the St Denis street they came to the bridge leading to the square of Notre Dame. Here all the prelates of Paris and the members of the learned University were assembled. The King and the Dauphin dismounted. The University orator, Nicolas Midi—he who had judged Jeanne d'Arc

61

and persecuted her so cruelly — celebrated the virtues of Charles VII and described the long widowhood of the University during the absence of her lawful King.

Then King Charles took the oath, swearing on the holy Gospels. He and his son entered the majestic parish church of France to hear the *Te Deum*. Then they passed on to the Palace,[1] where the Kings of France were wont to spend their first night in the capital. Cries of "Noël" were heard on every hand in honour of the Parisians' lawful lord, the King, and his son, the Dauphin. Night fell. Fires were lit in the streets. In the flickering light there was dancing, drinking, and playing on divers instruments. Everyone forgot his misery. Time enough to return home to the cabbages and turnips which so long had been the starving Parisians' only food. Everyone had a good day, including the cutpurses sneaking in and out of the crowd.

On the morrow, Louis made the round of Paris and worshipped the holy relics at la Sainte-Chapelle. The King took up his residence at l'Hôtel Neuf near the Bastille, and Louis at Les Tournelles.[2]

But in spite of all the machinations of magistrates and corporations, Louis and his father had no intention of residing permanently in Paris. At the end of three weeks, on the 3rd of December, and, under the pretext of saving the capital the expense which their residence in it would involve, the King and the Dauphin set out for Tours, where they were joyfully welcomed by the Queen and the Dauphiness, who had not seen them since the Battle of Montereau

The valour of King Charles, the "brilliant beginning" of My Lord the Dauphin, the good fortune God had vouchsafed unto him, and his magnificent entry into Paris were the talk of all the ladies. But the King soon let it

---

[1] Now le Palais de Justice.

[2] Only a short distance away, in what is now called le Faubourg Saint Antoine.

be known that he was leaving them for the siege of Montargis.

The stay of the King and the Dauphin in their midst had been a bitter disillusion to the Parisians. They went about saying that the royal capture of Montereau and visit to the capital had cost the city 60,000 francs. During that hard winter of 1438, robbers from the valley of Chevreuse had penetrated as far as the Porte Saint Jacques ; they had beaten a sergeant to death and killed several poor people, crying : " Where is your King ? Is he in hiding ? " As a result of the royal visit the prices of wine and bread had risen, and few were able to eat as much bread as they needed. The poor could not afford to drink wine or eat meat : turnips and cabbage-stalks cooked on ashes were their only food. And day and night men, women, and little children might be heard crying : " I am dying, alas ! sweet Jesus, I am dying of cold and hunger "

CHAPTER V

LOUIS' COMMAND IN LANGUEDOC

The King's Financial Difficulties.—Louis in Limousin.—Death of his
pet Lioness.—At fifteen Lieutenant-General of Languedoc.—
Magnitude of his Task.—Vigour and Intelligence with which he
set about it.—Revolutionary Character of his Administration.—
Intervention in the Quarrels of Nobles.—Prepares an Expedition
against the English in Guyenne.—His sudden and inexplicable
Recall.

CHARLES, like everyone else, was short of money ; for war
never enriches, not even when it is victorious. The
English in Guyenne were giving trouble ; and the King
was planning an expedition against them. But first he
went into Poitou, taking the Dauphin with him, in order
to replenish his treasury. He found this province no more
prosperous than the other parts of his kingdom. The
price of victuals was as high as everywhere else. And the
Estates of Saintonge refused to vote any contribution.
Jean Majoris, who was now the Dauphin's steward as well
as his confessor, told Louis that he could not meet the
expenses of the Dauphin's household. So Charles doubled
his salary.

The King and his son returned to Touraine. Then
Louis went into Berri and stayed there till the end of
1438. The few notes we possess in his own handwriting
dating from this period show that he was already a clear
thinker and capable of expressing himself with decision
and simplicity.

In the early days of 1439, Louis and his father set out
on another progress, this time directed to Languedoc,
where things were going badly. On their way they
visited Limoges, arriving on the 2nd of March. While
Charles was received at the Château of La Bonardière,

Louis accepted the hospitality of the Abbot of Saint-Martial, who placed the finest rooms in the monastery at his disposal. In the room next his own, Louis lodged a little eight-months-old lioness, given him by Tanneguy du Châtel, and of which he was very fond. But one night, the lioness tried to jump out of the window and broke her neck, much to Louis' distress.

The Dauphin went round the town. He visited the church containing the head of the Blessed Saint Martial, and accompanied his father when he presided over the States General of Limousin. At the request of his physician, Guillaume Leothier, he intervened on behalf of a certain friar, who had been unjustly deprived of his office of almoner. Parting from his father, the Dauphin went to Saint-Symphorien, where he stayed for a while with a well-known citizen, Guillaume Piédieu. Then he rejoined his father at Guéret, accompanied him to Riom, where the Auvergne Estates were meeting, and went on to Puy, arriving in time for the meeting of the Estates of Languedoc, at which the King had to listen to the numerous grievances of his subjects. By the way they had made a pilgrimage to one of the King's favourite shrines, the mountain sanctuary of the Black Virgin.

Languedoc, always a disturbed province, had in those days fallen into dire poverty. Charles realised that something must be done. But instead of going himself he sent his son. He appointed the fifteen-year-old Louis his Lieutenant-General, to act with the assistance of nobles, prelates, and other counsellors. The Dauphin was also to be accompanied by his governor and the other officers of his household. Having made these arrangements, Charles continued his progress in the direction of Lyons.

The weight of the burden imposed on these young shoulders might have alarmed a youth of fifteen less vigorous and intelligent than Louis. This vast province, with its four commands of Toulouse, Carcassonne, Beaucaire and Béziers, was in those days a prey to every kind of misfortune—pillaging, pestilence, and inundations.

There were disputes everywhere, in the Church, between the nobles. Rodrigo de Villandrando was a perpetual menace, and so were the English in Guyenne. In spite of all this, the King demanded large contributions. He had but one reply to every grievance of the Estates : the Dauphin will see to it.

All the people expected Louis to be their deliverer. He was known to be brave and clever.

On the 17th of May he entered Albi, advancing in state, beneath a canopy of cloth of gold, accompanied by divers bishops, by the Vicomte de Lomagne, the Seneschal of Rouergue and other nobles. The town was hung with tapestry ; processions of children bearing pennons and his standard followed him. Louis drank the strong wine of the city. On the 25th of the month he made his state entry into Toulouse. There the *capitouls*[1] on horseback received him, escorted him through the streets, and gave gifts to his foragers. All presents were eagerly accepted. Toulouse granted 2,000 crowns. Beaucaire and Carcassonne signified their willingness to help defray expenses. And Louis, who was already well aware of the value of money, required even the poor shepherds of barren Gévaudan to pay their share in the expenses of his journey.

For Louis fully realised the importance of sound finance. Those who served him for the first time found themselves well provided for. At this early stage he adopted a practice, continued later, of choosing his officers of state from among his personal servants, his scribes and secretaries. His government was already essentially personal. But he announced his intention of ruling in accordance with the wishes of the Estates, of making every effort to relieve the sufferings of the province, of waging war on oppression and wrong-doing. He insisted on seeing the country with his own eyes, travelling everywhere, listening to the grievances of everyone. The fairly numerous decrees and other documents of this time that we possess show a spirit of initiative and resource in dealing

---

[1] Town magistrates.

with these grievances, and a keen sense of the situation which are surprising, even in this precocious youth. Though during his six months' government of Languedoc, Louis may not have succeeded in ridding the country of the scourge of freebooters, it must be admitted that he took up the task seriously and worked at it with all diligence.

With regard to social—especially hygienic—measures, Louis, even at this early age, was strangely in advance of his day : he appointed inspectors to visit the sick and prevent infection, especially those poor creatures, accused —wrongfully in many cases—of being afflicted with leprosy and proscribed by civil and religious law.

The free-lances who infested the country round Toulouse Louis contented himself with buying off ; but to ordinary thieves, incendiaries and other criminals he showed no mercy.

Louis frequently intervened as judge in the scandalous disputes between the litigious nobles of the south : as, for example, when he summoned before him one Mathieu de Foix, who was keeping his aged wife in captivity, because her previous husband, Jean IV, Count of Armagnac, demanded her, or rather her inheritance.

Louis commanded the Seneschals of Toulouse and Carcassonne to summon their vassals and lead them against the English of Guyenne.

This was a very grave matter. The Dauphin sent word of it to the King, who had summoned him to Brie to discuss the affair. But Louis, without waiting for his father's reply, had commanded a watch to be kept on the frontier near Bordeaux, while he himself was directing the first hostilities. He carefully superintended all the preparations. In order to raise the necessary funds, Louis persuaded the provincial Estates, which met at Castres, of the necessity of paying men-at-arms, of provisioning and repairing fortresses. At Castres on the 10th of October, the young lieutenant-general held a great council at once judicial and military. At Albi, he nominated as his generals the Comte de Foix, the Sire

d'Albret and the Vicomte de Lomagne. For though the
Dauphin employed mere scribes and secretaries in his
domestic administration, he knew full well the value of the
great feudatories when it was a question of fighting
against the enemies of France.

Why had the Dauphin suddenly to leave Languedoc?
We do not know. But King Charles must have had some
reason, seeing that he repeatedly recalled him in urgent
letters, saying that it was his pleasure to employ him in
another part of the kingdom.

The Dauphin started, but without haste, and all the
way to Albi he was sending instructions to those over
whom he had ruled. The King seemed to be undoing
the whole of his son's work; and although Languedoc
was not actually invaded, the freebooters had everything
their own way, and the quarrels between the nobles broke
out again.

Louis returned to Tours in no very amiable mood.
There was great excitement at court. For the King had
just taken the first step towards the establishment of
a standing army, by publishing an ordinance forbidding
the nobles to raise troops. The measure was highly
unpopular. For the life of a mercenary was much to be
desired; and it hardly seemed just to disband men for
whom war was a profession. Bandits they were, no doubt,
but very useful in certain circumstances.

CHAPTER VI

THE PRAGUERIE

Reason for the Dauphin's Recall.—The Duke of Bourbon.—Louis intrigues with the Discontented Nobles.—The King appoints him Lieutenant in Poitou, Aunis and Saintonge.—Louis conspires with the Duke of Alençon.—Establishes himself in the Auvergne Mountains.—Poses as the Deliverer of the Kingdom.—The King takes the Field against the Rebels.—Able generalship of the Constable Richemont.—Defeat of the Rebels.—Louis' Insolence.—Outrageous Demands.—Final Submission and Humiliation.—Deprived of his Household.—Appointed Governor of Dauphiné.

It was not only to those petty tyrants who were in command of the free companies that the King's decree applied. After their leader, Rodrigo de Villandrando, had gone into Spain, the chief fomenter of discontent in France was the young Duke of Bourbon. This valorous knight, as handsome as Absalom or Paris of Troy, and the greatest athlete in France, had just married King René's daughter. For years he had dallied with the English. He was a friend of the Duke of Brittany and of the mad young Duke of Alençon. He had even involved the brave Bastard of Orléans in his machinations, by persuading him that the King had abandoned his intention of delivering his half-brother, Charles Duke of Orléans, from his English prison. The Dauphin was well aware of all this. Rodrigo had already held out a hand to him, as we have seen. And there is no doubt that the cause of the Dauphin's sudden recall must have been his father's discovery of certain intrigues, the thread of which has now been lost.

The Duke of Bourbon met Louis at Tours, when he was with his father. He can have had no difficulty in fanning the flame of discord between an embittered son and a suspicious parent. Then the King went to Angers to reorganise his army and prevent war from spreading across the Loire. He was furious at the failure of his troops before Avranches. He summoned the captains who were responsible. "How did it happen?" he inquired. "Why were they such cowards?" The King made much of one of Rodrigo's comrades, Antoine de Chabannes, Comte de Dammartin, and tried to retain him. But when he insisted on going: "Farewell, Captain of brigands," he cried. Whereupon Chabannes retorted: "If I acted as a brigand, it was only towards your enemies, and if I slew them, it was more to your advantage than to mine."

Charles must have known of the conspiracy of the malcontents. Their idea was to make the Dauphin their chief; and Bourbon intended to capture the château of Angers and to take the King prisoner. Charles anticipated him: he appointed Louis lieutenant-general in Poitou, Aunis and Saintonge. His energy would be well employed in those miserable provinces where freebooters preyed on the land, occupied castles and churches, held the peasants to ransom and plundered merchants. So Louis went to Poitou, somewhat perturbed, no doubt. But now, as always, this youth of sixteen did his work conscientiously, administered justice, repressed pillage and punished oppressors severely. Charles had reason to be pleased with the results of his son's government.

But there was something behind this fine outward semblance, this diligence in the public service. At Niort, in February, 1440, Louis was visited by his godfather, the Duke of Alençon, who had just signed a treaty of alliance with his handsome cousin, Bourbon, and who was a regular traitor, mad enough to offer to send his men to help the English in their siege of Avranches.

The interview was kept secret; that it lasted long is all that is known about it. But it marks a complete change in Louis' conduct; he now threw over the control of his Governor, le Comte de la Marche; and the good Count reported at Angers that the Dauphin would henceforth refuse to obey his father ; that he intended to have his own way and not to be a subject as he had been hitherto, and also that he thought he might render great service to the kingdom.

Shortly afterwards Charles learned that my Lord the Dauphin intended to take the government of the kingdom into his own hands and to hold the King in tutelage.

Any sense of filial duty Louis may once have possessed had now deserted him. Consumed with energy, he was doubtless convinced of his ability to deal with the ills from which the unhappy country was suffering more effectually than his lethargic father.

But King Charles had realised the gravity of the situation. He started for Amboise, whence he addressed a circular letter to the good towns warning them against the rebels, among whom was his own son. The Constable Richemont, accompanied by Gaucourt and Saintrailles, was despatched to the Duke of Bourbon with orders to summon him to give an account of his conduct, and to represent to him that it would inflict great suffering on the poor people of the kingdom. My Lord of Bourbon's reply was an insult. But he allowed the men-at-arms to pass. On the morrow, however, when the King appeared before the Château of Loches, he was refused admittance.

Was King Charles to suffer the fate of King Richard whom his cousins had deposed and imprisoned ? Charles wondered. But the good Constable soon returned. That hardy Breton, ugly and blobber-lipped, was a good general and one who knew how to reduce an army to obedience. Taking the Constable with him and also his brother-in-law, Charles of Anjou, and Louis' dismissed tutor, the King went down into Poitou. He was marching against his son, whom he had determined to take prisoner.

Louis was at Niort, making himself popular with the neighbouring towns by promising to deal with their grievances, and beginning with the suppression of aids. The Duke of Alençon, having thrown two large garrisons into Melle and La Roche, was now besieging Saint-Maxent. But the vigorous Richemont had recaptured Melle, occupied Mirebeau, Sainte-Néomaye and the Island, and was now at the gates of Niort. Then the Dauphin and the Duke of Alençon began to open negotiations. They wanted to gain time, to wait for the help of the Duke of Bourbon, of Chabannes' freebooters and perhaps also—the traitors!—of the English and Huntingdon. While the King, leaving everything to his negotiators, was keeping Easter at Poitiers, the Duke of Alençon took the castle of Saint-Maxent. The news was brought to the King as he sat at table ; he rose hastily, went to Saint-Maxent and recaptured the château. There were a few executions. But most of the traitors had fled to the Dauphin at Niort.

Then the Duke of Alençon carried off Louis in all haste to the Auvergne Mountains, where the Duke of Bourbon's forces had assembled. There were strong fortresses in Auvergne, as Louis well knew. He convoked the Estates at Clermont, entreated their support, and induced the nobles to take an oath to oppose the King. Then he turned astutely to Languedoc, and addressed the people of Dauphiné as if he were their independent lord.

Everywhere Louis gave himself out to be the saviour of the kingdom, who would abolish aids and make peace with England. He fixed a date for the assembling of the Estates at Lyons. He may have approached the Duke of Burgundy. He was capable of it ; and about this time, we find the Duke, through one Bertrandon de la Broquière, offering his mediation between father and son, with the object of procuring pardon for the Dauphin and indemnity for the rebels.

The King was not disinclined for peace. In his letters and despatches to the good towns he endeavoured to minimise the Dauphin's share in the rebellion. But Richemont was going on with his successes. And Louis meanwhile was waiting for the free companies to come to his assistance. More and more strongholds were being

captured for the King, who was about to besiege his own
son in the fortress of Saint-Pourçain. First, however, he
announced to the rebels the conditions on which he would
accept their submission : the rebel lords must return to
their obedience to their natural sovereign, they must
disband their archers and men-at-arms, for to the King
alone belonged the right of making war ; they must
surrender to the King " my Lord the Dauphin and
those who had given him bad advice " ; and if the Dauphin
refused, they must not " favour him, nor comfort him,
nor receive him and maintain him in their towns and
fortresses against the will of the King." Then King
Charles gave a list of the persons and fortresses which were
to be delivered up to him.

The rebels sent messengers to Charles with their reply ;
they had always held the King to be their sovereign lord ;
as to the disbanding of the men-at-arms they agreed, but
they demanded that Charles, on his side, should cease his
pitiless oppression of the people ; the clause concerning
the Dauphin's surrender they would accept, but with
considerable reservations—they would counsel him to
present himself without delay before the King his father,
and in all humility, as was meet, to do him honour and
reverence, and promise him obedience. But the clause
demanding the surrender of Louis' counsellors they
considered too hard. It might delay the Dauphin's
submission for " he is," they said, " the chief of us all and
of our whole company."

Here we have Louis' true position. His own reply to
his father's conditions displayed his impatience, his passion
for dominance, and his feigned humility : " the said Lord
Dauphin asks the King to permit him to continue in his
good grace and favour, as it hath ever been his chief desire
so to do ; further he asks the King not to bear him ill-will
for things that have happened, to grant him pardon and
to put them out of mind." Louis meant these conditions
to include his confederates, for whom he asked letters of
indemnity. Then abruptly he came to the point : " In

order that the said Lord Dauphin may keep up his estate, may it please the King to grant him Dauphiné, for it seemeth to him unjust that he hath not possessed it hitherto, seeing that in time past it hath been granted to other Dauphins before they arrived at the said Dauphin's age." But the province of Dauphiné would hardly suffice to keep up Louis' estate. The King therefore was asked to make further provision for it and to appoint his son to the governorship of Guyenne, Gascony, or l'Isle de France. Neither did Louis forget Madame la Dauphine. Charles was reminded that she still lived in the King's household and that her list was insufficient. Then, considering that in any undertaking, however unfortunate, one must always remember one's associates, and seeing that one must always be regarded as chief even by those whom one has led to defeat, Louis demanded absolute pardon and reinstatement in office as well as restoration of confiscated property for all his fellow rebels.

To these exorbitant demands, Charles replied firmly and kindly : " When my Lord the Dauphin comes before the King with the humility that is his due, the King will treat him as his son and provide for his estate, as well as for that of Madame la Dauphine, in such manner as shall content him. As for the other requests here set forth touching the associates of My Lord the Dauphin, measures shall be taken to content him when he appears before the King."

Such moderation wounded the young Dauphin's pride. He insisted as posing as the defender of the public weal and as his father's counsellor. In order to avoid such dangerous divisions in the future the King must cease to oppress his people and unite all classes in war against England, the country's greatest enemy. My Lord the Dauphin offered to place himself and his supporters at their head. Or the King might adopt another course : he might convoke the Estates General of the kingdom. Louis and his partisans were prepared to submit their cause to the decision of that assembly. The Duke of Burgundy himself might appear as witness before it, or he might send an ambassador. Or, if the King preferred, the Dauphin would enter into direct communication with Duke Philip.

The impertinence and irony of this reply were character-istic of the Dauphin, who was practically accusing his father of being incapable. It is not surprising that the negotia-tions, which had been going on through the heat of June in the glowing little lava town of Montferrand, set like a jewel among the dark mountains of Auvergne, were abruptly broken off. Hostilities were resumed. The royal troops captured Vichy, Cusset and Varennes, then penetrated into le Forez, and took Roannes and Charlieu by storm. The rebel princes were done for ; their army melted away ; and Louis remained without money and without troops. What was he to do ? Should he, with his few remaining supporters, take refuge with the Duke of Burgundy ? No doubt he was thinking of it. But Duke Philip replied to the Dauphin's messengers that though he was prepared to receive him and to try to reconcile him with his father, he would not help him to make war.

Accordingly Louis was driven to make peace. In company with the nobles who had been most deeply compromised by this adventure, the Duke of Bourbon, the Lords de La Trémoille, Chaumont and Prie, Louis set out for Cusset, where the King had just arrived. But when they were about half a league from the town, a messenger met them, saying that the King would not receive the three nobles, but only the Dauphin and Bourbon. Then Louis swore a great oath, and turning to Bourbon, exclaimed : " Comrade, would you ever have said that things would have turned out thus, and that the King would have refused his pardon to my followers ? " The Dauphin swore again and declared he would not return to the King his father. But Bourbon remon-strated, showing that no other course was possible, seeing that the King's vanguard barred the way of retreat. But Louis refused to listen to reason. No, he would return with his followers to Moulins. They dissuaded him, however, so the Dauphin and Bourbon resumed their way to Cusset and alighted at the King's residence.

It was the prodigal's return. Three times the two rebels knelt in the King's chamber. The third time they most humbly sued for pardon. Then the father addressed his son : " Louis, be welcome. You have been long in coming. To-day, go to your house and rest there. I will talk to you to-morrow." Then, not unkindly, but at great length, Charles reproached the Duke of Bourbon.

The next day, after mass, the two conspirators were brought before the King and his council. Again they craved pardon for their comrades, La Trémoille, Chaumont and Prie. The King refused, saying he was glad they had returned. " But," remonstrated the Dauphin, " would you have me, Sire, take back my word that I have pledged to them ? " Then the King replied gravely : " Louis, all doors are open to you, and if they be not wide enough, then will I make a breach in the wall, so that you may depart wheresoever you will. You are my son, and you may not grant favours to anyone without my permission. But if it please you to go, then with God's will we shall find some other prince of the blood to do us better service than you have rendered."

Thereupon the King left his son, and went to the Duke of Bourbon, who took the oath to serve him loyally henceforward.

On the 17th of July, Charles announced by letters patent that the Dauphin and the Duke of Bourbon had come to him in all humility and obedience and had received his pardon. But as for the obstinate son, whose embittered mood Charles was endeavouring to hide, he was deprived of his household, of all his officials and servants, save only his confessor and cook. It was dangerous, however, to keep such a devil in idleness ; and, after a few days, the King assigned Louis the government of Dauphiné, with a pension of eight hundred *livres* a month. Thus through his error and ill-doing Louis had won the administration of a fine domain.

CHARLES VII OF FRANCE
(Father of Louis XI)
(*From the portrait by Jean Fouquet in the Louvre*)

CHAPTER VII

LOUIS IN COMMAND AGAINST THE ENGLISH

The Dauphin as Husband.—Charles and Louis march against the English.—Diversion in Champagne.—Punishment of the Dauphin's Confederates.—The King and Louis visit Jeanne d'Arc's Country.—Louis' secret Mission to Paris.—The Storming of Pontoise.—Narrow escape from Drowning.—Meeting with Charles of Orléans.—With the King in the South.—The taking of Tartas.

BEFORE returning to Touraine, the King made a long progress through Auvergne, in order to assure his own victory and his son's defeat. The shamefaced Dauphin had to accompany his father, before returning to his wife at Tours.

The year after her arrival in France, Margaret had lost her father, James I, who had been assassinated by his nobles (1437). What kind of welcome Louis received from his consort we do not know. She must have been surprised at the story of her sufferings circulated by the rebel lords. For this bright and cheerful young person had nothing whatever to complain of at the hands of the good Queen, and of King Charles, who adored her.

The strange husband, whom she seldom saw, can have played but a small part in her life. He was certainly not in love with her. Later his avidity made a grievance of her failure to bear him a son. Louis also reproached her with being too free in her behaviour, too fond of dress, and too extravagant ; and he complained that her breath was not as sweet as it might be.[1]

In those days King Charles was perpetually on the move. What with the freebooters and the English, he never had any peace. In September 1440, the English

[1] See Pierre Champion. " La Dauphine Mélancolique," p. 58.

besieged Harfleur. The King left Tours in all haste, taking the Dauphin with him, and travelling by way of Orléans, in order to organise two armies—one to march on Harfleur, the other on Conches and Louviers. Still accompanied by his son, the King made Chartres his headquarters. But, after a few months, the news that freebooters were laying waste Champagne compelled him to give up the idea of a campaign against the English, and to hurry eastwards, in order to anticipate Philip of Burgundy, who was only too eager to play the policeman in that part of France. In January 1441, we find Charles and Louis at Bar-sur-Aube. And there Charles arrested a score of brigand chiefs, among whom was that famous plotter and plunderer, the Bourbon Bastard, Alexander. The chiefs were tried. The Bastard was put in a sack and thrown into the Aube : a punishment which must have afforded Louis food for thought, seeing that among the crimes Alexander thus expiated was that of having set the son against his father. From Alexander's fate another of Louis' associates, that gallant adventurer, Antoine de Chabannes, took warning, and fled to a place of safety.

From Bar, Charles and the Dauphin went on to Langres and the Jeanne d'Arc country—to Domremy, her birth-place, to Vaucouleurs, where she had made her first appearance before Captain Baudricourt. The ostensible object of Charles's visit was to inquire into the claims of Antoine de Vaudemont to Lorraine, which he was disputing with the King of Sicily. But Louis may well have thought of the Maid, whom he had seen at the Château of Loches when he was a child. Passing by Châlons, they went on to the coronation town of Reims, which Louis now visited for the first time. At Laon, they opened negotiations with Burgundy, represented by the Duchess Isabelle. The Duchess, who was then forty-seven, was a very great lady, a Braganza, with grand and grave manners, and so good and reasonable that her flighty husband was glad to entrust her with matters too delicate for his professional diplomatists. It was Isabelle who had negotiated the liberation of Charles of Orléans from his English prison. Now the subject of discussion was that famous project of a peace with England, of which Louis had been so enamoured during his rebellion. Though the Dauphin now appeared reserved and submissive, we know that he was all the while corresponding secretly with the Duke of Burgundy, who had for a while kept him at a distance ; but Louis never nourished a grievance when it was against his interest.

Then the King and the Dauphin went down the Oise valley, revictualling the fortresses of Soissons, Noyon and Compiègne. The English still held Creil in the teeth of a prolonged bombardment.

The great enterprise the King had in mind was the siege of Pontoise, another town occupied by the English. And with the object of providing the sinews of war, Louis was despatched on a secret mission to Paris, where he succeeded in raising a heavier *taille* than the unhappy capital had paid for half a century.

During the spring of this year, 1441, Charles and Louis took up their quarters sometimes at Saint-Denis and sometimes at Paris, in the château of Saint-Antoine. The Parisians regarded them as foreigners, for whom they had no liking, seeing that they never came to the capital except to raise money. Louis spent the fine days of June and July in besieging Pontoise, where he took up his position in the redoubt he had constructed in the monastery of Saint-Martin. The tide of war ebbed and flowed : at one time the English, under York and Talbot, succeeded in crossing the Oise, and the French had to retreat to Conflans. Louis was ever at the King's side, inspecting outworks and reviewing troops ; and, when, on the 19th of September, the signal for the assault was given, the Dauphin, at the head of the attacking party, and accompanied by the Constable and Charles d'Anjou, fought from morning till night, and was one of the five or six assailants who, driving the enemy before them, were the first to enter the town.

There is no record of the Dauphin being present when Paris celebrated this victory. He must have been there, however. Possibly, after the failure of his great rebellion, he may have thought it prudent to keep in the background. Or it may simply have been that he did not like the Parisians ? We know that he considered them loquacious and quarrelsome.

Louis was modest and amenable in those days. And when Charles returned to Saumur to inquire into the condition of Poitou and to see how he could alleviate the sufferings of the people which *la Praguerie* had intensified, he could have had no better collaborator than his son.

Louis had learned that it may sometimes be expedient to forget promises. He had learned also that patience is often rewarded, and that he must curb his natural eagerness. He resolved to show himself worthy of some high command.

It was during this journey that Louis had an accident, which was to exercise considerable influence over his life. King Charles had decided to keep the Easter of 1442 at Ruffec ; and Louis had gone off alone for a walk in the country. On his way he met his uncle, Charles of Anjou, and the Lord of Tillay. The three embarked in a boat on the Charente, which was in high flood. As they approached a weir, their little craft overturned, and the pleasure-seekers were all precipitated into the mill-stream, head foremost. Neither of them was a good swimmer ; but they prayed devoutly to the Holy Virgin, and soon found themselves safe and sound on a little beach in mid-stream, whence, after having taken off the long gowns they were wearing in honour of St Friday, they were able to reach the bank, much to the astonishment of the good folk who had come to their rescue. In after years, Louis was to make an offering to the beautiful chapel of Notre-Dame de Béhuard on the Loire, in gratitude for her deliverance of him by virtue of the " bitter grief and anguish she had endured when she beheld her beloved Child, the Author of Life, hanging from the cross."

Thus the Virgin, so often indulgent to the wicked, had saved a bad son.

It was at Limoges that Louis saw his uncle,[1] Charles of Orléans, for the first time. The Dauphin, it will be remembered, had made his entry into the world in a bed, curtained with hangings, borrowed from the captive Duke's palace. Now, after twenty-five years of imprisonment in England, Charles had been liberated through the intervention not of France, but of Burgundy.[2] Consequently the Duke of Orléans was not one of the most contented of King Charles's subjects. Possibly for this reason, the Dauphin, though he did not like his uncle, made every effort to be agreeable.

In June, Charles and his son were at Toulouse. Thence they went on to the town of Tartas, which they captured from the English, taking the fortress of Saint-Sever by the way and storming Dax, where the Dauphin led the assault.

January and February (1443) they spent at Montauban. On the 26th, the King presided over the States General of Toulouse. And a few days later Louis entered the town in state beneath a canopy borne by eight *capitouls*, riding a white horse, and with his mother, Queen Marie d'Anjou on a pillion behind him.

But it was in Normandy rather than in these remote provinces that the English power in France could be vitally assailed.

---

[1] Or, as we should say—first cousin once removed.
[2] Cf. *ante* p. 79 and Pierre Champion. " Vie de Charles d'Orléans " (Paris, Honoré Champion), pp. 272-312.

CHAPTER VIII

LOUIS AT DIEPPE

Capture of the Port for King Charles.—The English Blockade.—Louis prepares to raise it.—His Progress through the Somme Towns.—Reception at Amiens.—Relief of Dieppe.—Return to Tours.—Expedition against John of Armagnac.

THE English imported their wine from Guyenne and a considerable part of their food from Normandy. After having occupied it for twenty-six years, they were now about to make a supreme effort to retain the province, though it had always been French at heart.

Soon after the Treaty of Arras (1435), a bold pirate, one Charles Desmarets, had taken Dieppe and handed it over to King Charles. A rising of the peasants in the neighbourhood of Caux and Vire alarmed the English at Rouen; and, in the beginning of 1442, Talbot was sent to capture Dieppe with a well-drilled and disciplined force. As he could not blockade the town from the sea, he erected a powerful fort on the land side. The French contrived to revictual Dieppe from the sea; and Dunois even succeeded in getting in one hundred and forty knights. The English would never succeed in taking Dieppe unless they could complete the blockade. It was with the difficult task of preventing their accomplishing this that the King now entrusted his son, whom he appointed lieutenant of the country north of the Seine and the Yonne. Louis' first act was to draw four thousand of the twelve thousand livres assigned to him. He reached Paris on the 25th of July 1443, and took the opportunity of raising a heavy *taille*. Three days later, he further asserted his authority by convoking the Presidents of the Court of Parlement and commanding them to delete from the conveyance of certain fiefs to Charles of Anjou the formula *de expresso mandato domini regis per dominum Delphinum.* The Presidents objected, Louis insisted, and declared he would not leave Paris until he had had his way. In the end they were obliged to give in, since the Dauphin declared that if his expedition were delayed the King would be displeased and great injury to the country might ensue.

Louis was at Compiègne on the 27th, escorted by the President of la Chambre des Comptes and the Provost of Paris, receiving a present of a cask of red wine, and being welcomed by the nobility of the district, who were courageous and intriguing, fond of war and eager to curry favour with the heir-apparent.

Louis of Luxembourg, Count of Saint-Pol, brought the Dauphin six hundred well trained men-at-arms. The Prince made the round of Vermandois, visiting the towns and winning over vacillating nobles. He rejoined his army at Corbie. There he was in a country belonging to the Duke of Burgundy, since, by the Treaty of Arras, Charles VII had surrendered to him all the towns on both banks of the Somme.

As he passed through the territory his father had given up, Louis must have gazed with envy on its woods, pastures and rich corn lands. He was invited to Amiens, where on his entrance into the city the aldermen presented him with eight casks of wine and four oxen garlanded with wreaths of periwinkle. The Dauphin was touched by this reception. He thanked the citizens for the help they had sent the King and for the interest they took in the relief of Dieppe. Amiens was gaily decorated. The guards of the gates saluted. There were games and mystery plays, in one of which figured a great ship, representing Noah's ark. Louis must have been cut to the heart at the thought that his father was making no effort to regain possession of this fine city, one of the brightest jewels of the crown, which he so passionately desired.

The citizens were delighted with the Dauphin; and after his departure they made inquiries as to the expedition he was about to undertake. Louis passed through Abbeville, which must then have been poverty-stricken, seeing that its inhabitants had to sell securities in order to make suitable presents to the Dauphin. Here Louis obtained valuable information from one Théodal le Bourgeois, who had tried in vain to relieve Dieppe. He told the Dauphin that the English occupied all the fortified châteaux in the neighbourhood, and he described the formidable fort of le Pollet, the artillery of which wrought terrible havoc. Charles Desmarets, he said, was at his last gasp. There was no time to lose. Louis straightway organised his troops in one compact company and, marching by way of Eu, arrived beneath the walls of Dieppe on the 11th of August, and encamped in the suburbs. The day after his arrival the Dauphin summoned the defenders of the fort to depart if they wished to save their lives. The English replied that they would hold out to the end.

Then Louis held a council of war and decided that he would make the assault in a few days, as soon as his artillery and other engines of war should be ready. In mid-August, on the day of Notre-Dame, about ten o'clock in the morning, after having had several casks of wine broached in order to hearten his people, who were well rested, the Dauphin commanded the trumpets to sound the assault. The attack lasted three hours. The fort was strong, well provided with large cannon, and stoutly defended.

The besiegers had to climb down into a deep moat and then up again on to the ramparts, which were defended by four to five hundred English. Three hundred were put to the sword; the remainder were taken prisoners.

Then the Dauphin took off his shoes and went barefoot to the church of Saint Jacques in Dieppe, and there in all humility thanked God his Creator, and blessed Saint Jacques, the patron of knights, for the good fortune vouchsafed to him in his combat with his ancient enemies, the English. The fort was demolished, and after the

Dauphin had stayed three days at Dieppe, he departed for Abbeville, where the townsfolk received him with joy and honour.

Thence Louis returned to Paris, spending three days with the discontented Parisians, who could not forgive him for the heavy *taille* he had imposed on them. That caustic writer, the "Citizen of Paris," remarks that when Louis was at Meaux he did not attend church but occupied himself with hunting "and such frivolity or worse."

King Charles had just summoned his son to Tours. He obeyed in all haste, for Count John IV of Armagnac was giving trouble in the south. This insolent feudatory had trafficked with the English, and boasted that he was going to marry his daughter to Henry VI.

The King, we are told, received his son right royally, and with all the nobles of his train fêted him nobly for the grand victory he had won over the English. Charles commissioned Louis, during his expedition against Armagnac, to take captive a notorious freebooter, one Severac, who held the people of Guyenne to ransom. The Dauphin arrived at Toulouse, where he received the submission of numerous nobles from whom he exacted contributions.

John of Armagnac was holding out in the strongly fortified town of l'Ile-Jourdain, where Louis blockaded him so that he gave in, in January, without any great resistance. He made as if he would come and do homage to Louis. But this humble attitude did not deceive the Dauphin, who was as wily as a fox. Armagnac found himself a prisoner, and, with his wife and two daughters, conveyed to Carcassonne.

L'Ile-Jourdain, the great stronghold of la Garonne with all its precious jewels and other treasures, was now in the King's hands. And after an expedition into Rodez, where he confiscated the estates of the Bastard of Armagnac, and a stay at Toulouse, where he received subsidies, the Dauphin, now well in funds, returned to his father's hunting-lodge of Montils-lez-Tours towards the end of April.

Bernard of Armagnac, Comte de la Marche, Louis' former tutor, had been fighting with him during this expedition; for the Dauphin, as we have seen, was not one to nourish resentment.

CHAPTER IX

PEACE WITH ENGLAND

Arrival of the English Ambassadors in France.—Their Reception by
Charles of Orléans at Blois.—Their Meeting with the King and his
Court at Tours.—Letters from the King of England.—Notable
omission of the term " Adversary " as applied to France.—Jousts
and Feasting.—A Two Years' Truce sealed by Margaret of Anjou's
Betrothal to King Henry VI.—Rejoicing throughout France.—
The Dauphin's Fears for the Future.—His Mistrust of the Influence
of Agnes.

WHILE relieving the French defenders of Dieppe, King
Charles had been making up his mind to reopen negotiations with England. For he knew that his enemies were
exhausted and that every Christian heart was longing for
peace. The English on their side appeared inclined to
avail themselves of the mediation of their ally, the Duke
of Brittany. But to make peace was as difficult and
dangerous as to make war. The French wondered how
they could humble English pride and bring a well-ordered
nation like the English, depending for its very food on
French supplies, to renounce its occupation of French
territory.

A matrimonial alliance was of course considered the
best expedient for bringing the two nations together.

On the 11th of February 1444, Henry VI appointed,
with powers to negotiate, William Pole, Earl of Suffolk ;
Adam Moleyns, Dean of Chichester, Keeper of the Privy
Seal, and others who knew Charles of Orléans well and
were his friends.

That delightfully human person, Suffolk, a noble of
merchant descent, had been the Duke's indulgent gaoler.
Suffolk himself had suffered a long term of imprisonment
in France. He knew the country well, adored its language,

G   87

and wrote love poems in it. The Earl's mission was to negotiate a marriage between the young King of England and the niece of the King of France, Margaret, the winsome daughter of King René of Anjou. Suffolk depended for success on the intervention of his quondam prisoner, Charles.

On St Valentine's Day, 1444, the Duke of Orléans and Margaret's father, the good King René, were together at Blois.

They had much in common ; for they were both men of letters and lovers of fine pictures and beautifully illuminated manuscripts. They had both known adversity and imprisonment. René had just lost his kingdom of Naples, and Charles at fifty was a confirmed invalid, whom his doctor, Nonchaloir, ordered to recline on a cushion and take a daily nap.

The Duke of Orléans must have been pleased to be able to announce to the King of France, by his herald, Valois, that the English Ambassadors were on the point of landing at Calais, and that they would be met by the Duke of Burgundy.

The Ambassadors proceeded by way of Harfleur, Rouen and Le Mans to Blois. Thence King René escorted them in state to Montils, where the King was holding his court. The letters the Ambassadors brought from their royal master " to his very high and excellent prince, our very dear uncle of France," were courtesy itself. For the first time since the beginning of the Hundred Years' War, the word *adversary*, as applied to France, was omitted from documents coming from an English chancellery.

The white-haired Charles of Orléans presented his friends to the Queen, the Dauphiness, Margaret of Scotland, and the great feudatories, who had gathered from all parts of France. Anjou was represented by the King of Sicily and his son, the Duke of Calabria ; Brittany by the Constable, Richemont, and his nephew, Duke Francis ; Burgundy by a veritable embassy, at the head of which was Jean de Croy, Count of Chimay.

Such gallant knights were not likely to lose an opportunity of ushering in the new era of peace by feasting and festivity. People in those days knew how to appreciate simple joys—the song of a bird, the green grass in the meadow, the pearly whiteness of the hawthorn flower.

On May Day, Queen Marie and the Dauphiness Margaret, with their lords and ladies, some three hundred knights and squires, rode out into the country to gather may.

On the morrow the great Duke of Burgundy himself arrived at Montils, with two hundred horse. Then two days later came Yolande, Queen of Sicily, with her daughter, the bride elect, who was another Margaret. They had come from Angers; and they took up their residence in the Abbey of Beaumont, a mile and a half out of Tours. There Margaret, the future Queen of England, then an attractive maiden of fifteen, received the English Ambassadors, and charmed Suffolk by her girlish grace and beauty.

Another wedding in this " merrie monthe of Maye "— that of the Comte du Maine with Isabelle de Luxembourg—gave occasion for high festival, jousting in the meadow and an archery contest, presided over by Pierre de Brézé and the Earl of Suffolk, at which the Scottish guard won a prize of a thousand crowns.

The peace negotiations, however, were not going smoothly. The English refused the conditions insisted on by the French—that they should renounce their claim to Normandy and Guyenne and evacuate those provinces. Finally a compromise was arrived at in a two years' truce, during which the two countries were to trade freely with one another.

The betrothal of Margaret to King Henry VI was celebrated on Sunday, the 24th of May, in the church of St Martin at Tours, by the papal legate. King Charles was there, giving his hand to his brother-in-law, King René, the bride's father. The princes of the blood followed, and after them came the Queen of France, hand in hand with the Queen of Sicily, who was accompanied by her daughter-in-law, the Duchess of Calabria. It was the Dauphin Louis who escorted the beautiful *fiancée* up the aisle to King Charles. Taking off his hood, the King gave his hand to the Princess and led her to the legate. Then the nuncio read the Pope's provisional dispensation, while the people in the nave, who beheld peace coming down from heaven like a dove, clapped their hands and cried " Noël, Noël." The Queen of France advanced to the future Queen of England and set her by her mother's side. Whereupon the procession started for the Abbey of St Julien, where a brilliant banquet had been laid out in honour of the little Queen of England. At dessert two giants appeared, bearing huge trees in their arms and two camels, with towers on their humps and men-at-arms inside, who waged a mock combat. Dancing went on well into the night.

The joy that spread through France at the news of this truce is almost indescribable. The negotiations had been eagerly followed at Paris, where all the sacred relics of the capital had been borne through the streets at the head of a procession of forty thousand people. Up and down the country the poor, whom the terrors and dangers of war had imprisoned within the walls of towns and châteaux, felt they had been delivered from the direst slavery. Along the country roads crowds of men and women were seen making pilgrimages, enjoying the woods and fields for the first time in their lives.

What part the Dauphin took in this general rejoicing we do not know. At Tours he escorted the future Queen up the aisle. But Louis was no lover of pomp and pageantry. Beneath all this noise and glitter he saw things as they were. And during those days of feasting he was having long interviews with the ambassadors of Burgundy and other foreign representatives. He was moody and grave ; for his eye was on the future ; and there were many things in his father's triumph that did not please him.

That girl Agnes, of the household of the Queen of Sicily, to whom Charles at forty seemed to have lost his heart—who was she ? Very attractive no doubt, and as fair as a Madonna. Her father was but an obscure Picard gentleman, one Jean Soreau, and the extravagance of her attire shocked everyone, especially the Dauphin, who loved simplicity. At court she was always surrounded by young men, and especially by those of the House of Anjou. Agnes's charms had bewitched that gentle knight and brilliant talker, Pierre de Brézé. Was he or she to rule the King in his middle age ? And all these people, plunging with such childish delight into rejoicing over the peace—had they a thought for the morrow ? What would happen, when war ceased, to all the mercenaries for whom war was a profession ?

CHAPTER X

Louis leads an Army of Free-lances against the Swiss Confederates.—
Cosmopolitan character of Louis' Army.—Ravages by the way.—The
Dauphin in disguise conducts a Reconnaissance at Bâle.—Battle
of Saint-Jacques.—Hand to hand fight in a Leper-house.—Defeat
of the Swiss.

WHAT was to be done with the professional soldiers, some
twenty or thirty thousand, who, ever since the Treaty of
Arras had thrown them out of employment, had lived on
brigandage ? Flayers (*écorcheurs*) they were often called,
because they flayed their victims alive, and stripped them
of everything, even to their shirts. In Alsace and Lorraine, the freebooters passed for Armagnacs. They were
to be found also in the centre of France—in Forez and
Auvergne—but more especially in Languedoc, where
Louis had encountered them. Burgundy had not escaped
this scourge. In the Somme marches they were sometimes
employed against the English. And at Dieppe Louis had
been glad to make use of certain of their captains and of
their free companies. Now, after the Truce of Tours,
their services were not needed. But how was France to
get rid of them ?

The King's Council prided itself on having solved this
difficult problem ; the Emperor Frederic,[1] whose son was
betrothed to Charles' daughter, Radegonde, needed troops
to march against the Swiss Confederates who were attacking
his ally, the town of Zurich. Why should not the freebooters be sent to his assistance under the leadership of
the Dauphin ?

[1] Nicknamed " Frederic of the Empty Purse," who reigned 1440-
1493.

They could have no better general. For Louis knew their ways and was eminently qualified to lead them to victory. The rumour soon spread that the Dauphin was at the head of an army of from sixty to seventy thousand horse. As a matter of fact, about half of these were freebooters, and, among them, including their women were hardly more than four thousand men-at-arms and six thousand bow-men. A formidable army, all the same, in those days.

Their march, all the way from Langres, where they had assembled, struck terror into the people. They represented all nations—Lombards, Gascons, Spaniards, English—they spoke all the dialects of France, all the languages of Europe. Their artillery consisted of two large cannon, firing stones weighing sixty pounds each, six field-pieces and six culverins firing leaden balls. They carried in their train ladders, grenades, powder-casks, every kind of engine of war. At the head of one of the strongest of the companies rode Louis, surrounded by his household, and accompanied by Jean de Bueil, a hero of the Norman War and one of the most capable generals of the time. Bueil was Louis' lieutenant and standard-bearer. He had three hundred Spanish veterans of the very worst reputation for his guard. Under his direct command were one hundred and forty captains, most of them men with a famous, if not an infamous, past, some of them ordinary thieves. For to eat one must live on the country, even if one belongs to a regular army.

Louis had no definite plan of campaign. As he approached Montbéliard he either heard or invented the story that a certain Henry, a Montbéliard bastard, had made war against the King of France. Louis declared that the King had charged him to avenge this war. And, as the townsfolk of Montbéliard were not organised for defence, the magistrates delivered the castle, which belonged to the Count of Wurtemberg, into Louis' hands. The Count's people were glad to make their escape, taking with them their papers, plate, and precious stones. On the 19th of August, 1444, Louis entered the town, and received messages there from the town council of Dijon, complaining of the ravages his freebooters were perpetrating in Burgundy. Duke Philip offered Louis 10,000 golden *saluts*, and his generals 3500 if they would restrain their followers. Louis did not refuse the money, but there is no evidence of his having taken steps to repress the disorderly conduct of his soldiers. How could discipline be imposed on such a rabble, crying, as they passed through the villages : " Where is your lord and master, the Duke of Burgundy ? He sleeps and you think there is none other in France."

As for beating the farm labourers, holding them to ransom, crucifying, hanging, suspending poor wretches by the feet and roasting them till they gave information, flogging them till they produced their money ! why, all freebooters did these things, not in Burgundy only, but everywhere. It was odd of the Duke to imagine that any restraint could be put upon such people. They made firewood of ploughs and fences ; they robbed mills of their iron-work, and only went to church to open reliquaries and see if they contained money.

Frederic's ambassadors arrived to ask Louis to make haste ; and, on the 23rd of August, his council decided that they would march to Bâle. The Dauphin took up his quarters near the town, in the château of Waltighoffen. On the 25th, in disguise and with only two or three companions, Louis made a tour of the walls and went right up to the gate, whence, having been greeted by a volley from an arquebus, he hastily made his way back to the château. The Swiss Confederates, who were besieging Farnsbourg, hearing of the approach of the freebooters, sent an army to intercept them. By forced marches four thousand Swiss, all picked men, fell unexpectedly on the invaders, who were encamped in the plain of Prateln, on the opposite side of the Birse, which is a little river flowing into the Rhine above Bâle. The Dauphin's Armagnacs resisted stoutly. None the less

94

Chabannes and the Spanish captain, Salazar, had to withdraw and rejoin their main body, which was strongly entrenched at Muttenz. Nothing now prevented the brave Swiss from driving the Armagnacs from their position to the opposite bank of the Birse, and taking possession of their camp and all their belongings. Then, in the teeth of the Dauphin's fire, the Swiss tried to cross the river. They endeavoured to draw up in battle array in the Saint-Alban meadow. But the Armagnacs, supported by a considerable body of German cavalry, attacked them on every hand. Some tried to cross the river, others went up the bank as far as Bâle, in order to join the citizens of that town, who were advancing to meet them, under the leadership of the Burgomaster. But the Armagnacs were upon them ; and all the Swiss could do was to take refuge in the leper-house of Saint-Jacques, entrenching themselves behind the garden walls, while every man of their compatriots on the river bank was massacred.

The slaughter in the leper-house was terrible. The French artillery having destroyed the walls, the Armagnacs burst in ; a tower, in which some of the Swiss were holding out, was set on fire ; and, suffocated by the smoke, both Armagnacs and Swiss perished in a hand to hand fight. Faithful to the words they had uttered on the previous day : "We give our souls to God and our bodies to the Armagnacs," not one of the Confederates was left alive.

The battlefield was a gruesome sight, strewn with the corpses of eight thousand Armagnacs, which were carried into the surrounding houses and burnt.

In the evening, as the freebooters were returning to their quarters in the villages, they passed a château, and one of their trumpeters blew his horn. The lord of the château came out and inquired what they wanted at so late an hour. The trumpeter replied : "We have wrestled and fought all day." "Who conquered ? " asked the lord. "The Swiss were defeated," answered the trumpeter. "And how many of you were killed ? " "At least four hundred," was the reply.

95

CHAPTER XI

ON, TOWARDS THE EMPIRE

The Results of the Battle of Saint-Jacques.—Louis' Designs on Bâle.—
Receives Envoys from the City.—Offers his Protection to the Holy
Council.—Enters the Empire.—Negotiations with the Emperor
Frederic.—Wounded at Dambach.—Claims the Rhine frontier for
France.—Signs the Treaty of Einsisheim with the Swiss.—Menaces
Strasbourg.—Dreams of the Empire.—Returns to France, having
rid the Kingdom of the Freebooters, whom he had left in Alsace.

NEWS of the Battle of Saint-Jacques reached Louis in
the little château of Waltighoffen, three leagues from Bâle,
whither he had returned after his reconnaissance of the
city. Fifteen hundred Swiss had perished, and all the
survivors were wounded. The Grand Master of the
Order of St John, Robert de Brézé, great German nobles
like Dietrich von Rathsamhausen and Burckard Munch,
lay on the battlefield. The Confederates, who were
besieging Zurich and Farnsbourg, fled in panic, abandoning
their baggage and artillery, leaving the corpses to be
stripped by plunderers.

The Dauphin thanked his captains and others who had
taken part in the battle. His counsellors advised a rapid
advance on Bâle. But Louis hesitated. For the moment
his chief concern was to give honourable burial to the
bodies of the fallen French and medical aid to the
wounded. This commander of twenty was perfectly
self-possessed. Two friars came to entreat him to be
merciful; and he received them. If Bâle were taken, he
knew that his freebooters would sack the wealthy city and
spare no one. How could the son of the Very Christian
King be a party to the ruin of the archiepiscopal city, the
seat of the Council of the Church? A campaign in the
barren Swiss mountains would be futile. Obviously the

citizens of Bâle feared him, seeing that they sought his alliance. He resolved to seek theirs. They were brave and trustworthy, people among whom mercenaries might well be recruited. An alliance with Bâle would involve an understanding with the Duke of Savoy, and the extension of the protection of France to several countries. Louis hesitated no longer. He resolved to constitute himself the protector of the Holy Council.

Meanwhile he deemed it expedient to withdraw his freebooters from the Swiss cantons and to lead them into Alsace, into the territory of the Empire. This was not exactly King Charles's idea. Only two or three days' march away from the battlefield of Saint-Jacques, Louis was on imperial ground. He himself was the Emperor's Viceroy in the province of Dauphiné and the kingdom of Arles.

Things happened much as the Dauphin had foreseen. On the 31st of August, illustrious envoys from the Council waited on Louis at Altkirch. They represented to the Dauphin that for the eldest son of the King of France to attack the seat of the Holy Council, a city so good, so peaceful, so virtuous and just, would be to strike a blow at the Christian religion and the Catholic Church, and to brand with infamy the royal House of France.

Louis declared that the object of his coming had not been to put God's Church to confusion. On the contrary, treading in the footsteps of his ancestors, he was prepared to defend the Church with his life-blood ; his object had been to destroy the adversaries of his brother and ally, the Archduke of Austria, who was affianced to his sister. Let the city of Bâle break off its alliance with the Swiss and submit to him, let it undertake not to attack the House of Austria, and Louis asked for nothing better than to leave it in peace.

Thereupon the ambassadors returned to Bâle, having concluded a truce for eight days. In order to facilitate the ambassadors' task, Louis sent envoys to Bâle, instructing them to deal faithfully with the lordless city and to impress upon the citizens that from time immemorial it had been under the protection of France. But this was mere by-play. Ambassadors from the Council, accompanied by the Bishop of Bâle and envoys from the chief Swiss towns, returned to Louis, who was then at Einsisheim. The Dauphin granted them a truce for twenty days, expressing a wish that a similar agreement might be made between the House of Austria and the Confederates. In order to prepare the way for a definite agreement, Louis formally took Bâle under his protection and sent his envoy, Gabriel de Bernes, to confer with the representatives of the Swiss towns.

The Emperor, too, had sent ambassadors to the Dauphin. United by faith and friendship to the royal House of France he had been astonished and dismayed, he said, to see Louis leading on to imperial territory an army of barbarians as numerous as they were terrible, and who were already beginning to ravage cities of the Empire. He added that he was prepared to make any agreement with Louis that would seem to him just. But the Dauphin replied that though he had come in order to assist the Emperor, he had also come to recover territory which had from time immemorial belonged to France and which had renounced allegiance to the Empire. A few days later he sent an ambassador to Nuremberg.

Meanwhile Louis had despatched his own ambassador to the Emperor ; and, while awaiting his return, he had thoughts of attacking Mulhouse. But this would have been a gross violation of international law. And Louis changed his mind and decided to wait on events at Einsisheim.

Here he was visited by numerous Alsatian notabilities, town councillors and petty nobles in search of adventure. Already the Dauphin had his eyes on Strasbourg ; and, through the influence of its Bishop, he hoped to impose his protection on that city also. But the citizens, who were very jealous of their liberties, were warned of his intentions.

Already certain strongholds in the neighbourhood were in his possession. And now, with the whole of his artillery train, the Dauphin attacked Dambach, a small fortress at the foot of the Vosges. Having made a breach in the walls, he was about to lead the assault when, on the 7th of October, an arrow, shot by one of the besieged, pierced his knee right through to the saddle. His wound was dressed at Chatenois, near Schlestadt, and thanks to his physicians, he made a rapid recovery.

But Louis did not resume active command. He spent his convalescence at Einsisheim, where an embassy from the Emperor and Duke Albert of Austria waited upon him. The Dauphin refused to be moved. He had risked his life and sacrificed his soldiers : he was fully determined to claim the Rhine frontier and to spend the winter in Alsace. In the little fortress of Einsisheim, he re-read his treaty with the Confederates, had it sealed with the great equestrian seal, and signed it with his own hand.

King Charles was growing anxious about his son's wound, and still more about the plans he was making. He urged Louis to return to court. The Dauphin, however, persisted in remaining in Alsace, and even asked that the Dauphiness Margaret should be sent to him there. The freebooters were appearing to the Alsatians in their true character. Strasbourg was up in arms ; so were the Imperial forces ; and Duke Philip was on the point of intervening.

There is no doubt that Louis was thinking of the Empire. But, before risking such an important enterprise, he decided to go to his father, who was bombarding him with letters. So he marched into Lorraine, leaving his freebooters in Alsace, where the Duke's people insulted them at every turn and refused to let them enter their cities. With a small band of horsemen Louis entered France, where the poor—and indeed all the King's subjects—might now live in peace, seeing that the Dauphin had emptied the kingdom of all those adventurers and professional soldiers who had kept it in a perpetual state of perturbation.

Louis had accomplished his mission. Now he was thinking of an alliance with the Swiss, and dreaming of becoming Emperor.

CHAPTER XII

NEGOTIATIONS AT NANCY AND AT CHÂLONS

Fighting round Metz.—Winter quarters at Nancy.—The Wedding of Margaret of Anjou.—The Dauphin's moodiness.—He conducts Negotiations with Isabelle, Duchess of Burgundy.—His strained Relations with the Duke.—Further complications.—The Affair of *l'Eveillé Qui Dort.*—Intervention of King Charles.—The Treaty of Sarry.—Gaieties at Châlons.—Return of Jean d'Angoulême from captivity in England.

WHILE the Dauphin had been leading his freebooters into Switzerland and Alsace, King Charles and King René had been fighting on the latter's behalf in his duchy of Lorraine, where René was being opposed by one of the Emperor's allies, the Count of Vaudemont. After occupying Epinal and summoning Toul and Verdun to open their gates, Charles, with an army of no fewer than thirty thousand men, marched to the aid of René, who was besieging Metz.

The operations that ensued hardly amounted to a regular siege; they were little more than a series of skirmishes and negotiations, which dragged on for several months, until Charles retired to René's court at Nancy, where he spent the winter.

At last King René was established in the capital of his duchy, where he was delighted to do the honours and to give full expression to his passion for pomp and pageantry. King Charles, too, who had spent so many years in poverty and sorrow, was now a powerful and victorious sovereign. He also began to take a pride in his appearance, donning fine clothes and hiding his bow legs beneath long robes. He was in love and anxious to please.

The Queen and the Dauphine with their ladies joined him. The Queen of Sicily came too, accompanied by the

King of England's betrothed, escorted by Bertrand de Beauvau. The Earl of Suffolk, who had recently been made a marquis, was there also, the centre of a brilliant little group of English lords and ladies, including the Earls of Salisbury and Shrewsbury, Alice Chaucer, Marchioness of Suffolk [1] and Margaret Beauchamp.

Here at Nancy, the final touches were being given to the preparations for Margaret's wedding, at which the Bishop of Toul was to officiate. During the jousts, which lasted for a week, the King of France was frequently to be seen in the lists, where the most dashing figure was that of one of the Duke of Burgundy's barons, Bertrand de la Tour. Bertrand, accompanied by his ten gentlemen, all in white satin, would parade up and down the lists, on his magnificent horse, accoutred in cloth of gold with gold tassels. These festivities went on until the departure of the young Queen of England. When Charles kissed her for the last time, the poor child was convulsed with sobs.

The Dauphin Louis, at his age—which was twenty— ought to have enjoyed such amusements; but he took no part in them. They had never appealed to him much, and now he was tired and ill. We find him writing in person to ratify the treaty between the people of Metz and their King René, and following the negotiations which were to place the bishoprics of Toul and Verdun under the protection of the King of France. Louis had also to deal with the complications that had arisen out of his campaign in Alsace.

He had heard that his main force had disappeared in an ambush at Val-de-Liepvre; but that mattered little. The placing of the royal army on a new footing was the most urgent matter, and Louis attended councils held with this object. The little Princess Radegonde, who had been affianced to the Emperor's son, was dead. Consequently her betrothed, having no longer any reason for sparing the kingdom of France, demanded from the

---

[1] Daughter of Thomas Chaucer, who was in all likelihood the son of the poet. (D.N.B. Thomas Chaucer.)

Dauphin an indemnity of 600,000 florins for his Swiss campaign.

The Court left Nancy towards the end of April. The Queen with the Dauphiness went to Châlons, where they arrived on the 4th of May. And while King Charles visited his towns on the Meuse, he left his son to open negotiations concerning the frontiers of France, with Isabelle, Duchess of Burgundy.

Queen Marie of Anjou gave the Duchess a ceremonious but cordial reception. Isabelle sat at Margaret's table; and the Dauphiness treated her with as much deference as if she had been a Queen, kneeling low when she rose from table. But the Dauphin, who at that time was not on the best of terms with the Duchess's husband, was cold and reserved with her. The autocratic and chivalrous Philip had no sympathy with a rebellious son. Besides, the Dauphin's soldiers had made too many incursions into Burgundian territory. The freebooters had emptied too many houses and burned alive too many people. Then there was the question of indemnity to be settled and the matter of the Montbéliard fortress, a constant menace to the county of Burgundy, occupied as it was by the Dauphin's men, under the command of his trusted follower, Joachim Rouault. King Charles endeavoured to explain and to curb the excesses of the freebooters. But the Dauphin continued to equivocate, to support and justify his followers. As far as he himself was concerned, he refused to ratify the Treaty of Arras, thus revealing one of the main objects of his policy. And at the very time when he ought to have been promoting friendship between France and the Duke, Louis was making common cause with his friends, the people of Dieppe, who were involved in a serious dispute with Burgundy.

A little whaler, *l'Eveillé qui dort*, lying in wait for English vessels, had captured one of them off the Flemish port, Sluys, was making for Dieppe with its prize in tow, when the prize was reft from it by Flemish vessels and carried off to Bruges, where the English sailors, who manned it, were executed. Charles Desmarets of Dieppe was inclined to settle the dispute by recourse to arms. But the Dauphin adopted more pacific means. On behalf of the people of Dieppe he had written to the aldermen of Bruges. He addressed them, however, as if they were the vassals of the French crown.

This incident was not calculated to promote an understanding between France and Burgundy ; and the moment for the opening of negotiations—apparently desired by the Dauphin—between the two Houses seemed to have been ill chosen. They covered an immense field : Burgundy demanded respect of the Artois and Burgundian frontiers, freedom for the Flemish ports, ratification of the Treaty of Arras by the Dauphin, evacuation of Montbéliard, payment of King René's ransom and of an indemnity for the ravages of the freebooters, the foundation of obits for the repose of the soul of Jean-sans-Peur.[1] For three weeks the Dauphin, by turns sarcastic and suave, supple and violent, did his best to prolong the debate and prevent any settlement. Isabelle was patient and reasonable, but firm. This made Louis all the more bitter and violent ; and they had words. Meanwhile Charles Desmarets' sailors continued their piracy and captured two fishing-boats at Nieuport. Finally, on the 29th of May 1445, the intervention of Charles VII changed the course and the spirit of the negotiations.

Charles took up his residence at Sarry, in the Bishop's charming castle. Those spring days were delightful, and it was pleasant to saunter along the green banks of the Marne, gathering flowers in the meadows, and to see the churches of Châlons, glittering in the sunlight behind the ramparts, half concealed by trees.

In this bright atmosphere difficulties soon vanished and an agreement was arrived at : René recovered his fortresses of Clermont-en-Argonne and Neufchâteau without paying his ransom, but Louis lost Montbéliard,

---

[1] Duke of Burgundy, assassinated on the Bridge of Montereau in 1419.

which returned to the Counts of Wurtemberg. The Dauphin, tricked, was compelled to ratify the Treaty of Arras. This was a triumph for the House of Anjou—but, as was often the case in those troubled times, a triumph of short duration.

Charles of Anjou, Count of Maine, who had just married into the House of Luxembourg, was the life of that brilliant party, in which another striking figure was the gallant knight le Comte de Saint-Pol, his brother-in-law. One evening when the Kings of France and Sicily were amusing themselves in the fields, gathering grasses and wild flowers, they met Charles of Anjou and Saint-Pol with a troop of knights and squires ; and they all fell to talking of ladies and of the magnificence of the Duke of Burgundy, who understood so well the ordering of feasts and festivities, and who was of all French princes the most courteous, debonnaire, wise and generous. Then the Counts of Maine and Saint-Pol withdrew a little and talked apart. " Why should we not devise something to make a stir ? We have heard our ladies being told of the feasting, dancing, jousting and carolling which goes on every day at the Duke of Burgundy's court, while we at the King's court do nothing but sleep, drink and eat, without practising the noble profession of arms. Surely it is in no way seemly that we should spend our time in idleness." So they resolved to hold a tournament and challenge all comers for the space of eight days.

The master of the ceremonies was to be Jacquet de Lalaing, a squire of twenty-two in the service of my Lord of Clèves, and trained in the Burgundian tournaments. He was good and brave, tall and fresh coloured as a rose. He took Marie de Clèves as his lady. " Whoever serves the brother should serve the sister also." She gave him a rod of gold set with a fine ruby. And Jacquet, at the tournament, appeared with a beautiful collaret trimmed with pearls presented to him by Jean d'Anjou's young wife, the Duchess of Calabria ; for she also desired to be his lady. And both Mme de Clèves and Mme de

Calabre wished their husbands resembled Jacquet. At the banquet they sat one on each side of him. And while Mme de Clèves, all unknown to Mme de Calabre, was stealthily presenting him with a diamond, Mme de Calabre, all unknown to Mme de Clèves, was secretly slipping a ruby ring on to his finger. He accepted these gifts in all honour, not forgetting the advice his father had given him when he left Burgundy, to refrain from anything for which God or society could reproach him. Then they danced to the accompaniment of melodious instruments and drank spiced wine.

At dinner there appeared Jean d'Angoulême, the brother of Charles d'Orléans, who had just been delivered from his long captivity in England. A hearty welcome was accorded to this sad and pious man, with reeved brow and emaciated hands. He also joined in the dance, a slow Burgundian step, dancing with the Queen of Sicily, the playful Mme of Calabria, and the Dauphiness, who was always attractive and always extravagant.

Meanwhile the Dauphin looked on, grave and jealous.

CHAPTER XIII

THE DEATH OF THE DAUPHINESS

Failure of her Marriage.—Kindness of the King and Queen.—Monotony of her Life at Court.—Her Love of Poetry.—The Dauphin's Jealousy.—He sets Jamet de Tillay to spy upon her.—A Fatal Pilgrimage.—Sudden Illness.—Forsaken by the Court and her Husband.—Death in the Convent of Saint Étienne at Châlons.

LOUIS' marriage was a complete failure.[1] While the King and Queen, charmed by Margaret's vivacity, indulged her in her love of dress, her husband neglected her ; and they were seldom to be seen together. Though everyone else found her fascinating, Louis complained that her breath was offensive and that she bore him no children. His real grievance was, however, that Margaret had not been the woman of his choice, but the wife his father had forced on him ; and Louis never liked anything of his father's choosing.

For Margaret was much more the child of King Charles and Queen Marie than the wife of the Dauphin. She spent her time with the pious Queen, who was a docile wife, very plain and very simple. Day after day passed in unrelieved monotony, in telling of beads, attendance at church, keeping of accounts, needlework, sometimes accompanied by the reading aloud of historical chronicles, while the listeners ate nuts and sweetmeats.

The books of la Tour Landry and Christine de Pisan give a faithful picture of the grey monotony of a young girl's life in those times. Devoutness and chastity were the first things required of her. Her demeanour must always be correct. She must speak seldom, laugh with moderation, always submit to the wishes of her lord and master, her husband.

[1] See " la Dauphine Mélancolique." Pierre Champion (Paris).

Margaret was not at all like that. Hers was a strong personality, not in the least French. She was a petulant Stuart, a gay and lively Scottish lassie. Delicate in health and consumptive, her tendency was to be excessive in everything, too confidential, too fanciful, too exuberant. A devotee of fashion, at a time when slim figures were in vogue, she determined to make herself as thin as possible ; so she wrapped her gowns tightly round her, and for fear she should grow stout, ate green apples and drank vinegar. She had the lively imagination of her romantic father, the poet King, who had recently suffered such a tragic death. Hers was a world of fancy, the world described in that poem of Master Alain Chartier, *la Belle Dame sans Mercy*, which was both admired and detested at court. Margaret, who had learned the tongue of her adopted land, was charmed with the French language and bewitched by French poetry. They helped her to forget her misfortunes, just as they helped men to forget their troubles in those hard times. The most fashionable poems in those days were those elegant little rondeaux about the feast of St Valentine and the affected sorrows of love-lorn knights and ladies. They were not difficult to turn, and everyone wrote them—Margaret better than anyone. So absorbed did she become in this pastime that dawn often surprised her at her desk.

Unfortunately not one of these compositions has come down to us. Her prosaic husband had them all destroyed. But the ladies of her household wrote verses, and some of these have been preserved, the following, for instance, by Jeanne Filleul, who writes to her lover :—

> *Hélas ! mon amy, sur mon ame,*
> *Plus qu' aultre femme*
> *J'ay de douleur si largement*
> *Que nullement*
> *Avoir confort je ne puis d'ame.*[1]

[1] Alas ! my friend, on my heart, I suffer more than any woman, and my grief is so great that my heart knows no consolation.

And Margaret too, like Jeanne Filleul, suffered *largement*. Another of her ladies, Mademoiselle de Salignac, sang of her mistress's charms. Among the young nobles who shared her love for poetry was the captain of the cross-bowmen, Jean d'Estouteville, Lord of Torcy and Blainville, cultured and brave, a typical man of fashion of that day. Her poet-in-chief was Blosseville, who may doubtless be identified with Jean de Saint-Maard, a Norman captain who was in touch with the Grand Seneschal Pierre de Brézé. Blosseville, who collaborated with Charles d'Orléans, used to declare himself the devoted servant of her whose initial he wore embroidered on his coat :—

> *Et serviray mieulx qu'aultre fame*
> *Celle pour qui je porte l'M.*[1]

All this philandering made a bad impression on a court as strict as that of Marie d'Anjou. Preachers, theologians and old people began to shake their heads and say : " All this extolling of beauty, this kissing at dances, this courteous love-making may be quite innocent, but where will it lead ? " Doubtless to something worse. The Dauphin agreed with the moralists. He hated his wife and detested all this choosing of knights by ladies, this dancing on into the small hours, this drinking of spiced wine.

We have seen that Louis, though young, never took part in the Nancy revels. Standing aloof, he looked on while his middle-aged father played the dandy and ran after that Agnes, whose low necks and startling gowns disgusted the young Dauphin. But the person Louis observed most keenly was his own wife, and to help him spy upon her he employed one of his own men, Messire Jamet de Tillay. The creature was a member of the lower Breton nobility, brave but unscrupulous. Louis made him his counsellor and chamberlain. Margaret disliked Jamet. She knew him for a spy and a chatterbox,

---

[1] And better than any other lady will I serve her for whom I wear the M.

bent on making bad blood between her and the Dauphin.
For Jamet had already represented her to her husband as
frivolous and imprudent. Jamet was one of those who
listen at keyholes and sneak into rooms where they are not
expected. One evening at Nancy, about Christmas time,
he entered Margaret's apartment with his steward Regnault de Dresnay. A bright fire was burning on the
hearth, but there were no torches or candles. Jamet, by
the light of a taper he held in his hand, groped his way
to Margaret's couch. There he found that gallant
soldier poet, M. de Blainville, leaning on his elbow at her
side, and another knight whom he did not recognise.
Jamet left the room with a highly indignant air. It was
scandalous, he said, of the steward not to have put torches
in Margaret's chamber. He went about saying that the
Dauphine was more like a harlot than a great lady.

During the Châlons festivities, while the ladies of
Orléans and Calabria were giving jewels to Jacquet de
Lalaing, Margaret was emptying her caskets for the
benefit of another knight, Charles Morillon. Her
generosity, duly reported to the Dauphin, drove him into
a fury. He accused one of the ladies of her household,
her favourite, Pregénte of Melun, of encouraging the
Dauphiness in her frivolity and of persuading her to
sit up at night writing rondeaux. But Louis detested all
Margaret's ladies—the young women, like Pregénte,
who was accused of keeping love-songs and ballads in her
coffer, and Jacqueline de Baqueville, who was twenty-five,
and the duennas of forty, like la Dame de Saint-Michel
and Marguerite de Vaux.
Towards the end of July, 1445, Jamet de Tillay's evil
genius began to do its worst.
As the King had brought his negotiations with Burgundy to a successful close, he began to think of returning
to the Loire, and to make preparations for departure.
The removal of the court with all its furniture and
baggage was never an easy matter. The King consulted

Jamet de Tillay, and then decided that on account of the
lack of sufficient accommodation on the way for such
immense trains of wagons and carriages, it would be
advisable for the court to split up—for the King and Queen
to travel by different routes. Queen Marie was to start
first and to proceed by shorter stages than the King.
Charles, of course, may have wanted to be left alone with
Agnes. Margaret was accustomed to travel with the
Queen. But Jamet confided her husband's plans to
Marie d'Anjou, and suggested that Margaret should
travel by yet a third route, because she had so much
baggage and so many ladies. The Queen, though reluc-
tant, agreed like a humble and docile wife. The King's
steward, Jean de la Haye, however, soon made it known
that Jamet had anticipated, and that none of these plans
had been definitely settled. Margaret was not pleased
with this ordering of her journey; but the journey she
was eventually to take was a very different one.

On the eve of departure it was customary to make
a pilgrimage. King Charles resolved that before leaving
Châlons he would visit the shrine of Notre-Dame de
l'Epine. It was an ancient sanctuary, which was being
rebuilt, in honour of the perpetual virginity of Mary,
symbolised by the thorn or the burning bush. Margaret
went with the King. It was a hot August day; and when
she returned to her icy cold room in the ancient Bishop's
palace, la Dauphine took off her frock and sat in her
petticoat. She caught cold; and the next day she was
very ill with a hacking cough. To ensure her being
kept perfectly quiet, she was taken to the cathedral
convent; and an order was given for all the church bells
in the town to cease ringing.

This sudden illness surprised everyone. For Margaret
had seemed brightness itself. The Dauphin's physician,
Guillaume Leothier, a man of fifty-six, who had been with
Louis since he was a child, pronounced her to be suffering
from a severe cold and said that her lungs were affected.
But the malicious Jamet, ever on the watch, gave a very

different report. Margaret had sat up too late, he said, had written too many rondeaux, and—he added in a whisper—had had too many love-affairs.

Suddenly every one abandoned the Dauphiness. It was not etiquette for the King and Queen to go to her. But her husband did not visit her either. Margaret was left alone with her ladies and her physicians; and they tormented rather than consoled her. For they were bent on reconciling her with God, and they knew that Margaret was resolved not to forgive the wicked calumniator whose slander was the cause of all her trouble. In the intervals of her fits of coughing Margaret would assert her innocence: " I call God to witness," she would say, " and I swear on my soul and the holy water with which I was sprinkled at the font, that I have never wronged my Lord." Pierre de Brézé, who was present at this doleful scene, came forth sadly from the room, saying: " The sorrow and the anger of this lady are piteous to behold." Then, with his mind full of Jamet, the Seneschal cried: " Ah! you false, wicked scoundrel, you are the cause of her death! "

Madame must forgive Jamet before she dies. All who are with her are resolved on this—her ladies and the King's physician, Master Robert Poitevin, who is also a priest and who comes to hear her confession. Madame says she forgives every one. But Jamet's name does not cross her lips. Meanwhile she makes no effort to live; she remains sunk in melancholy. Why must they plague her with all these questions? " Madame, are you thinking of God? " asks Master Robert. " Yea, Master." " Do not forget Him, Madame." And in a weak voice comes the answer: " Nay, I forget Him not." Then the priest puts the all-important question. " Is it true that you have forgiven everyone? " Whereupon Margaret, with one last effort, exclaims energetically: " No, in truth! " " But, Madame, you ought to; you must! " Still he dares not utter the hated name. A taper is put in the hands of the dying woman. Can it be that she has followed in her Saviour's footsteps and has forgiven ? Will the Heavens open and will the Virgin and her saints receive her soul when it issues from her forehead in the form of a little child borne by angels ? Those who listen most intently catch a murmur. The Dauphine, looking back over her life, is muttering that, were it not for her faith, she would regret having ever come to France.

Then Master Jean Boutet, the Dauphin's apothecary and valet, perhaps one of his spies, draws near to Margaret's bed and catches her last whisper, the last words of a young woman of twenty-one : " Fie upon the life of this world. Speak not of it, for it wearies me more than aught else."

CHAPTER XIV

Court Intrigues.—Louis plots to overthrow his Father.—Betrayed by his Confederates.—His Banishment for four months to Dauphiné prolonged to ten years.—His able Rule a foreshadowing of what he will do as King.—Creation of a Standing Army.—Organisation and Centralisation of Government.—Financial Measures.—Protection of Industry.—Establishment of Fairs.—Upkeep of Roads.— Foundation of a University.—Happiness of Louis' Bachelor Life in Dauphiné.

THE inquiry, which the King ordered to be made at Tours, and other incidents following Margaret's death, show clearly that Charles was surrounded by plotters and intriguers, who were endeavouring to manage him.

Louis had no confidence in his father. Nevertheless, he served the King intelligently and energetically in the various missions entrusted to him. Meanwhile he was trying to gather into his hand the tangled threads of the numerous court intrigues, which were ramifying all round the King. Sometimes Louis seemed as clay in his father's hand, at others he would appear to be trying to usurp him. The Dauphin's impatience and loquacity were his ruin. For example, at one time he even attempted to curry favour with Agnes, and gave her presents; then disputes arose. One day, it would appear, Louis actually brandished his sword at the King's favourite and gave her a box on the ear. Though we cannot vouch for the accuracy of this story, of three things we may be certain : that Louis had resolved to be master, to ruin Pierre de Brézé, the Seneschal of Normandy, who stood in his way, and to disband King Charles's Scottish body-guard.

In order to carry out these designs Louis sought the aid of a certain captain, one Antoine de Chabannes, Comte de Dammartin, an ambitious and unscrupulous soldier, who had served with him in Switzerland. But Chabannes, somewhat alarmed by the far-reaching scope of the Dauphin's plans, was from the first a rather unwilling agent. "The thing is easier said than done," he remonstrated, when Louis was describing how with twenty cross-bowmen, thirty archers, and the gentlemen of his household, he would turn out the King's Scottish guard and take possession of his person. To one of the Dauphin's advisers, Amaury d'Estissac, Chabannes said : "I do not think my Lord the Dauphin is acting wisely. Speak to him and try to dissuade him. He will listen to you and take your advice more than that of anyone." But d'Estissac was not in the least anxious to play this part. He knew his young master to be the most suspicious of men ; and he told Chabannes that Louis actually suspected him, Chabannes, of being a spy in the Seneschal's service.

At any rate the King and the Seneschal were perfectly aware of all Louis' projects. On the 27th of September 1446, the Chancellor heard the evidence of Antoine de Chabannes, and a little later that of the Sire de Bueil and of the archers of the Scottish guard.

The fox had been caught ; and, as we learn from the chronicles of the House of Chabannes, it was Antoine de Chabannes himself who had set the trap.

Then Charles sent for his son and reproached him. "Louis," he said, "I know you dislike the Seneschal, who is my loyal servant, and I know that you have plotted to take his life. But that you will not do." "My Lord," replied the Dauphin boldly, "all that I have done in this matter was by the counsel of the Comte de Dammartin." "By St John," said the King, "I do not believe you." And he sent for Chabannes. "Count," he said, "have you advised the Dauphin to compass the death of the Grand Seneschal of Normandy ? " Chabannes denied it.

"Saving my lord's honour, you lie!" cried the Dauphin. "My Lord," answered Chabannes, "were you not the King's son, I would answer that accusation with my own person against yours." The King intervened, and, addressing his son, said: "Louis, for four months I banish you from my kingdom. You will go to Dauphiné."

Then the Dauphin went out bareheaded, saying: "By this head, now uncovered, I will have my revenge on those who have driven me forth."

Louis started for Dauphiné a few days after the birth of his brother, Charles, who was to become his bitter enemy.

Louis' four months in Dauphiné, intended by the King to be a short term of punishment during which he would merely have time to receive the homage of the province and to carry out the royal policy with regard to Genoa, was to be prolonged into ten years of admirable government in face of very great difficulties. Whenever Louis took up a task, he never failed to carry it out conscientiously and with all the resources of his extraordinary intelligence. Here in Dauphiné we find him foreshadowing what he will be as King.

As we have seen, he had first visited this disturbed province with his father in 1437. Since then his government, carried on chiefly by means of admirably chosen jurists from Lyons, had done him great credit. But now, in January 1447, the Dauphin was to enter into much more direct relations with his appanage.

On the 7th of the month he was at Lyons, on the 15th in Dauphiné, at Saint-Symphorien-d'Oson, accompanied by a numerous train, most of whom remained his faithful servants.

Louis was resolved to play the part of King, consequently he needed ministers. These he found for the most part among the lower nobility.

He acted as a sovereign from the first. He summoned all holders of fiefs to come within the space of one month to do homage and take the oath of allegiance to him. He made a progress through the Rhône valley, halting at the most important centres—Romans, Valence and Montélimar. Here he saw nobles who had come from all parts of the province. We find him providing for the working of mines, confirming the religious foundations of his predecessors, appointing to offices, confirming the privileges and liberties of towns and religious orders, endowing certain monasteries. Always a sportsman, he adjured his counsellors to forbid hunting without permission in the Dauphin's forests, woods and warrens (except in the case of bears, wolves, foxes and chamois), and the cutting and removing of wood in the said forests, save dead and dry wood—and that must only be removed with the permission of the foresters. Louis also odrered the owners of castles to keep up and preserve warrens, and he regulated grazing rights in the forests.

Like a regular sovereign, he organised his chancellery at Romans on the lines of the great chancellery of France. He appointed twelve secretaries, who were to write the letters signed by his chancellor. They were all reliable men; and most of them were to become rich and important; for Louis always paid well. One of them, Jean Bochetel, the Dauphin had stolen from his father; he came from Reims and had married Jacques Cœur's sister; another, Jean Bourré, whom he had met at Paris, at the University, was to be his lifelong friend.

After going on a pilgrimage to the monastery of La Sainte-Baume and to the Abbey of Saint Antoine-en-Viennois, the Dauphin made his state entry into his new capital, Grenoble, on the 17th of August 1447.

Louis' main concern was to concentrate in his own hand the powers exercised by certain feudal lords—ecclesiastical especially. Earlier in the century one village in Dauphiné had owed allegiance to no fewer than twenty-four suzerains, each independent of the other. A great part of the province was allodial, which generally meant that it was seized by the strongest; and in 1449,

Louis caused the Assembly of the three provincial estates to decree that henceforth all allodial lands should contribute to the voluntary contributions, aids and subsidies of the province. He succeeded, by means of an exchange, in acquiring a part of the town of Montélimar which belonged to the Roman Empire.

Finally, in 1450, after difficult and prolonged negotiations, Louis succeeded in doing something that none of his predecessors had been able to accomplish—in constraining the Archbishop of Vienne and the Bishops of Gap, Valence, Die and Grenoble to recognise his sovereignty. Thus ended the temporal power of the ecclesiastical dignitaries erected on the ruins of the kingdoms of Arles and Vienne. In 1452, Louis even checkmated his father by nominating his protégé, Antoine de Boissieu, to the archiepiscopal see of Vienne. An ordinance of 1453 separated the judicial, military and executive powers, and the Council of Dauphiné became a kind of Parliament, an imitation of the Parlement of Paris. The province bristled with lawyers. Louis organised them. And the Grenoble Chambre des Comptes became a well-ordered revenue office.

The Dauphin, again in the capacity of sovereign, established a standing army of five companies of men-at-arms and artillery, to which he added a few companies of cross-bowmen ; and to promote recruiting he promised exemption from taxation to any of his subjects who would enlist. The nobles who owed him military service were to serve at their own expense. Numerous commoners who enlisted were rewarded by patents of nobility.

In disputes between nobles the Dauphin prohibited any recourse to violence. In the large towns he encouraged the formation of companies of knights-archers, recruited from the *bourgeoisie*. At Grenoble all games not tending to promote efficiency in the defence of the country were prohibited. Louis saw that the roads were kept in good repair, and instituted open fairs on the ancient high road to Italy, at Gap, Montélimar, Valence and Briançon. Taxes interfering with the free circulation of merchandise were reduced. The office of factory inspector was created for the inspection of the famous linen manufactures of Dauphiné. By stationing horsemen from his stables at intervals along the principal roads, Louis instituted something like a post. He took Jewish bankers under his protection. His province must be a source of revenue ; consequently it must be prosperous ; and in districts that had suffered from pestilence, fire or devastation by war, subsidies and aids were reduced.

Nothing escaped the Dauphin's vigilant and resourceful attention, neither parts nor the whole, neither things spiritual nor temporal. Thus, on the 26th of July 1452, he founded a University at Valence and granted great and special privileges to its students. In his preamble to the decree establishing this foundation, Louis, who was then in the town, praised its delightful situation, its fine climate, its delicious air and its facilities for communication with other towns and the surrounding provinces. He prescribed every detail of the organisation of the University, the object of its studies, its constitution and privileges. It was to consist of four departments : theology, civil and canon law, medicine, and letters. And this infant University was to be placed on an equal footing with the ancient Universities of Orléans, Montpellier and Toulouse.

Louis' praise of Valence would seem to indicate that he was happy in his Dauphiné. It was indeed his work. There he was master. In its green forests he loved to hunt game, big and little, deer, boars, and even bears. Sport was a relaxation to him. Not only did it discipline his body, but it brought him into contact with the trees, the fields, and the simple folk of his domain. One, Etienne Cyvers, who plunged into a pond and was nearly drowned when chasing a stag, Louis exempted from taxation. The same exemption was granted to Pierre François, who presented him with several birds of prey, and to his falconer, Deniset Branchart.

Photo : A. Giraudon

THE DAUPHIN LOUIS
(*From the Arras Collection*)

Louis in his bachelor life at Grenoble must have been much happier than at his father's court at Montils-lez-Tours. His mistress was the daughter of a respected notary of the capital, Guyette Durand, whom he married successively to Charles de Seillons, one of his secretaries, and to Grâce d'Archelles, his equerry. He had two daughters by Noble Félise Reynard, daughter of a noble house and widow of Jean Pic, squire and captain, and lord of the castle of Beaumont-en-Trièves. Louis legitimised these children and gave them princely dowries; one married Louis, Bastard of Bourbon, Admiral of France; and the other Aimar de Poitiers, Lord of Saint-Vallier, one of his chamberlains.

Dauphiné prospered under Louis' rule.

CHAPTER XV

I.—ALLIANCE WITH SAVOY; II.—FLIGHT TO GENAPPE

I

Louis' opinion of his Father's Governnment.—The Death of Agnes.—
Treaty of Arbitration and Free Trade between Savoy and Dauphiné.
—Marriage Negotiations.—Charles's Disapproval.—Wedding of the
Dauphin and Charlotte of Savoy at Chambéry.—Disputes between
Father and Son.—Refusal of Louis' request for the Governorship
of Guyenne.—He is superseded in his Negotiations with Savoy.—
His Terror of his Father.—His Flight from Dauphiné.

WHILE at work in Dauphiné, Louis never lost sight of
his interests in France. He kept himself well-informed
of all that was going on at court. His spies were in his
father's household, as they had been in his wife Margaret's.
He used to say of Charles in those days : " The King is
behaving as badly as possible ; but I will change all that.
When I go back I shall get rid of Agnes ; I shall turn the
King from his follies; and everything will be much
better." The King, he would say, is occupied with
such trifles as the recapture of Genoa and the establishment
of his control over Asti, when he ought to be thinking of
reconquering Normandy. Pierre de Brézé must be got
rid of. He will never understand anything, for he is
a mere echo of Agnes.

The Duke of Burgundy was in the plot, and was to
provide 100,000 crowns or more. For Duke Philip had
told Louis that it was with him he wished to deal and
not with the King, that the kingdom would be better
in Louis' hands, and that Charles ought to retire to
a hermitage like the Duke of Savoy.[1] These at least were

---

[1] Amadeus VIII, then the anti-pope, Felix V. He was father of the
reigning Duke of Savoy, Louis, whose daughter the Dauphin married.

the revelations of a certain Guillaume Mariette, the King's notary and secretary, later the Dauphin's Master of Requests : a man who played a double part, and ended by being arrested at Lyons, imprisoned in the Bastille, beheaded and quartered at Tours. But the Dauphin was not to have his money. For Agnes died suddenly in 1450. And in the following year began the trial of Jacques Cœur, the famous banker, who had financed the campaign in Normandy, and who was now accused of having poisoned the King's mistress. But in Charles's opinion his chief offence had been " conspiring against the King's person." This can only have been by means of funds supplied to the Dauphin, in the plots he was for ever hatching against his father. Jacques Cœur, like many another great financier, was probably not averse to risking considerable stakes on political adventures and revolutions.

One of Louis' most powerful neighbours in Dauphiné was Louis, Duke of Savoy, the keeper of the gates of Italy, who ruled over the fertile valleys of Piedmont. The Dauphin was anxious to keep the peace with Savoy. In 1446, there had been a treaty establishing free trade between Savoy and Dauphiné. And now—on the 2nd of August 1449—Louis signed another treaty, as modern in spirit as was the mind of the Prince who conceived it. There was to be absolute free trade between the two countries, peaceful settlement of all disputes by four counsellors, extradition of criminals, refusal to receive in the respective countries the enemies of either, but in case of war with other powers mutual aid of certain specified military forces, including 2000 horse.

In compliance with the terms of this treaty, in May 1450, Louis sent the Bastard of Armagnac to offer the Duke of Savoy assistance in his war against Sforza of Milan. Louis also expressed a wish to visit the court of Savoy, provided he should find the Duchess and her daughters there.

For Louis was thinking of marrying Charlotte of Savoy, who was then eleven years old. It would be, of course, a merely diplomatic alliance. Louis seemed to be establishing himself in Dauphiné permanently. But in reality he had other irons in the fire. After the Norman campaign he had endeavoured to obtain the governorship of that province; and with this object he tried to win the support of Thomas Basin, Bishop of Lisieux. But the Bishop betrayed him to Charles VII; a piece of treachery for which Louis was to repay him a hundredfold.

Louis' main concern in these marital negotiations with Savoy was Charlotte's dowry: he demanded 400,000 crowns down; or, if the money were not immediately obtainable, the county of Nice and its dependent territory as security. The Duke was not averse to these proposals; but he was as crafty as the Dauphin, and he fully intended to haggle over the terms. He began by submitting them to his father, Pope Felix V.

While sending one ambassador to the court of Savoy, the Dauphin had been despatching another, his steward, Geoffrey Chausson, to Normandy. All this time he was apparently on friendly terms with his father. They were sending one another presents at the New Year: Louis' had been a leopard. He was very fond of wild beasts. Whether his father shared this preference may be doubted. But of one thing we may be sure; that the King thoroughly disapproved of the Savoy marriage. Charlotte was not yet of marriageable age; and it was highly necessary that Louis should have children. The Dauphin, on his side, reminded the King through his ambassadors, that it was high time he married, and that, while formerly it was the King who selected the Dauphin's consort, it was now for Louis to take to himself a wife of his own choosing. Charlotte would bring a substantial dowry. Moreover, the Savoy alliance would further Charles's designs on Milan, Genoa and other territories, in the conquest of which he would be aided by Duke Louis. The Dauphin now, as always, dilated on his poverty; he

had not sufficient to keep up his state as the son of a king.
He must have some new source of revenue. He asked
for an additional domain, Guyenne for instance, a province
of no great value, which he might win from the English.
He hoped his father would pay no heed to the evil reports
concerning him. He was innocent. He had been banished
without cause, and would never cease to protest against
the accusations of his enemies.

Such fine words never deceived Charles. He was in
no haste to reply. But he sent his son gifts and also one
of his counsellors, Thibaud de Luçay, charged to make
known the King's intentions. A marriage with a daughter
of Savoy could be of no advantage to the French crown,
which was already allied to that power. A marriage with
Eleanor of Portugal or the King of Hungary's sister would
be much more advantageous. As for Louis' request for
Guyenne, that was flatly refused.

The King added that he had not banished his son,
but had merely sent him to Dauphiné for a short time,
long enough to receive homage and collect aids. Louis,
however, had shown no desire to return, and he had
annoyed the King by his attitude towards the Church in
Dauphiné. It was even said that he was on the verge of
taking possession of the papal County of Venaissin. The
King's ambassador was instructed—should occasion arise—
to remind Louis that he had dismissed the four counsellors
whom the King, at the time of his leaving France, had
appointed to advise him, and that more recently he had
got rid of other members of his household on the plea
that they kept the King informed of his doings. Louis
was to be told that his behaviour was causing great anxiety
at the French court, and that the King was sending his
herald, Normandy King-at-Arms, in all haste to the Duke
of Savoy, to inform him of Charles's surprise that this
marriage should have been arranged without his consent.

But before the 8th of March 1451, the day on which
the Herald reached Chambéry, where the Duke was
holding his court, the contract had been signed, and the

marriage was about to be celebrated. On the 14th of February, at the Franciscan convent at Geneva, Louis had agreed to receive as Charlotte's dowry 200,000 crowns, 15,000 of which the Duke paid immediately, and Louis had received the Duke's undertaking to pay Charlotte 15,000 gold crowns annually until she should have attained marriageable age. The Herald was recognised as soon as he arrived at Chambéry. Louis asked him for his papers in order that he might give them to the Duke, and offered to pay Normandy's expenses if he would go off to Grenoble and amuse himself there for four or five days. But the Herald refused; for he had heard that the wedding was to take place the next day. So he went to the castle instead; and there in the chapel, he saw the Dauphin, wearing a long crimson robe, lined with ermine, married to the Princess Charlotte, who wore a brocaded petticoat and a cloak of crimson velvet.

There was now nothing for the King-at-Arms to do but to return to France. He took with him a despatch from the Duke of Savoy to King Charles, in which the Duke excused himself on the ground that the wedding had taken place before he received the King's letters. Let not the King mourn, wrote the Duke, but rather rejoice in that great good would accrue from the marriage. The bride's brother, the Prince of Piedmont, had recognised the Dauphin as his lord and master and undertaken to support him against all his enemies, including the King himself, in the event of his displeasure causing him to take measures against his son.

The King was furious. The Dauphin was delighted. His capital, Grenoble, had welcomed the little bride with all manner of rejoicing. His chief towns had voted him subsidies as wedding gifts. He had rewarded the Duke's counsellors handsomely, and now, in conjunction with his father-in-law, he was preparing an expedition into Italy, directed against his father's ally, Sforza, Duke of Milan. But Venice formed a league against Milan. On all sides there was intrigue, treachery, lying: and, as the result of the imbroglio, the expedition of the two Louis came to nothing.

The Dauphin was now at liberty to renew his offers to his father concerning Guyenne, where, as he happened to know, a large army of English had landed near Bordeaux. But Charles was inexorable. He circulated letters, explaining his relations with Louis, announcing that he was about to take Dauphiné from him, that there were fourteen counts, on any one of which a father might disinherit his son, and on no fewer than seven of which the Dauphin was guilty.

Meanwhile what the Dauphin was precisely aiming at no one knew. *Louis è homo inquieto et cupido de nove cose*, wrote the Milanese ambassador. At any rate he seemed to be preparing to resist his father : buying arms, fortifying strongholds and keeping in touch with the Duke of Burgundy, the Duke of Alençon, the Count of Armagnac and the Duke of Milan. At one time he thought of marching on Genoa, at another of turning against Bresse.

II

But events were rapidly taking things out of the Dauphin's hands. In August 1455, the King despatched Dunois and the Constable to Geneva to settle all questions in dispute between the Duke of Savoy and the King. Chabannes was sent to Lyons to direct military operations there, should they be needed.

The Dauphin was seized by that wild fear which came over him from time to time. He saw himself a prisoner in his father's hands. Panic-stricken, he appealed to his fellow-conspirators, Brittany, Armagnac, Burgundy. To the Duke of Alençon he wrote : " Kinsman, fail me not in my hour of need." Louis had heard that the King had established himself in Bourbonnais. He sent a friar to him with a verbal message imploring pardon in abject terms. But the friar had also letters signed by the Dauphin's chancellor ; and these, while undertaking that Louis would not cross the Rhône without his father's permission, and that he would renounce all his alliances, demanded freedom for himself and his followers to come and go in Dauphiné without molestation.

Charles did not think it right for a son to bargain with his father in this way.

Matters had come to a deadlock. The King had no faith whatever in his son. Louis was terrified of the parent who represented himself as "a kind and pitiful father." He felt that he was being encircled in Dauphiné and caught like a mouse in its hole. The earth did not seem big enough to cover him. He heard that he was to be disinherited in favour of his little brother, Charles.

He resolved on a secret flight. On the 30th of August 1456, accompanied by a few intimates, he took the road to Saint-Claude, as if he were going on a pilgrimage. At Saint-Claude, he had three masses said, and wrote a note to the King. His uncle of Burgundy,[1] he said, intended to march against the Turk in defence of the Catholic Church. Louis was going with him in obedience to a summons from the Pope's standard-bearer. He would entreat his uncle to endeavour to restore him to his father's favour, which was what he desired more than anything in the world. "My greatly feared lord," he concluded, "I pray God to grant you a long and happy life."

But this "very humble and obedient son" did not breathe till he found himself at Vers, well out of his father's reach and in the domain of the Prince of Orange, who was greatly surprised to see the son of the King of France. From Vers, Louis continued his flight northward, escorted by the Marshal of Burgundy through Lorraine and Luxembourg, fearing all the while that his father was on his track and that Torcy and Tristan l'Hermite would tie him in a sack and throw him into the river. Speeding on, barely halting for sleep or refreshment, he felt sure they were at his heels, until, when neither steed nor rider could go another step, the fugitive rode into Namur.

[1] Duke Philip's first wife, Michelle de France, had been Charles VII's sister.

CHAPTER XVI

AT THE DUKE OF BURGUNDY'S

The Dauphin's Reception by the Count of Charolais, the Duchess Isabelle and Philip of Burgundy.—The excessive politeness of their Greeting.—The Dauphin takes up his Residence at Genappe.—His occupations.—Hunting and Reading.—His Relations with the Ducal Household.—Mediator in the Quarrels between the Duke and his Son.—He takes Charlotte of Savoy to wife.—Birth and Death of Joachim of France.—Birth of Anne.—King Charles's attitude towards his Son.—Deprives him of Dauphiné.—The Duke's Generosity.—Charles's Exasperation.—The Course of Louis' Life at Genappe reflected in " Les Cent Nouvelles Nouvelles."—Character and Appearance of the Count of Charolais and the Duke.—The Duke's Château at Hesdin.

At length, in September 1456, the Dauphin's headlong course ended in Louvain, the capital of Brabant. Here, for a while, Louis amused himself with hunting and flying his birds. Duke Philip was on the Frisian frontier with his army. He sent his son, the Count of Charolais, to welcome Louis; and with him came Adolphus von Ravenstein, Antoine, Bastard of Burgundy, the Bishop of Cambrai, and Jean, Sire de Croy, Counsellor and Chamberlain. The town offered the fugitive wine.

About St Martin's Day, at eight o'clock in the evening, with a suite of some ten horsemen and escorted by the Marshal of Burgundy, Louis entered Brussels. The Duke was then reducing the town of Deventer to obedience to his natural son David. And there remained at Brussels to receive the Dauphin only the Duchess Isabelle and her daughter-in-law, Mme de Charolais, pregnant with a child who was to be the famous Mary of Burgundy, Archduchess of Austria. These ladies welcomed the Dauphin most humbly—the Duchess and Madame de Ravenstein on their knees.

Louis played the part of a gallant prince. He kissed the hands of the court ladies. He took the arm of the Duchess and would have placed her on his right had she not objected that he did her too great an honour. Then followed a discussion which lasted a quarter of an hour, and in which Louis protested that he was the humblest in the kingdom of France, a poor fugitive whose only refuge was with her and her husband the Duke. Finally the Duchess had to give way ; and the Dauphin was escorted by her to the Duke's apartments, which had been placed at his disposal.

Philip was in an awkward position ; he waited to receive his instructions from the King before welcoming Louis in person. But Charles gave no sign. And, on the 15th of October, Philip returned to Brussels. Here was another opportunity for the Dauphin to display excessive politeness. Instead of awaiting the Duke in his own apartments according to etiquette, Louis, with the Duchess and her daughter-in-law, went out to meet him at the palace gate. And there the Duke dismounted and knelt before the Dauphin, who would have hastened towards him, had not the Duchess retained him by the arm, allowing her husband time to give a second salute and to kneel again. Louis bowed low, took his uncle's arm, and they went up the palace steps together. The Duke had refused to allow his grand equerry to bear his sword before him in the Dauphin's presence. Duke Philip was then a man of sixty, a French prince, for whom there was nothing higher than the crown of France, though he had spent a great part of his life attacking it, and though he still remained its enemy. His vanity and conceit were stupendous ; and it was as his protector that he welcomed the Dauphin. No doubt he dreamed of holding the French crown in tutelage and constituting himself the umpire in the quarrel between the King and his son. Consequently he regarded Louis as a hostage.

He replied to the Dauphin, who had explained the reasons for his flight, saying : " My Lord, your coming here is a great joy to me ; I praise God and you for the honour and the good luck which have befallen me in this matter ; you are as welcome to me as was the angel Gabriel to the Virgin Mary, for never have I felt such joy or received such an honour as to see you and receive you in my dominions, which are at your service."

Louis was overwhelmed by this affectionate greeting. He tried to raise the Duke, saying : " By my faith, Uncle, if you will not rise, I must go away and leave you. You are the only man in the world whom I have long desired to see, and I come to you from afar, through great dangers. I praise God that I find you safe and well. The sight of your person is the greatest joy I have ever experienced. If it please you, kind Uncle, we will make good cheer together. I will tell you my adventures and you will tell me yours."

Tears were in the eyes of both Philip and Louis. Then the Duke greeted his wife and daughter. And the Dauphin said : " Good Uncle, you must change your clothes. Let us go up." The Dauphin went first, and the Duke followed him bareheaded. In the Dauphin's apartment, which was Philip's, they conversed secretly together.

The rejoicings in the city of Brussels, far-famed for its pomp and pageantry, were magnificent. But that which struck everyone was the subservience of the Duke to his royal guest. Everywhere, in town and country, Philip followed the Dauphin bareheaded, his hood thrown back. He required from all a like subservience, and showed the same to the Dauphin's followers.

Philip assigned the castle of Genappe to Louis for his residence ; and he granted him a pension of 36,000 francs, which was a considerable sum in those days.

Genappe was not far from Brussels, situated in a well-wooded, well-watered country, abounding in game, with fine horses and cattle, a country well adapted for the Dauphin's favourite sport of hunting. In this pursuit, in company with the romantic young Comte de Charolais, Louis indulged freely, staying out all day and sleeping in the villages. But the Dauphin was a reader as well as a sportsman. He studied at the University of Louvain ; and it may have been there that he imbibed the doctrine of Aristotle. There, at any rate, he met the learned Jean Wessel, whom Louis was to transfer to the University of Paris when he became King. He mixed with the country folk, among whom he discovered his barber, Olivier le Daim, a native of Thielt in Flanders. He was also on intimate terms with certain of the nobility, especially with Les Croy.

Louis was constantly in the Duke's household ; and when, in 1457, Madame de Charolais' little daughter, Mary, was born, the Dauphin stood sponsor at the magnificent christening in the church at Caudenberg.

By a strange turn of the tables Louis played the part of mediator in those disputes which were constantly arising in the House of Burgundy between father and son. Charolais was passionate and utterly lacking in self-control. Philip regarded Louis as his own son, but a submissive son. One day, when Louis and Charolais had been out hunting together, and Charolais returned alone, Philip was furious and ordered his son never again to come back without the Dauphin.

In company with the Duke, Louis visited the rich and well populated Flemish cities. They filled him with wonder, for never had he seen so many people in one town.

Then it occurred to Louis that he was married and that it was time his marriage was consummated. Charlotte had remained in Dauphiné. And the court of Savoy had been surprised that Louis had been in no hurry to live with his bride. In 1456, the Duke of Savoy had sent to remind him that he had a wife. She was a sweet, plain and insignificant woman, destined to be a Queen of whom there would be nothing to say. Now Louis sent to Grenoble for her. She arrived at Namur in

January 1458, and she was delivered of a son on the 15th of July 1459. Four months later, on the 29th of November, the child, Joachim, died and was buried at Brussels. A daughter, Anne, was born two years afterwards. And the Duke required a triple aid from the Estates of Artois, to meet the expenses of the Dauphin's household.

For King Charles had taken possession of Dauphiné, from which province Louis had hitherto derived his revenue. Although the Dauphin had formally submitted to this deprivation, we find him from time to time acting as sovereign in Dauphiné, distributing pensions and offices to those who had been faithful to him, and actually nominating the Armagnac Bastard governor of the province.

Throughout Louis' residence at the Burgundian court King Charles never concealed his annoyance, making it felt in various ways. Philip, on the other hand, was always perfectly correct and chivalrous.

When the King's ambassadors urged him to surrender the fugitive, he replied that it was not through any persuasion or encouragement from him that Louis had come to Burgundy, but entirely through fear of his father ; that it was because of his respect for the King that Philip had received his son and given him all the assistance in his power, and that as long as Philip possessed a penny, Louis was welcome to half of it. Never had the Duke forbidden the Dauphin to return to France : indeed, if it were necessary, he was ready to go with him, to see that he suffered no hurt.

But of course Philip was well aware that his conduct exasperated the King of France.

From one of the most famous books of the day, " Les Cent Nouvelles Nouvelles," we may learn the manner of Louis' life at Genappe, the character of his Burgundian host, and the kind of society in which he moved at Philip's castle of Hesdin. Although the Dauphin did not, as many have thought, figure among the tellers of these hundred new stories, which were first printed three years after his death (1486), three members of his household were among the narrators : and the setting of the book, one of the numerous imitations of Boccaccio's " Decameron," is the scene in which the Dauphin spent five of the most important years of his life.

Louis' residence at Genappe was an unpretentious little château, encircled by the River Dyle, a comfortable house with fine gardens and orchards in the midst of a well-cultivated country. The Dauphin was fond of associating with the peasants—with one of them especially, Conon by name, in whose house he enjoyed many a well-cooked meal of vegetables. When the Dauphin became King of France, Conon set out to wait upon his royal friend with a basket of turnips so delicious that Conon could not resist eating them by the way, so that when he arrived at court only one turnip remained, and for that the King paid a thousand gold pieces in memory of the days of his youth.

Louis' most intimate friend of his own rank was the Duke's son, le Comte de Charolais, who was ten years the Dauphin's junior, and one of the handsomest knights of his day, tall and strong, with red lips, black hair and keen, laughing eyes, passionately fond of music, a great reader of romances, good at games, chess especially, and at all feats of arms. This gallant knight was abstemious, drinking little wine, for fear it should rouse his wrath, and faithful to his wife—which was unusual in those days, and more especially in his case, because his marriage with Catherine de Bourbon had been against his will.

Charolais' father, Duke Philip, did not resemble his son in this respect, being known to have had thirty mistresses. At this time the Duke was a man of sixty, spare and bony. The veins stood out on his full forehead, his lips were thick and red, and his eyes started out of his head from beneath their heavy eyebrows when he was angry. In his youth Philip had worn his hair over his forehead, cut round like a soup-plate. But, when he began to grow bald he had his head shaved, and all the court flattered him by following his example. Philip's whole aspect was princely. He seemed to be made to love and be loved. With the humble he was humble, with the proud proud, with men courteous, with women gallant. He was rich, accumulating great treasure, but disdaining to ascertain the extent of his wealth. The citizens of the towns loved him because he did not grind them down with taxes. Of the details of government he took no account, delegating them to others. He himself was entirely occupied with high politics. He posed as a Knight of the Round Table. All his life he dreamed of going on a crusade to the Holy Land, but it was not until after his death that his heart was taken to Jerusalem. This was the duke, the gallant knight who had bought Jeanne d'Arc and sold her to the English.

Philip was no longer of an age to dance and tilt, but he still hunted furiously and far into the night when some anxiety oppressed him. He used the dramatic and elaborate ritual of the Order of the Golden Fleece to kindle the ardour of his followers, and always with some political object. He himself took more pleasure in the practical jokes of his curious château at Hesdin, which was more like the abode of some conjurer than the castle of a powerful prince. The walls were hung with distorting mirrors, in the ceilings were contrivances to sprinkle water on you when you walked under them, mysterious devices shut windows when you opened them, the books on the reading-desks spurted ink at you when you tried to read them, boxes spoke, manikins beat you, bridges precipitated you into the water.

Philip, as he advanced in years, preferred this kind of jest to the romances of Alexander and Jason, just as he preferred the society of his valets and his bastards to that of his proud nobles, who were always prostrate before him. Grand ceremonial and rich banquets bored him. He would put off going to mass till two o'clock in the afternoon, taking a liberty with the ordinances of the Church, for which he received papal dispensation. The poet, Georges Chastellain, who, like the Dauphin, knew all the secrets of the Duke's household, has represented him fleeing from Brussels, and, cold and hungry, finding calm and peace in the house of a charcoal-burner. " By my faith," said the good man, " the fare I have to offer you is poor indeed, being nought but a pasty, cheese from the Abbey, and clear water." Tranquillity and simple fare like this Philip sought and found in the house of his gamekeeper at Halsenberghe.

CHAPTER XVII

THE DEATH OF KING CHARLES VII

Quarrels between the Duke of Burgundy and his Son.—Louis as Peacemaker.—Affairs at the French Court.—Ill-health and Senility of
King Charles.—An old Dandy governed by Women.—His Distress
at his Son remaining with Burgundy.—The Embassy of 1459.—
Reported Preparations for War with Duke Philip. The King's
Illness and Recovery.—Louis' Correspondence with the King's
former Mistress.—His impatience for his Father's Death.—The
King's Suspicions of Treachery.—His Last Illness.—Letter from
the King's Council to Louis.—The Dauphin starts for Reims and
summons Burgundy to join him with his Army.—The Death of the
King, 22nd of July 1461.—Funeral Ceremonies.

WE have seen that if Charles and Louis were not on good
terms the relations between Philip and Charolais were hardly
better. On one occasion the Duke threw the regulations
his son had made for his household into the fire. "Dare
you disobey me ? " cried Philip. " Get out of my sight ! "
And with his usually rubicund face as white as a sheet,
he drew his dagger and threatened his son. The Duchess
of Burgundy took Charolais' hand and dragged him out
of the room. They shut themselves up in a little chamber,
opening into an oratory, of which a priest-chorister had
the key. The voice of the Duke was heard outside : he
was pursuing them in a furious rage, with flashing eyes
and face distorted with passion. " Unlock the door, my
friend," cried the Duchess, " or we are dead ! " The
chorister turned the key, and Isabelle and her son rushed
through the oratory into the Dauphin's room, entreating
him to intervene on their behalf.

Philip was ashamed that his foreign guest should be
involved in family quarrels. " I crave your pardon, my
Lord," said the Duke. " And I entreat of you not to insist
on your request. For I am not yet inclined to be pleased

with Charolais. I will show him that I am his father
and that I can make him nothing better than a lackey.
Do not be anxious. I know how to deal with my
son and with his mother, who has done no good by
mixing herself up in this quarrel." Then Louis fell on
his knees, put his arms round the Duke, wept and
entreated.

But Philip behaved like a madman. He had his horse
saddled, and rode at full gallop through the park out into
the open country. Without cloak or gaiters, he wandered
in the rain and mist, while his broken sword knocked
against his thigh, and his horse stumbled and fell.
Dragging it by the bridle, the Duke took refuge in a
charcoal-burner's hut, which he discovered by the barking
of a dog. Having warmed himself there, he went on to
a hunter's lodge, where he passed the night and the
following day. Not until evening did he return to
Genappe, whence Philippe Pot, one of the gentlemen of
his bedchamber, had gone out to look for him. It was
the Dauphin who calmed him and brought to him
Charolais, whom he pardoned.

This quarrelsome father and son were a lesson to the
Dauphin, who was inclined to be impulsive and quick-
tempered, and who saw that he must learn patience and
self-control.

Louis learned all the secrets of this Burgundian family,
in which he played the part of peacemaker. He saw the
father posing as a knight of chivalry, for ever talking of
going on a crusade to the Holy Land, but staying at home,
regarded as a prince who loved ceremony and pomp,
and yet in reality never so happy as when telling gross
stories, surrounded by his servants, mistresses and bastards.
Louis saw the mother withdrawing to the Nunnery of
the Grey Sisters, which she had founded at Nieuport.
The Dauphin played the father to the little Mary,
Charolais' daughter, to whom he had stood sponsor, and
who was to be the heiress of those dukes whose power he
was to destroy.

Photo : A. Giraudon

PHILIP THE GOOD
(Duke of Burgundy)

CHARLES THE BOLD
(Duke of Burgundy, son of Philip)

At the French court the situation was equally sad and dramatic. King Charles, who had had a serious illness in 1457, had aged prematurely. According to the Milanese ambassador he was completely in the power of women. Agnes's niece, Antoinette de Villequier, who had succeeded her aunt, and was younger and quite as beautiful, was treated as a queen. Then there were Mme La Régente and Mme des Chaperons, and five or six more, all of whom the King dressed sumptuously and took about with him to those châteaux, in which, while he left Pierre de Brézé to carry on the government, he sought relaxation from his kingly duties, but not, as in earlier days, in order to pray. At that time Charles was a regular old beau, decked out in fashionable clothes, in green or red silk and velvet.

Among all the vicissitudes of his foreign policy—his break with Duke Philip, his intervention in Scotland and in Luxembourg, his attempted occupation of Genoa and descent on Sandwich, where he lost his fleet—his great preoccupation was the presence of his son at the Burgundian court. The embassies and remonstrances which had been unceasing for five years culminated in the great embassy in 1459, in which Charles represented himself as a noble and virtuous father, sorrowing over the absence of his son, and to which Louis, through Jean de Croy, replied in the tragic tone of a banished but obedient son, unjustly cut off from his beloved family, to which he had rendered brilliant service.

One of Sforza's agents, who had every opportunity of being well informed, wrote on the 2nd of July 1459, that the King was on the verge of going to war with Burgundy. At any rate he was negotiating with the Duke's rebel city, Liége, and making an alliance with Henry VI of England and Margaret of Anjou, the enemies of the Duke, whose sympathies were with the House of York.

At this juncture, however, King Charles was taken ill. And Francesco Sforza's agent wrote that astrologers had told Philip that nothing short of a miracle could prolong the King's life. But Charles recovered and presided over his council. Louis was feverishly watching all these incidents from Flanders. Mlle de Villequier was keeping him informed of them. For she had now exchanged her infirm and aged lover for the Duke of Brittany. " My good lady," wrote Louis, " throw my letters into the fire, and let me know whether I ought to remain in my present situation."

Louis was impatient for his father's death. It may have been intentionally that he allowed one of his letters to Mlle de Villequier to fall into the hands of the King's valet. In this letter, after having thanked his correspondent for the information she had given him, Louis added : " I have also received letters from the Comte de Dammartin, whom I pretend to hate, and which are in the same strain as yours. Tell him to continue to serve me by writing to me as he has done. I will consider the matter concerning which he wrote and he shall hear from me."

The letter was shown to the King, who was again ill. Charles felt surrounded by traitors. Was the Comte de Dammartin false ? The King would find out. So in all haste he sent a Franciscan friar to Genappe to question those whom the King employed to spy on Louis. They said the letter was a blind, only one of Louis' tricks.

But this report did not altogether dispel the suspicions of the King and of those who surrounded him. His doctor, André Fumée, was imprisoned in the great tower at Bourges. One of his surgeons fled to Valenciennes to be near Louis.

Charles's death was thought to be imminent. He had some strange disease in the mouth, a swelling and an abscess. A tooth was extracted. There was talk of poison. Masses were said for his recovery. Louis also had Masses said. But to what intention? The King's council were growing anxious and beginning to pay addresses to the heir. On the 17th of July, they sent a letter to Louis telling him of the nature of the King's illness, that he was growing weaker, and asking the Dauphin to inform them of his good pleasure.

At Genappe this letter was regarded as the King's death-knell. The Dauphin immediately started for Avesnes, on the road to Reims. There was no longer any question of preparing for war, but rather for the coronation. Louis wrote to the Duke of Burgundy : " If by any chance you hear that he is dead, we pray you straightway to take horse, you and all your people, in habiliments of war, and come to meet us in the marches of Reims."

Such were the son's commands, while the father over at Melun was dying, and for a whole week refusing to take nourishment for fear of being poisoned. In only one of his retainers, le Comte de Foix, had he any confidence. And from his hand alone Charles took anything he was capable of swallowing. But his powers were failing, though he lived on and retained consciousness until the 22nd of July. " What day is it ? " he asked of the religious who were with him. " Sire, it is the day of the glorious Mary Magdalen." " Ah ! " he cried, " I thank God for granting to me, the greatest of sinners, to die on the day of that sinful woman ! "

Charles made his confession, received extreme unction and asked to be buried at Saint-Denis, in the chapel in which his father and grandfather rested. He adjured Chabannes to serve *le petit seigneur*, his son, faithfully, seeing that he was not a bad son, like his brother. And when Chabannes entreated him to take food, saying that, if he mistrusted anyone, he would prosecute him and have him torn asunder by four horses, the King replied : " I leave vengeance to God." Charles passed away between twelve and one o'clock, at the age of fifty-eight.

During the closing days of July 1461, a procession wound its way towards Paris. A jolting cart, drawn by five horses, bore the waxen image of the King, dressed in his royal robe of blue velvet lined with ermine and miniver, his mantle embroidered with fleurs-de-lys, on his head the golden crown. The image was adorned with jewels, and in its hands were the sceptre and the silver wand of justice. The white-haired Charles of Orléans led the procession. He had had so few opportunities of appearing in public. He walked as if in a dream. Then followed his brother, the bent Comte d'Angoulême, the Marquis of Saluces, Charles of Gaucourt, Rochefort, the Bailiff of Touraine, the Provost of the King's household and the servants of Charles, " the well served." There was a service at Notre-Dame-des-Champs. Another procession accompanied the body to Notre-Dame, where Master Jean de Chasteaufort preached the funeral sermon on the text : *Memento judicii mei, Domine,* extolling the piety of the dead King. At Saint-Denis the nave was hung with black satin ; and there Master Thomas de Courcelles, doctor in theology, the unrighteous judge of Jeanne d'Arc, praised the King who owed everything to the Maid.

Then the body was borne to the chapel in which Charles V and Charles VI lay buried. And when the priest had sprinkled the first handful of earth over the coffin, the Herald-at-Arms approached and, lowering his mace, said : " Pray for the soul of the very excellent, the very powerful, the very virtuous prince, King Charles, seventh of the name." A moment's silence ensued. Sobs were heard. Then the Herald raised his mace and cried : " Long live the King ! " And the secretaries responded " Long live King Louis ! "

PART II
KING LOUIS

CHAPTER XVIII

THE CORONATION AT REIMS

Louis leaves Flanders.—Reception of the new King in France.—Burgundy's intention to play the part of his Protector.—Change of Ministers.—Funeral Service in honour of the late King at Avesnes.—Louis at Saint-Thierry.—State Entrance into Reims.—The Anointing.—The State Banquet.—Louis' Return to Saint-Thierry.

Now the Dauphin Louis was King, an uncrowned King, master of the kingdom for which he had been waiting for twenty years. He set out from Genappe in all haste, to take possession of his domain. With carts and baggage wagons, he crossed through Hainault, on his way to France. The death of his father, who had been his enemy, did not sadden him in the least. During his father's lifetime, Louis had scandalised everyone by inquiring of astrologers the precise hour of the death for which he might almost be said to have longed.

Charles's death affected Duke Philip almost as much as his nephew, seeing that war had been on the point of breaking out between France and Burgundy. While Louis had stood on the tiptoe of expectation, Philip had been waiting under arms. Consequently his army was ready to escort the Dauphin to his anointing. Philip was relieved of a serious embarrassment; and his vanity was flattered; for he had always dreamed of being the protector of France. Now he would accompany Louis to Reims with an army described as " terrible and marvellously great." He left Hesdin without delay, and went to Lille, where he spent five or six days, assembling his nobles and men-at-arms. He gave a look to his coffers, filled to overflowing with gold and silver, against the day when he should take part in some vast enterprise. Meanwhile he had sent his trusty messenger, the Lord of Croy, to reassure Louis, who was perturbed by the assembling of what seemed to him an unnecessarily great Burgundian force. " My good Uncle need have no fear, seeing that he is with me and I with him. Am I not King ? Of whom can he be afraid ? " The Lord of Croy replied that Philip was assembling his army, not because he was afraid of anyone, but in order to serve and honour the Dauphin should occasion arise. Louis made a wry face. He had put himself entirely in his Uncle's hands. That ought to give him confidence. Then he changed the subject. But it was plain that the King was not going to allow anyone to be his protector.

Louis was at Avesnes, waiting for his uncle. He had the great seal with him ; and he used it to confirm the privileges of the Knights of St John of Jerusalem ; for it was seemly that his royal majesty should take those who fought for the Catholic faith under his protection.

The French were beginning to feel anxious about their new master, especially those who had carried on the government during King Charles's last years. Pierre de Brézé, his former enemy, had not ventured to go to the King, but had sent him one of his servants, whom Louis had refused to receive. For Pierre de Brézé and Antoine de Chabannes, the Master of the late King's household, were the two persons whom Louis most cordially detested. Naturally they were both afraid.

And Louis, too, seemed almost afraid of his own power, that very power which he had so earnestly desired. " What a curious world it is," he said to Jean de Croy, " a world in which God deals strangely with men, sending them one fortune one day and another the next ; so that when one thinks oneself the most unhappy of creatures one is on the verge of prosperity, and when one deems oneself firmly established in prosperity, then the wheel turns again. This is true of myself ; for yesterday I seemed the poorest of kings' sons, one who from childhood upwards had suffered nothing but sorrow and tribulation, poverty and hunger, having been cast out of my patrimony, cut off from my father's love, a borrower and a beggar. Neither my wife nor I would have possessed a rood of land, nor a house to live in, nor a single penny, had it not been for the kindness and charity of my uncle, who kept me for the space of five years. And now, suddenly, as in a dream, God hath granted me prosperity; and, in the place of my past poverty, hath made me the richest and the most powerful king in Christendom, more puissant than the King, my father, who was reputed marvellously powerful and who was feared by all nations."

But though Louis could be loquacious, and though he could moralise, as on this occasion, he did not care to listen to others. And when Jouvenel des Ursins, Archbishop of Reims, came to address him in the name of the city, the King three times commanded him to be brief. Prelates and delegates came from other towns. Not the least adroit of these was Joachim Rouault, Marshal of France, who waited to appear before the King until Louis came out to mount his horse, when the Marshal, pushing another squire aside, presented the King with his spur, crying: "Give way, all of you, and let me perform my office." The King burst out laughing and promised to make the Marshal his first equerry. One the King did not forget was his kinsman, the Duke of Alençon, whom he liberated from the château of Loches, where he had been imprisoned as a traitor. No one was ever the worse for having served Louis.

The reign opened with a veritable revolution. For Charles's ministers and officers were substituted those who had supported Louis; some of them were Burgundians, like the Lord of Croy, who was appointed Master of the King's Household.

The Duke of Burgundy himself came to greet the new King, and to present at once his condolence on the death of King Charles and his congratulations on Louis' accession to power. For Philip was always correct. The King received him cordially, avoiding any allusion to the Duke's conflicting emotions.

Philip and all his suite were dressed in black. Louis and his household did not wear mourning until the funeral service, which was not held until the 3rd of August. It took place in the church at Avesnes; and the King for the first time wore the customary black cloak and mourning hood. The Archbishop of Bourges officiated. Five hundred candles burned round the image of the dead King, clothed in rich crimson and cloth of gold. Three hundred masses were said on that day, and a hundred francs were given to the poor.

Philip had opened his coffers and offered the new King three to four hundred thousand crowns. Louis seems to have been in no hurry to accept this advance. He was growing restless, and, dismissing the Burgundian army, he retained only five hundred lances as an escort for the Burgundian nobility, and left Avesnes for Reims. He did not even stay to bid farewell to the Countess of Charolais; and he left the Queen to follow him as best she could, so that she was reduced to borrowing horses and conveyances from the Countess.

Having reached the environs of Reims, Louis took up his residence at Saint-Thierry, where his Uncle Burgundy awaited him. He lost no time in arranging the ceremonial of his state entry. A brief command to the aged Archbishop, Jean Jouvenel des Ursins, sufficed : "It will be next Saturday. Have everything in readiness and see that nothing is lacking."

The Burgundians had just entered the city in great pomp. The King had received the keys at Saint-Thierry and had at once presented them to the Duke. Then he mounted his horse. It was late in the day, but still light. And in the midst of a vast crowd surging in the streets, pressing to the windows, he entered Reims. Never in the memory of the oldest inhabitants had so many people been assembled.

The procession, all in red and white—the King's

colours—went by. Torches flared. It was seven o'clock in the evening when Louis, in red and white satin, riding a horse accoutred in cloth of gold, and preceded by his grand equerry, rode into the city beneath a canopy. The Duke of Burgundy was with him, and his archers and pages. At Notre-Dame the King dismounted to pray; and then withdrew to his palace. An oratory had been prepared for him at Notre-Dame, and there at midnight he went to hear mass, to confess, and partake of Holy Communion.

On the day of the anointing the Duke, in royal array, took his place among the peers of the realm and was the first to enter the cathedral, where the King awaited them. The holy ampulla was brought in, while trumpets sounded. The great doors were opened; and Louis proceeded from the choir down the nave to the parvis. There he knelt with clasped hands while the ampulla was borne down the aisle from the high altar, followed by all the people. The Bishop of Laon took it and presented it to the King to kiss. Louis, still kneeling, gazed long on the sacred vessel and prayed. Then, following the time-honoured ritual, the peers of the realm stripped Louis to the waist. There, in the midst of croziers, mitres and pontifical robes, was the half-naked King. He was anointed with the sacred oil on the eyes, the mouth, the navel, the armpits, the shoulders and loins. Then, while the ampulla was borne back to the high altar, prelates and princes clothed the King, first in a red shirt and then in his royal robes, embroidered with fleurs-de-lys. He majestically took his seat on the throne, and the Duke of Burgundy, as first peer of the realm, presented him with his cap. Then Philip took the crown, raised it in both hands and held it up for a while for all to see, after which he placed it gently on the King's head, crying in a loud voice: " Long live the King ! Montjoye Saint Denis ! "

The crowd took up the cry, shouting " Noël." Trumpets and clarions made a deafening noise.

This mystic ritual of the coronation of the King of

France impressed even the Burgundians, accustomed as they were to the pomp and pageantry of Philip's court. But there was something else which might well have impressed them and made the Duke anxious : that was the oath Louis had just sworn with great solemnity—an oath he was frequently to renew in ordinances and despatches. The King had sworn to regain all his lands, even those which had been sold, alienated or pledged by his predecessors. That oath he was to keep, like many another sworn to the saints.

The Duke of Burgundy was occupied in arming his young knights ; but they were so numerous that Louis grew impatient and went into his palace to rest. Later on a State banquet was held, presided over by the King, who wore his crown. But it was rather too large for his head, so Louis took it off and put it on the table by the gold and silver plate borrowed from the Duke of Burgundy. Louis talked familiarly, often addressing Philippe Pot, who stood behind him ; the same Philippe who was one of the narrators of " Les Cent Nouvelles Nouvelles," and with whom Louis had often enjoyed a hearty laugh at Genappe.

Such good cheer and such elaborate ceremonial must have delighted the Duke. He appeared eager to place not merely the treasures of his well-filled coffers at the King's disposal, but the treasures of a heart, which Louis mistrusted. On the very day of his anointing the King quitted Reims and returned to Saint-Thierry, where, in the absorbing interest of state affairs, all thought of festivities passed out of his mind. Leaving the Duke of Burgundy to receive the congratulations of the Chapter, Louis took the road to Meaux.

The King's subjects were well pleased with their sovereign's devoutness and Christian humility. After having suffered so much, he was now, wrote the Milanese ambassador, " more powerful and more implicitly obeyed than any king since Charlemagne."

CHAPTER XIX

THE KING AND THE DUKE OF BURGUNDY AT PARIS

Arrival of the Duke.—The King's State Entry.—Reception at Notre-Dame.—Banquet at the Palace.—Philip at the Hôtel d'Artois.—Louis at Les Tournelles.—Disillusionment of the Burgundians.—Philip begins to see Daylight.—His Popularity.—Louis' Jealousy.—The King and the Duke leave Paris

MEANWHILE Paris was preparing to welcome the King. Never had so many foreigners been seen in the city—more than three hundred thousand, according to Thomas Basin. They climbed on to the roofs of houses and perched in gutters. Every window was booked for Louis' state entry ; and the prices were very high.

At Paris, as at Reims, the Duke of Burgundy played the part of introducer. He arrived on the 30th of August, and made an imposing entry into the capital, which he had not visited for twenty-four years, though he had practically ruled the city at one time, when his English allies were in power. The streets were crowded ; and some cried " Noël " as the Duke passed, although they had been strictly forbidden to do so. Philip took up his residence in his Hôtel d'Artois, near the Fish Market, where he had once made himself so popular with the market-folk that the French party, instead of accusing people of being Burgundians, would say : " You smell of herrings."

In the royal procession which started from la Place des Porcherons, it was the Burgundians who led. Philip rode a white horse with jewelled accoutrements, in his plumed hat gleamed precious stones, his cloak was of black velvet. The Comte de Charolais, his son, wore an Italian robe of crimson velvet. Their pages were dressed in black damask. A procession of nobles, French and Burgundian, was followed by the King's guard in chain armour and helmets. Behind the trumpeters, heralds and marshals of France and Burgundy, two knights bore Louis' mantle and his beaver hat lined with ermine. The royal helmet was also carried before the King, who, in a robe of white damask, rode a white hackney, accoutred in his colours, red and white. Six Parisian citizens in violet held a canopy of blue satin embroidered with fleurs-de-lys over his head.

A symbolical show in the King's honour had been prepared at each stage of this magnificent procession through the city: at St Lazare, five women robed like queens in cloth of gold, each representing one of the letters of Paris; at the St Denis Gate, the silver ship of the arms of the city and figures in it representing the three estates; in la rue St Denis, a fountain pouring forth wine, milk and hippocras. All tastes were catered for: for the frivolous there were dances of savage women and beautiful girls personating sirens; for the serious, at the Trinity Hospital, a representation of the Passion and Jesus on the Cross between two thieves. The King, as conqueror of Dieppe, was especially honoured by a fort, which the besiegers stormed, cutting the throats of the English defenders, just as the King passed.

All day the procession defiled through the streets and squares of the city until, at six o'clock, the King arrived at Notre-Dame, where the Bishop of Paris, assisted by the Archbishop of Bourges, received him with all the clergy at the doors of the cathedral. There Louis took the oath—with a bad grace—why, we do not know. A grand procession escorted him up the brilliantly lighted aisle to the high altar, while the *Te Deum* was sung. Then the organ played, the bells pealed and the crowd cried: " Noël! Noël! " After a short prayer, Louis armed four new knights, and left the cathedral for the usual supper at the Palace.

There the marble table was furnished forth with that

magnificent gold and silver plate which the Duke of Burgundy had already lent for the royal banquet at Reims. On the King's left sat the Duke of Orléans, on his right, the Duke of Burgundy. Heralds and Kings-at-Arms cried largess and received 200 francs. Mummers opened the ball, which continued until midnight, when the King withdrew to his palace of Les Tournelles.

While the Duke of Burgundy lived magnificently and kept open house in his Hôtel d'Artois, Louis at Les Tournelles lived as simply as he had done at Genappe.

He was already immersed in work, plagued by all those to whom he had made promises during his exile, but with whom he was well able to deal : " Certainly, my friend. Then I was Dauphin. But now I am King," he would say. He consulted the Duke of Burgundy about his resolution to change the members of his Parlement ; and he decided to keep the officers of the Treasury whom his father had appointed. But, as a rule, he was hard on all who had served the late King.

Louis was often to be seen making good cheer in various houses of the city. The Duke of Burgundy was doing his best to make himself popular, presiding at dances, and dispensing hospitality in his vast hall, hung with tapestry of high warp, representing the story of Gideon, the Patron of the Golden Fleece. There he received the Duchess of Alençon, whose husband the King had just pardoned. Those who served the Duke of Burgundy did so because they liked him, whereas Louis was served through fear or hope of reward. No wonder the King was jealous. Meanwhile, the Burgundians, who had hoped so much from Louis' accession, began to be disillusioned. And Louis tried to assert his influence over the Comte de Charolais, who had been his friend at Genappe, and whom he knew to be a bad son, as ambitious as himself.

There was a certain Guillaume de Bische, whom Duke Philip more especially mistrusted. He seemed to rule Louis' household, going in and out by day and night ;

and he was often to be seen arm-in-arm with the King, visiting the ladies of Paris, with whom he was well acquainted. Bische was very useful to Louis, who took his pleasures secretly and who was said to be amorous. The King offended the Duke of Bourbon by depriving him of the governorship of Guyenne.

Citizens from the Duke of Burgundy's rebellious town of Liége had arrived in order to effect a reconciliation with the new King. And Louis seemed to be trying to pick a quarrel with his uncle over his truces and conventions with the English.

Philip was beginning to see daylight ; he had harboured a fox ; he almost regretted the days of good King Charles : his one thought was of returning to his dominions.

But as yet there was no open rupture between uncle and nephew. The King declared, in the Duke's Hôtel, to the assembled representatives of the Estates of Paris, of the Church and of the University, that he owed both his crown and his life to his uncle. Philip was about to return to his dominions and Louis to Touraine. But first the King confirmed the privileges of the various corporations of notaries, barbers, archers and cross-bowmen who drew up in procession before him, and also of the wine merchants, fishmongers and dealers in butter, eggs, cheese, apples, pears, onions and leeks, including the costermongers. Neither did he forget the blind in the Quinze-Vingt Hospital, nor the Carthusians of Vauvert ; for the King always had a place in his heart for the religious. So the villagers went home pleased : those of Fontenay, near Vincennes, for example, for the King had exempted them from the obligation to serve as beaters when wolves were being hunted.

Louis knew his people.

CHAPTER XX

HOME AND FOREIGN AFFAIRS

1461–1463

Louis' Delight in his Kingdom.—His Attitude towards the Middle Class
and the Nobility.—Matrimonial Alliances.—Reduction of Expenditure.—Relations with the English.—Louis narrowly escapes
Capture.—Arrival in France of Margaret of Anjou.—The Conference of Hesdin.—Truce with Edward IV.—Recovery of the
Towns on the Somme.—Annexation of Roussillon.

LOUIS was glad to leave Paris. He never had any liking
for the Parisians, whom he regarded as idlers, prone to be
dazzled by Burgundian ostentation, given to fine words,
but stingy as soon as there was a question of paying taxes.
He was pleased to return to Touraine, where he had spent
his childhood. Louis' heart was in Touraine—in Touraine
the heart of France. The King, who in temperament
was a peasant, could never be at his ease in towns; and
when he could not escape from city walls, he chose to
reside in the humble home of some citizen who was his
friend. But Louis liked to be for ever on the move,
coming face to face with his subjects, doing business on
the spot.

Now that he had parted from his uncle Burgundy
he could begin to settle his own affairs as he liked.

His mind radiated over the whole of France. He
knew it well already. Had he not been King Charles's
lieutenant in Languedoc? Had he not passed through
Auvergne, fought in Normandy and ruled in Dauphiné?
Had he not visited the towns on the Somme? Had he
not fled through Burgundy to Flanders? Had he not
even entered into an alliance with the Swiss and cast his
eyes on Alsace? He knew the wealthy cities of the north.

He was perfectly at home with the nobles and peasants of Brabant and Hainault. But of all countries he was most pleased with his patrimony of France, the country with a temperate climate, equally divided between six months of summer and six months of winter ; a country that it took twenty-two days to traverse from Sluys to Saint-Jean-Pied-de-Port, sixteen days from Saint-Mathieu-de-Finistère to Lyons ; a country abounding in corn, wine and fruit, a wool-producing country, rich, too, in metals—iron, lead and copper—well watered, with rivers flowing to the Ocean or to the Mediterranean, with the Loire right in the centre. Even more blessed in her people than in her natural resources : those good folk of the centre, simple-hearted and obedient to their lord, those robust mountaineers of Auvergne, those hearty Poitevins, those Gascons, courageous and light-hearted, those loyal dwellers in Champagne, those frank but choleric dwellers in Artois, the industrious Normans, lovers of good cheer, the seafaring, butter-making Bretons, the ploughmen of the centre, the folk of Anjou and Maine, of the lands round Orléans and Chartres, and those speakers of good French, the inhabitants of l'Ile de France, who were also pious Catholics.

Louis was the good shepherd of all this flock, knowing his people well and loving them, especially those of the middle class. That expression, "the common weal" (*la chose publique*), which was frequently on their lips, was often on his also.

The barons, more numerous in France than in the other two Christian kingdoms, pleased him less. He began by strictly defining the game laws and depriving the nobles of certain hunting rights.

Though, on Louis' accession, the English, who had occupied half of France, from Guyenne to Picardy, had been driven out of all their former possessions, except Calais and the neighbouring country, the great French feudatories remained. The King's personal domain comprised but one quarter of France. The great feudal lords were of royal blood. Family quarrels—between Burgundians and Armagnacs, for instance—were frequent. When Louis, at his coronation, swore to maintain and increase his royal domain, he meant to do so by the addition of these appanages, some of which were practically independent states.

Such was the case of Burgundy : a principality almost as powerful as the kingdom of France. With the rise of the Burgundian House, descended from Charles V, Burgundy proper had dwindled in importance, and the centre of Burgundian influence had come to reside in the northern provinces, Flanders, Artois and Hainault, which had grown rich through trading with England. Philip the Good learnt Flemish and spoke it. Brussels was his capital, Bruges his Venice. The Duke's ambition was to unite the two prongs of his dominion, which almost encircled the royal domain. At one time the English had granted him Champagne, but he had never dared to take possession of that province. Charles VII had been crowned at Reims. Philip had looked on sadly, never venturing to become the declared enemy of France, like the English, with whom he had so much in common.

The Duke of Brittany, too, was in close communication with the English, and did homage to the King of France reluctantly. Louis granted him merely the honorary title of King's Lieutenant in the lands beyond the Seine.

But now Louis himself must needs think of creating an appanage for his brother Charles, who was of an age to possess an establishment of his own. The King granted him Berri. Louis had also to please his uncle, King René. He gave him the county of Beaufort to round off his county of Anjou.

Louis, as we have seen, had delivered the Duke of Alençon from prison. He now gave him back his confiscated lands. And he did the same for Jean, Count of Armagnac.

But there were two persons whom Louis could not

bring himself to pardon : Pierre de Brézé and Antoine de Chabannes. He outlawed them both and offered a reward to anyone who could lay hands on them.

Antoine gathered his brave soldiers round him, and appeared before them, robed in cloth of gold ; then he retired, and after a while reappeared to bid them farewell, wearing a pilgrim's cloak of coarse cloth. Pierre de Brézé, brave, loyal and chivalrous, instead of going over to his English friends, as he might have done, entered Paris in disguise and there surrendered to the King's men. The King imprisoned him at Loches, and then relented and set him free ; for he found that, far from preaching discord, the Seneschal was inclined to speak well of his new King. Louis knew how to charm on occasion, as, for example, when Charolais passed through Tours. The King received his former comrade with great honour. He went out hunting with him as in the old days at Genappe, and sent to look for his guest when he was lost in the forest. He gave him the Hôtel de Nesle, and promised him the government of Normandy.

Louis was busy making matrimonial alliances, never taking into account the age and suitability of the parties, but always keeping in view dynastic and territorial objects. So he promised his daughter Anne, who had been born at Genappe, to Nicolas of Anjou, because he was the heir to Lorraine, and married Burgundy's great-nephew, Bourbon's son, to the Duke of Orléans' daughter.

Louis was making himself feared now that he was King, through that same restless and headstrong activity which he had displayed as Dauphin. But no one was grateful to him for reducing the national expenditure, for cutting down the expenses of his household, and for disdaining those royal silks and purples which his father had affected towards the close of his life. Charles VII's old servants, whose pensions he had reduced, complained loudly ; so did the University people, the ecclesiastics and those to whom the late King had granted the privilege of selling wine retail without paying taxes.

Though by no means ignorant of the life of his people, Louis was determined to see everything, and to see it as a private individual. Consequently, leaving Tours with six companions, dressed like pilgrims in coarse grey cloth, with wooden paternosters hanging round their necks, the King set out to visit the marches of Guyenne. The inhabitants of Tours, under pain of death, had been forbidden to make any demonstration on his departure. But a company of a hundred and twenty men-at-arms followed him at some distance.

One day, however, he narrowly escaped being taken prisoner. The King and a few companions were in a little boat on the Gironde. Some bold Englishmen saw them, sailed after them in a skiff and fired a volley to cut off their retreat. It was only by rowing furiously in the direction of Bordeaux, that the King and his comrades succeeded in reaching the bank, where Louis, hiding among the reeds, waited for the turn of the tide.

On his return to Tours, Louis received deputations from the Italian towns, Venice, Genoa and Florence, who came to offer their services. But the King had already decided on his policy. He had had some experience of Italian politics when he was governing Dauphiné; and now he decided to follow his father's example and to throw in his lot with the strongest power in Italy, Francesco Sforza, Duke of Milan, though by so doing he displeased the House of Orléans,[1] which had not relinquished its claims to the inheritance of the Visconti. So Louis gave a cordial reception to the Milanese ambassador, and inquired anxiously after his master's failing health.

With England, as with Milan, Louis seemed desirous to live at peace; and at that time, in his opinion, England was Edward IV. In August 1461 he had had the envoys of Henry VI and Margaret of Anjou arrested at Eu, while

---

[1] The mother of Charles, Duke of Orléans, was Valentine Visconti, whose father, the Duke of Milan, had, in the event of there being no heirs-male, bequeathed to her the territory then occupied by the House of Sforza.

he sent an ambassador to King Edward, requesting him
to fix a day for the settlement of the great question of
peace and war between them. But for the English, who
depended on France for corn and wine, peace meant
starvation. So Louis' peace negotiations came to nothing,
and his ambassador failed to persuade the English to
sheathe their swords against the French and join them
in a crusade.

It was to be war with England, then. And Louis
began to think how he could turn the English out of
France. An alliance with Burgundy would be necessary.
But Louis coveted Burgundy also. And he was not going
the right way to propitiate the ailing Duke when he
forbade his subjects to obtain their salt from Burgundian
salt mines.

Philip now knew only too well the kind of man with
whom he had to deal. And he was not inclined to listen
favourably to the proposals made to him on the King's
behalf by Dunois and the recently liberated Pierre de
Brézé. They sketched a vast plan of action. Margaret
of Anjou had asked for Louis' aid against Edward IV. The
King had promised it on condition that Calais should be
surrendered and that a hundred years' truce should be
made with France. The French would invade England,
with an army led by the Comte de Charolais. Philip was
to supply the funds for the enterprise, Holland and
Zeeland the ships.

Meanwhile Louis made a progress in Normandy,
entering the stronghold of Rouen, which had once been
English, accompanied by the Seneschal, Pierre de Brézé,
who was received with great acclamation.

Now with trumpet sound throughout the length and
breadth of his kingdom, Louis proclaimed mortal enmity
between himself and King Edward. Under penalty of
death he prohibited all trade with England. The English
retaliated : in August and September 1462, they landed
on the Island of Ré and in Brittany. They commandeered
the services of the people. They carried off casks of wine

and committed all manner of depredations, while a fleet of pirates cruised along the coasts of Normandy and Guyenne. When a French army was said to be on the point of invading England, King Edward sent word to Louis that it was unnecessary for him to take so long a journey, seeing that Edward would take it for them both, and come to the French King in France. Louis smiled and said he would be welcome. He admired the young King's courage, but such things were easier said than done.

King Louis, meanwhile, was bent on enriching his kingdom and filling the royal exchequer. He promised patents of nobility to all citizens who would engage in commerce ; he encouraged even the nobles to trade ; he sold offices for the profit of the Crown, but at the same time he cut down the number of officials ; he gave little and spent less. His heavy hand was felt everywhere. He was greatly feared, and so were those who served him.

In August 1463, Louis' cousin, Margaret of Anjou, landed at Sluys, with her son Edward, the little Prince of Wales, and seven women attendants. So reduced were they that they had not a change of raiment between them, and depended for their daily bread on Margaret's old friend, that charming knight and brilliant talker, Pierre de Brézé, who, with King Louis' associate, Philippe Pot, had come to meet them.[1]

Duke Philip was at that time at Boulogne on a pilgrimage. Margaret went to see him at Saint Pol and again at Saint Omer. Philip lent a sympathetic ear to her tale of woe, but did no more than furnish her with 2,000 crowns and an escort to her father's dominions.

The time was not propitious for Margaret, seeing that the Duke was ostensibly presiding over negotiations for a truce between her enemy Edward IV and her cousin

---

[1] In the previous year Margaret, leaving her husband, Henry VI, in Scotland, had gone to Brittany and seen Louis at Chinon, Tours and Rouen. The King had granted her a small force under the command of de Brézé, with which at first she had achieved considerable success in the north of England.

159

Louis XI. Ambassadors from France and England, the latter including the King-Maker's brother, the eloquent Archbishop of York, were then at the Burgundian court. Philip thought he was deciding everything, but in reality the whole matter was in the hands of that double-dealer, Antoine de Croy, who was playing the game both of England and of France. The French and English were very offhand with one another. The English, as usual, affected to treat King Louis and his subjects with contempt. The old Duke declared that if Louis would come to meet him, he would go to Hesdin. But the King remained at Paris ; and the truce with the English—which was merely one step back in order to take two forward—was concluded in his absence.

While these negotiations were proceeding, Louis was occupied in gathering together all his resources for the recovery of the towns on the Somme. By the Treaty of Arras (1435), these towns—Saint-Quentin, Amiens, Doullens, Montreuil, Rue, Saint-Valéry, Le Crotoy, Crèvecœur-en-Cambraisis and Montaigne—had been handed over to Philip, in return for 400,000 crowns. Louis, as his emissary told the people, had 200,000 crowns in hand. For the remaining 200,000 he looked to his loyal subjects, those especially who lived near the mortgaged towns. The people of Touraine responded by raising a loan of 20,000. The Parisians grumbled, as they always did, when it was a question of paying taxes. But Louis took no notice. There was no time to lose. For Philip, a licentious old man, would probably be easier to deal with than his successor, who was " young and green and hard to bend." From Paris, the King was able to send 200,000 gold crowns, with a strong guard, to Abbeville, where Philip's emissaries waited to carry them safely to Hesdin and deposit them in the ducal treasure chest. Louis himself entered Abbeville, where he waited for the last instalment of the money, concerning which the Paris Parlement was making difficulties. The municipality of Abbeville received him in great state. The town was sumptuously decorated ; bonfires were lit ; the school children cried " Noël " ; plays and mysteries were acted, casks of Beaune and Burgundy were broached and three oxen roasted. Meanwhile the Chancellor explained to the people in the town hall the terms of the mortgage and its release ; and Louis, beneath a canopy of damask, embroidered with fleurs-de-lys, held over his head by the notables of the town, paraded through the streets on the way to the house of his lawyer, Jean Vilain, on the Place Saint-Pierre.

From Abbeville, Louis went on to Hesdin, where Philip received him. They rode side by side, the King ill-dressed and ill-mounted, with a little hunting-horn hanging from his neck. The people did not recognise him. " Where is the King ? " they cried in a voice loud enough for Louis to hear. " Bless us ! " they exclaimed, " can that be the King of France, the greatest King in the world ? He looks more like a valet than a knight. Why, the whole of his equipment, his own and his horse's, is not worth twenty francs. Now, our Duke looks like a great personage."

These words had little effect on Louis. He may have looked nothing but an obscure hunter, but under his coarse cap he wore a crown which was worth millions ; and he was clothed in glory ; for he had satisfied his peasants' hunger for land, for the land of France, which he had redeemed. Louis, who loathed ostentation, had forbidden the troops to make any demonstration on his arrival at the castle. All the same, a princely guard accompanied him.

At Hesdin, the King received an ambassador from the King of Aragon asking for help against Barcelona, an emissary from the Duke of Denmark, and ambassadors from England, who came to obtain his ratification of the treaty.

It was the Duke of Burgundy who presented them to the King. Louis' words were too smooth to be sincere. He assured the ambassadors that Philip was a father to him, nay, more than a father. When the English bishop made a brief oration in Latin, Louis praised it and asked for news of King Edward, declaring that he wished him well, in spite of his being the enemy of his cousin, King Henry VI. Louis called Edward *un gentil prince* and protested that he was at his service. The astonished English went home with the impression that Louis was a dangerous monarch, too polite to be sincere.

This conference, like many another, pleased no one. They had all looked one another in the face and seen each other's faults. The French felt humiliated by Burgundian ostentation. Philip was furious with Antoine de Croy for trying to serve two masters and caring for no one save those of his own household.

But after all, Louis had the towns of Picardy; and Philip had lost the territory where he had recruited most of his men-at-arms.

The King's entry into Amiens was a triumph. The town was illuminated. The school children bore torches emblazoned with its arms. When the King and Queen arrived at Notre-Dame, Jonah stepped out of a whale and greeted them. Then the King, turning to the Milanese ambassador, said : " Do you not agree that this town alone is worth more than the 400,000 crowns I have paid to the Duke of Burgundy ? "

Meanwhile, on the other side of his kingdom, Louis— who claimed to have inherited rights to the kingdom of Aragon from his mother, the granddaughter of John I, King of Aragon—was intervening in the troubled affairs of the Spanish Peninsula. The attempt of Catalonia to assert its independence had brought on a war between John II, King of Aragon, and Henry IV, King of Castille. After playing a double, if not a triple, game, Louis succeeded in capturing Perpignan and annexing Roussillon to the Kingdom of France.

CHAPTER XXI

THE KING AT WORK

The Perpetual Pilgrim.—Land Hunger.—Daily Life.—Correspondence
—Dealings with the Towns.—With the Church.—Activities in
Normandy, Guyenne, Paris, on the Somme.—Renewal of Alliance
with Milan.—The King's Army of Secretaries.

For four years—from the time of his leaving Genappe
until the rebellion of 1465—Louis was constantly on the
road, dressed as a pilgrim, smiling his caustic smile. Only
in winter, when the roads became impassable, did he settle
down and take up his residence on the banks of the Loire.
On this perpetual pilgrimage he was working out his
salvation as King, just as he might have done had he been
a monk. Indeed, so he told the King of Portugal, a
monastic life would have been his, had circumstances
been different. This salvation for which Louis was
working was the salvation of the Kingdom of France, the
fulfilment of the great oath he had taken at his coronation :
the oath to recover all the lands " which had been separated
or alienated from his domain." And the King's first
important act was, on the 9th of September 1461, to
cancel the alienation of all those lands.

From one point of view Louis may be regarded as
a mystic, with eyes ever raised to the Virgin, his protectress and the protectress of France, in the attitude he
assumed for all time on his tomb at Cléry. But from
another point of view, Louis was of the earth : a man of
the land, his land, the land of France, which he was
resolved to visit incessantly and to know thoroughly.

His days were so full that it was difficult to obtain an
audience with him. He rose early, prayed, went to mass

and from his chapel passed into his dining-room, where he sat at work until the afternoon. Then, after taking exercise, either on horseback or on foot, he conferred with his secretaries until supper, which he took early. He went to bed late.

The King set the mark of his strong personality on everything he touched : on his ordinances, far more numerous than those of his predecessors, on the thousands of letters he dictated to his secretaries. Louis had no ministers, only secretaries, agents, commanders of his military forces, and spies. The chief thing he required of these agents was money, for money was the first necessity to a landowner rounding off his possessions, to a sovereign with a standing army of 12,000 paid soldiers, such as Louis had in the first year of his reign.

Louis' letters are among the most interesting of contemporary documents. We seem to hear his voice as he dictated them, now humorous, now facetious, often intensely serious and even menacing. We seem to hear him nicknaming Toison d'Or, the Burgundian herald, *Trahison d'Or*. But though Louis was a great letter-writer, he never committed matters of the greatest moment to paper. In such cases his emissaries, generally persons of humble rank, received verbal instructions, accompanied by a scrap of parchment authorising them to act in the King's name. And Louis considered himself at liberty to ratify their actions or to reject all responsibility for them. For those who betrayed him there were state prisons, dungeons, iron cages.

The King's mind moved with lightning swiftness, and he expected the minds of all around him to do likewise. He exacted complete and instant obedience ; and in return for successful service he gave rich rewards, land and money. But for those who failed he had hard words. "You have spoiled everything," he would say. His servants had need of all their wits in order to follow the double game he was constantly playing. "I can give you no precise instructions," he said to two of his ambassadors. " If the Burgundians lie, you must lie also. Do not believe everything you see."

Louis knew all that was going on. He had spies everywhere. He would despatch a servant to some prince with a greyhound as a present or to fetch a bird or a dog : that servant would be one of his secret agents.

Among the most trusted of his agents and the most frequent of his correspondents were the good towns of France. To them Louis opened his heart ; and they responded by confiding their needs and their aspirations to him. He knew exactly how to treat the faithful folk of Tournai, his friends at Reims or Troyes, the borderers of Amiens and the traders of Lyons. It was Louis who inaugurated the famous Lyons fairs as a means of economic warfare with Geneva, a town which had profited from the destruction of the French international fairs during the Hundred Years' War. Louis now forbade any Frenchman to go to Geneva, while he invited all foreigners to attend the Lyons Fair, and made all coinages current there. He definitely made Lyons the centre of that silk industry which he was later to extend to Tours. Louis was a regular merchant in his dealings with the towns. He exacted money from them, but he also gave them the opportunity of making it. The free fairs he established up and down the country promoted the circulation of commodities. The tolls he authorised the towns to demand provided them with an income for the upkeep of roads and fortifications.

Absolute monarch as he was, Louis converted a large number of towns into municipalities, governed by elected magistrates, many of whom he ennobled, preferring, no doubt, this new nobility to the old.

Living from day to day, learning from experience, without any preconceived plan, Louis, during these four years, made many mistakes and corrected some of them. His own impulsive and revengeful temperament was often his worst enemy.

We must now glance at Louis' work as organiser and

administrator, in order to judge whether his conduct justified the serious rebellion of 1465—a rebellion in which he narrowly escaped ruin.

We have already considered his attitude towards the towns. As to learning, he confirmed the privileges of the University which he had founded at Valence when he was Dauphin. As to his ecclesiastical policy, it can only be described here in the merest outline.

On Louis' accession, in 1461, the Church of France was almost completely independent of the papacy.

This Gallican Church was one of the results of the movement to establish the supremacy of the œcumenical councils. The famous liberty of the Church encroached on monarchical as well as on papal authority. But the papacy was the greater sufferer. In the domains of the Very Christian King all temporal matters were outside papal jurisdiction, while with regard to spiritual matters the rules and canons of the Councils strictly limited the papal power. The Church of France protested against contributions being exacted by order of the papal legates and sent to Rome. The famous Pragmatic Sanction, drawn up at Bourges in 1438, had constituted Charles VII Defender of the Church in France. This celebrated Assembly had adopted the decrees of the Councils of Constance and Bâle, which had established the authority of the œcumenical councils ; and it had instituted a system of election to benefices which had converted the Church into a republic of churches, monasteries and colleges. With regard to the bestowal of benefices, the power of the Sovereign Pontiff was limited to one in ten. This arrangement placed immense power in the hands of the King, the University, and the nobility. The Church's escape from papal authority merely meant that it had multiplied its masters.

It was naturally not long before the papacy began to resent the Pragmatic Sanction. Eugenius IV, in the reign of Charles VII, had endeavoured to replace it by a concordat, which would give the Pope the right to annul elections to monasteries and metropolitan churches and to nominate to benefices falling vacant during the odd months, while leaving the ordinaries power to appoint during the rest of the year. But Charles VII stood firm to the principles of that Pragmatic Sanction, which, for Pius II, was a wound in the side of the Church, and the most abominable of abuses.

Louis, who, as Dauphin, opposed everything his father did, allowed it to be understood that he desired the abolition of an arrangement which was so cordially detested at Rome. Consequently, when Louis came to the throne, Pius II expected to find an ally in the new King. The Pragmatic Sanction increased the power of the nobility, which Louis was determined to reduce. But though the Pope and the King seemed at one in their desire to abolish the agreement, their objects were different. The Pope's was the recovery of power that had once been his, Louis' the arrogation to himself of powers hitherto exercised by the nobility

An inevitable quarrel ensued. The very agreement which had been designed as a means for conciliation was now converted into a cause of friction. This friction was intensified when the Pope found that Louis, like himself, was dreaming of exercising hegemony over the Italian states.

A few days after Charles VII's death, Louis might have been seen praying at his father's tomb in St Denis. And the papal legate, Francesço Copini, might have been heard pronouncing the papal absolution of the dead King, as if he had been condemned on account of the Pragmatic Sanction.

The interests of Pius II at Louis' court were represented by the adroit Jean Jouffroy, Bishop of Arras, and a subject of the Duke of Burgundy. In the Bishop of Arras, the shrewd and discerning Pontiff had made a good choice. Under Jouffroy's influence Louis abolished the obnoxious Sanction; for the Bishop had persuaded the King that he would thereby deprive the nobles of any influence over ecclesiastical appointments; and he had promised Louis that the Pope would establish in France a legate charged to superintend the collation of benefices and to see that no French money was sent to Rome. This was precisely what the King desired, for he aspired to become the patron of all French benefices, which he intended to use as a means of rewarding his servants and winning numerous supporters.

Louis fervently kissed the letter, in which the Pope made these proposals, saying that he would enshrine it in a casket of gold. He showed it to the Parlement, asserting that he had abrogated the Pragmatic Sanction in order to quiet his conscience.

The aged Pius II wept with joy; the erudite Pontiff hailed in King Louis a second Constantine, a second Theodosius, a second Charlemagne. The Parlement, however, refused to register the royal edict. But Louis made light of this resistance. The King was determined to be master in his own house.

Meanwhile in Italy the Pope and the King were not on such good terms as in France. In the revolt which was going on in Genoa, the Duke of Calabria, son of King René of Anjou, was taking the French side, in the hope that Louis would support him in his claim to the crown of Naples. Pius II was on the side of Ferdinand of Aragon.

While the Pope was presenting Louis with a beautiful jewelled sword, while copies of the Pragmatic Sanction were being publicly burned in the illuminated streets of Rome, while in his most elaborate rhetoric he was celebrating the noble mind and the illustrious virtue of the monarch who had slain the monster, extolling the good fortune of the kingdom governed by such a sovereign, he was refusing to give satisfaction to Louis' ambassadors in the matter of Naples.

Then Louis began to perceive that he had been duped. He threatened to summon a council. He protested that French money sent to Rome was being used to oppose

French interests in Italy. A war of words followed. Finding threats to be of no avail, Louis tried persuasion and bestowed the magnificent gift of Diois and Valentinois on the papacy, at the same time proposing a marriage between one of his natural daughters and the Pope's nephew. Pius accepted the gifts, but continued to appoint to French benefices; and, in 1462, he declared himself supreme in all matters of investiture, threatening members of the Parlement and the King's counsellors with excommunication.

Louis was at that time involved in a dispute with Francis, Duke of Brittany, which, though ostensibly ecclesiastical, was in reality political. Francis, a friend of the English, was anxious to prevent the King of France from becoming too powerful. He had refused to put the brother of the Admiral of France, Arthur de Montauban, in possession of the Abbey of Redon, and he had forbidden his people to acknowledge Amaury d'Acigné as Bishop of Nantes. Louis intervened in favour of Acigné. Pius II appointed Jean Cesarini, his auditor, to act as umpire in the dispute. But Louis referred it to the officials of the Parlement.

Here was an open rupture. Louis, with all his Italian cunning, had been duped by the Italians. The Pope had kept everything and given nothing.

A religious war began which lasted from 1463 to 1465. Louis was now ready to listen to the Parlement when it complained of his annulling of the Pragmatic Sanction. With the support of Jean Jouffroy, likewise disillusioned —for he had been disappointed in his expectation of a plurality of benefices which he had hoped for from the Pope—Louis proclaimed the Gallican ordinances of 1463 and 1464. He prohibited the collection of tithes; he required churches and monasteries to give inventories of their possessions; and, finally, he restored the Pragmatic Sanction. In Italy he became more and more closely associated with the Duke of Milan, who was to be the umpire of the Peninsula; and he withdrew his support from the House of Anjou, whose chances of success were dwindling.

In 1464, the schemer, Pius II, died in the midst of organising a crusade.

His successor, Paul II, was a Venetian, a handsome man, whose mind worked slowly, and who was prepared to continue his predecessor's policy. Louis XI was not a king to start on a crusade. To the League of Rome, Naples and Venice he opposed a League of Milan, Florence and France. But the King of France had been too precipitate. He had hustled first the nobles, then the clergy. And suddenly he found himself confronted by the redoubtable Ligue du Bien Public. The Burgundian Coalition proved too much for him ; and one of the results of the treaties of Conflans and St Maur was that he had definitely to renounce the right of investiture and to confirm his restoration of the Pragmatic Sanction. Paul II now found him submissive, and Jean Balue[1] obtained a cardinal's hat. Then came the disaster of Péronne. Jean Balue was the scapegoat. The King, having discovered his treachery, had him arrested. For Paul II, Balue was the wonderful man to whose efforts had formerly been due the abolition of the Pragmatic Sanction, that horror which Louis had for ever been dangling before the eyes of the Pope. The King's ambassador, Cousinot, was received at Rome with great magnificence. But the pontifical comedy slowly dragged itself out in all its magnificence. Paul II concealed his stern determination beneath pleasant and amiable words. He regarded Cardinal Balue as within his jurisdiction, not the King's. The Pope imagined he could mollify the King by bestowing on him the title of " Very Christian," which Louis XI was the first French King to bear. But such an honour was no better than the fine jewelled sword Pius II had presented to Louis. And the King received nothing tangible. Venice, Naples, and Paul II, all joined Charles the Bold against him.

Another French embassy set out for Rome in

[1] See *Post*, pp. 193, 194, 196, 202, 206, 232, 284.

November 1469. They found Paul II dying, and as firmly set on another crusade as his predecessor had been. But Louis was still not in the least anxious to fight against the Turk. He was ill and sent a beautiful gold chalice to the Lateran Church. But it was the Pope who died— on the 26th of July 1471.

The Genoese, Sixtus IV, who succeeded him, was a strong man, austere and pugnacious. The Pope needed French tithes ; the King needed the Pope to support him against his brother, Charles of France, and to prevent the catastrophe of his marriage with Charles the Bold's daughter. Amiabilities were exchanged. Louis was made canon of Cléry. But by the time Cardinal Bessarion arrived in France the King's brother was dead. Consequently Bessarion received a cold welcome, being regarded as a friend of Burgundy. Nevertheless, he brought Louis what he had long coveted, the legation of Avignon. In August 1472, Gérard de Crussot, Bishop of Valence, was at Rome trying to arrange a concordat. The papacy and the monarchy were to share their powers. France installed herself at Rome.

Louis' friendship with Italy, however, was to bring him nothing but disappointment. Galeazzo Maria Sforza of Milan proved unreliable. Yolande of Savoy was inclining towards Burgundy. René's partiality for Burgundy was unmistakable. Peace in Italy was regarded merely as a way of gaining time, of restraining the King's allies—the Swiss, for example—until Charles the Bold had accomplished the maddest of all his undertakings. Charles's death at Nancy put an end to this imbroglio, and enabled Louis to play that part of arbitrator in Italian affairs to which he now aspired. After the conspiracy of the Pazzi, Louis took the part of Lorenzo di Medici. It was now the King's turn to threaten the Pope. In October 1478, the French clergy assembled at Orléans. The ordinance decreed at Selommes was a new kind of Pragmatic Sanction. Now it was the King who sermonised the Pope. Louis told Sixtus IV that he would be better employed in looking after the general interests of the papacy and in fighting the Turk than in fighting against the King's allies in Italy. Louis defended the Florentines, threatening to enter the Peninsula with a large army and oblige the Pope and Ferdinand to stop making war on the Florentines, who were the allies of France. The King gave himself the airs of a personage who, having been anointed with the sacred oil, was at once lay and ecclesiastical. He posed as the veritable sovereign of the whole of Italy.

Consequently the King could afford to appear generous when the papal legate arrived in France in 1480. His generosity took the form of the liberation of Balue. In Italy, in spite of the Sovereign Pontiff, Louis succeeded in reconciling Lorenzo di Medici and Ferdinand of Aragon. Now and again he declared that he was about to cross the Alps and establish peace. Having inherited Provence, he possessed Marseilles. The Pope offered him the investiture of Naples. He was made arbitrator in the dispute between Rome and Venice. Piety and politics mingled. Sixtus IV sent relics and the Saint, Francis of Paola, to the prematurely aged King, who was too ill to leave Plessis. Sixtus ordered prayers to be offered for the monarch whom he styled " the Zealous Defender of the Holy See." And after the King's death the Pope had a solemn service held for the repose of the soul of the King, who had been the veritable suzerain of Italy.

Thus, through suavity, strength, and patience had the King of France triumphed over the Pope of Rome.

The astuteness of Louis' dealings with Guyenne, which had recently been an English province, is beyond question. He granted privileges to La Rochelle, the great military port of France on the Atlantic, the centre also of trade with Holland, Flanders and the Hanseatic towns. The inhabitants of the Island of Ré, lately devastated by the English, were exempted from all taxation. The people of Bayonne, where many families had been ruined by war and plague, were also released from taxation and given two free fairs. The people of Bordeaux had all the rights they had possessed under the English confirmed. The duty levied on the export of wine was reduced, the municipality was organised, shoemakers and tailors were encouraged. It was Louis who instituted the Parlement of Bordeaux and gave it jurisdiction over Saintonge, Angoumois, Limousin and Le Quercy.

In matters of finance the King was not so well advised. For example, he suppressed the Court of Aids, which regulated the voluntary contributions of the kingdom, and invested its powers in the Court of Requests. Louis soon discovered his mistake. This attempt to simplify administration resulted in a serious diminution of revenue. And the King, who was never slow to realise his mistakes, before long re-established the Court of Aids.

In August 1462, Louis was in Normandy, on a pilgrimage to Mont-Saint-Michel, where he relieved of taxation the loyal defenders of the fort. He took Rouen on his way, and there re-established Pierre de Brézé as Grand Seneschal. He also instituted a mint, and renewed the statutes of the mercers, iron-workers and drapers. From Normandy his vigilant eye was surveying the whole of his kingdom ; he was reforming the order of Cluny, and taking the church at Metz under his protection.

In the beginning of 1463, we find him in the Bordeaux region, then in Les Landes and Languedoc, granting an act of indemnity to the people, and keeping an eye on the war in Catalonia. Returning north through Limousin, he confirmed the privileges of Limoges, whose magistrates (called consuls) were permitted to hold fiefs without being noble.

Back again in Paris, Louis as usual demanded money from the Parisians, this time for the recovery of the Somme towns.

Louis' cupbearer was Geoffroy Cœur, son of the famous banker, Jacques Cœur, who, after having rendered considerable financial assistance to Charles VII, had, by the machinations of his enemies, fallen into disfavour and been condemned in 1453 to imprisonment and the confiscation of his wealth. The King now restored the fortunes of the Cœur family, whose history probably he alone knew. He reversed the sentence against Jacques, took the family under his special protection, and restored his father's lands to Geoffroy.

In September 1463, the King was at Dieppe, superintending the repair of the city walls as a rampart against the English, and constituting himself the chronicler of his own earlier exploits, describing his storming and capture of the fort.

In November Louis was visiting the towns of the Somme, which he had recovered at such vast expense. With the object of quickening their commercial and industrial life, he established free fairs at Tournai, Tricot and Crèvecœur, authorised Rue to reclaim lands from the sea, with the object of creating another port on the Channel, and commanded Doullens to rebuild its houses, which were rapidly falling into ruins.

From these northern towns the King sent a ratification of his brother's foundation of a University at Bourges; and strengthened his alliance with Francesco Sforza of Milan. Louis extolled the virtues of his hero, Francesco, who, from being a condottiere, had risen to be Duke of Milan, and those of his aunt Bianca Maria Visconti. Sforza was now the most powerful ruler in Italy. His army was one of the finest in Europe. So Louis, foreseeing that he might be glad to appeal to the Duke for military aid—as his own subjects were not too keen on military adventures—determined to make him his lifelong friend by ceding to him the French claims to Savona and Genoa, which his father had conquered with no little difficulty. Louis realised, of course, that Sforza was the sworn foe of the House of Orléans, which laid claim to his town of Asti. But what did that matter, when it was a question of security on the French frontier?

Louis spent the summer of 1464 between Normandy

and Picardy. But his indefatigable activity radiated throughout the kingdom : he confirmed the customs of the Albigeois and certain rights of Verdun in the district of Toulouse ; he insisted that the nobles of Languedoc, both temporal and ecclesiastical, should pay *taille* when they acquired the possessions of commoners.

Indeed, the King found time to take an interest in everything.

He spent the January of 1465 at Paris. Finding the work of the Châtelet Law Court in arrears, he appointed four new commissioners, to the annoyance, naturally, of those who were dismissed. He also defined the functions of the Parlement and of La Chambre des Comptes, strictly confining the jurisdiction of the latter to financial affairs.

All this vast activity was, in the main, the King's personal work, carried out, as we have seen, through secretaries and military commanders, but without ministers.

Some of his assistants were old friends : Jean Bourré, the Angevin, for example, a middle-class law student, who had served him in Dauphiné as *clerc des comptes*, and had followed him to Genappe. On his accession, Louis appointed Bourré *clerc notaire* and royal secretary. His chief duties were to sign the nominations of officials. Louis shut his eyes to the fact that Bourré made no small profit out of this work. He served the King well, was industrious, shrewd, quick, and had the manners of a gentleman. What did it matter if, as the venomous Thomas Basin alleged, he received a commission of fifty crowns a letter ? In sexual morality Jean Bourré was beyond reproach. He was a family man. If he grew rich, so much the better, since the King might be glad to dip into his purse. So Bourré enjoyed all the privileges of the chase, and built himself fine residences in Anjou. He loved beautiful things—manuscripts, tapestry and jewels. He lived like a nobleman ; and the King made him one in 1465, admitting him also to the Order of St

Michael, and frequently, as we shall see, sending him on embassies. " M. de Plessis," as Louis now styled him, knew the King's business better than anyone.

Another of Louis' secretaries was Pierre Doriole, son of a mayor of La Rochelle. Because of his methodical ways and thorough knowledge of administration and of financial affairs, Louis appointed him Maître des Comptes and High Treasurer. He had the knack of raising money, and acted as Louis' agent in his dealings with Burgundy. Later we shall find him presiding as Chancellor over the great political trials of the reign, and concluding treaties of peace.

The Norman, Guillaume de Cérisay, was another of Louis' servants, who made a large fortune as Parlement Registrar. But generally the King had no liking for parliamentarians ; they were too long-winded and obstinate. Their one concern seemed to be to refuse to register documents. They could never make haste. But, though the King frequently wanted to muzzle them, he did not disdain to avail himself of their services : for example, he sent their First President, Jean Dauvet, on divers missions to Spain.

The King treated even his Chancellor, Pierre de Morvillier, as a mere agent. " Lord Chancellor," said Louis, " certain matters are reported to us, concerning which we have not been consulted. . . . Take care that it does not occur again."

In short, Louis, as we have said, had no counsellors, only servants ; and he dominated the whole band, even Commynes, one of the most intelligent men of his day, and a profound admirer of Louis' resourcefulness.

King Louis was essentially an autocrat, and, consequently, unpopular.

CHAPTER XXII

LA LIGUE DU BIEN PUBLIC

1465

Louis' Alienation of the Nobility.—His unpopularity throughout the Kingdom.—Origin of la Ligue du Bien Public.—Alliance between Francis of Brittany and the Count of Charolais.—The Question of the Duke of Brittany's Allegiance.—The Princes of the Blood summoned to Tours.—Meeting of the Confederates at Notre-Dame in Paris.—Programme of the Insurgents.—Charles of France leads the Rebels.—The King's Manifesto at Thouars.—Loyalty of the Towns and of René of Anjou.—Burgundy the Soul of the Rebellion. —Bourbon raises an Army against the King in the Low Countries.— Charolais marches on Paris.—Loyalty of the Capital.—The King's Attack on Bourbonnais.—Arrival of Italian Reinforcements.—The Battle of Montlhéry.—Both sides claim the Victory.—Louis in Paris.—Recruiting in Normandy.—Conference between Parisians and the Confederates at La Beauté.—Louis returns to Paris.— Negotiations with Charolais.—The Treaty of Vincennes.

Louis' conduct ever since his accession had been prompted by a desire for the well-being of his people. And yet it was ostensibly for the public good that, in 1465, a coalition was formed against him. Its aim was to arrest his great organising and unifying work and to ruin the King, with all that he had so marvellously accomplished.

Though the true origin of this League of Malcontents was Breton and Burgundian, Louis had provoked hostility in all directions. He had disappointed the House of Anjou by failing to support it as his father had done. He had behaved badly to the House of Orléans, by deserting its cause in Italy and allowing it to be calumniated in France. In Louis' eyes Charles of Orléans was nothing but an old fool, and Dunois more or less a traitor. After destroying the old independent Gallican Church and

177

compelling the ecclesiastics to make a statement of their possessions, Louis scandalised the clergy by the brutality with which he addressed the Pope. Nobles and clergy alike were compelled to contribute to the national revenue and to the maintenance of order in the towns. Louis' subjects loved ostentation and disliked his frugal way of living. A vast enterprise like that the King was endeavouring to carry out required money. In the beginning of the reign the levying of taxes had caused riots at Reims and at Angers. The Estates of Normandy and Languedoc, provinces which had not yet recovered from the devastations of the Hundred Years' War, protested against assessments, which they considered too heavy. The country took a long time to recover. Louis helped it to the best of his ability. But no one was grateful, no one liked him. An efficient ruler is seldom popular. The King was trying to form a nation, at a time when the province was the only unit. A shock was inevitable. It occurred first with Brittany.

The Bretons were proud and pugnacious, carrying on a prosperous trade with England. The stalwart Constable, de Richemont, who had devoted his whole life to France, had made difficulties about doing homage to Louis' father. His successor, Francis II, was a young man addicted to luxury and pleasure. He had his own Estates, as well as an independent court and university. He had come to Tours, soon after Louis' accession, and made the same difficulties as the Constable. Louis received him adroitly in the house of one of the citizens. The King would not insist on any particular form of words. If Francis objected to the term " allegiance," then he might simply pay his respects to his sovereign. That would suffice. But when it was a question of a secret alliance with Charolais and of a peace with England, which might be converted into an alliance against France, then Louis lost patience. A further difference arose over the homage of the Bishop of Nantes,

Amaury d'Acigné. When Francis required the bishop to do him temporal homage, Amaury informed the King. Thereupon his bishopric was seized and he was obliged to flee to Angers. The Nantes Estates took the Duke's side, and voted subsidies for war. The Duke of Brittany reviewed his troops, and renewed his alliance with Charolais.

These two young adventurers, as Louis well knew, were on excellent terms with one another. The King talked of " laying low the horns " of Brittany and Burgundy. Should occasion arise, he would make an agreement with the English and bring two or three of the greatest in France into bondage. For the nobles of France seemed more dangerous than his ancient enemies, the English, who were now reduced to the possession of Calais. The King was assured of the rights of the crown in the Nantes affair, and of the exorbitant pretensions of the Duke, who issued charters " by the grace of God," introduced a crown into his coat of arms, received papal bulls addressed to himself, and refused to take the oath of allegiance to his King. Francis meanwhile was circulating the groundless rumour that, in order to reduce the nobles of his realm, Louis was ready to buy the support of the English by ceding Normandy and Guyenne. The King wrote letters protesting against such an accusation. He appointed the Count of Maine arbitrator in the quarrel ; and Francis appealed to his Estates, who voted him a military aid.

Louis, on his part, convoked the Estates of Tours, in December 1464. He summoned all the princes of the blood—Sicily, Berri, Orléans, Bourbon, Nemours, Angoulême, Nevers, Saint-Pol, Tancarville, Penthièvre —to appear before him. The King resolved to sound the Princes, to plead his cause before them, and at any rate to prevent their joining the Duke of Brittany.

After the Chancellor, Pierre de Morvillier, had explained the rights of the crown in the Nantes dispute, Louis, realising the gravity of the situation, appeared himself and stated his case. He declared his affection for the princes of the blood, his concern for the public weal. On his father's death the kingdom had been poor. Louis could not let it be reduced still further. In his wanderings up and down the kingdom he had observed the loyalty of all classes. The nobles had done him homage. They were the pillars of the realm. The King relied upon them, as he did upon all his subjects. But he would resist any opposition. It was his duty to watch over them all, from the highest to the lowest. He had promised to do this at his coronation. Louis had added the counties of Roussillon and Cerdagne to his kingdom. He had recovered those bastions of France, the Picard towns. He had laboured tirelessly, dedicating himself and all he had to the public weal. He loved all his subjects, and was determined to be a good king. They, in their turn, must be his good kinsmen. He bore none of them malice, not even the Duke of Brittany. The Duke was a man of honour, who had been ill-advised. The King would do him no harm, but would bring him to reason.

So moving a speech brought tears to the eyes of those who heard it. After the princes had withdrawn to deliberate, King René spoke in their name, saying : " You are our King, our sovereign lord. We have none other. . . . We will serve you against every one." They all swore to follow him wheresoever he went. Louis thanked them. Let them go then, each of them, and remonstrate with the Duke of Brittany.

Some—Dunois, for instance—did go to Brittany ; but it was to join Duke Francis, who would not listen to reason. Bourbon went to Charolais and came to an agreement with him. All of them took up the cry of Francis II : " Louis' government is bad ; it must be reformed." One evening five hundred of the Confederates met in Paris at Notre-Dame, all of them wearing the rosette by which they were to know one another. One fine day it was said that Louis' brother, Charles of France, had fled to Brittany. He was a youth of eighteen, well-

meaning but weak and stupid. He was the King's
brother, however, and Louis had no son. Charles was
to be the nominal head of the conspiracy : he gave
himself out as the protector of his people. His reforms
included the suppression of a great part of the *taille* and
an order to the tax-collectors commanding them to
suspend operations. The sums they had collected already
were to be used to pay the army, of which John II, Duke
of Bourbon, was appointed the commander.

The situation was extremely grave. A programme of
reforms which includes the suppression of taxes is always
popular. The fury of Louis when he heard that his
young brother Charles had been declared Regent of
France may well be imagined.

On the 16th of March 1465, the King issued a manifesto at Thouars, denouncing the conspirators and their
wicked designs, which would sow dissension throughout
the kingdom and profit no one but the English, who would
probably invade the country, and once again put it to
fire and sword. Louis, however, would prevent such
disasters, such shedding of human blood. Now, preferring
mercy to justice, he offered to pardon all those who would
withdraw from his brother's confederacy within one
month. For Louis intended to be merciful, following
the example of Jesus Christ, "from whom we hold the
crown and this kingdom."

The towns responded to this pathetic appeal ; they
rewarded Louis for the protection he had accorded them,
and remained loyal. So also did René of Anjou. The
King empowered him to treat with the rebels, but they
refused to listen to him. Brittany and Burgundy lifted
up their horns. But Burgundy was the soul of the
rebellion.

Nothing had infuriated the Burgundians more than
the loss of the Picard towns. Not only did it restrict
their frontier, but it deprived them, as we have seen, of
recruiting ground for their best soldiers. Charolais
accused Antoine de Croy and his brother of having urged

Louis XI to recover this territory, and of having deceived the Duke by making him think that the King would grant him the usufruct. The Croy brothers, of whom it was said that they with the King constituted three heads in one sack, were banished and their goods confiscated. Shortly afterwards the Duke of Bourbon, Burgundy's ally, arrived at Lille. He came in the name of the princes to ask the Duke to allow him to raise an army in his territory, with the object of reforming Louis' government of France.

Thus opened the civil war, known as La Ligue du Bien Public, because the object of this second Praguerie was the reform of the government.

A reconciliation was effected between Duke Philip and his son. The Duke, worn out and senile, was content to leave everything to Charolais. The Count became commander-in-chief, gathering round him all who were hostile to France and to the House of Croy. The Count of Saint-Pol was his lieutenant. His army consisted of fourteen hundred men-at-arms and eight or nine thousand archers.

King Louis numbered his forces, calling out all who were liable for military service. The parts of France that supported him were the counties of Auvergne and Foix, the provinces of Dauphiné and Savoy, l'Ile de France, Normandy, Champagne and Languedoc, and the good towns of Paris, Rouen and Lyons. King René, too, remained with him, informing him of all that was going on. The vanguard of the royal forces attacked Berri. Then, hearing that the Bastard of Bourbon had entered Bourges, the King proceeded to march into Bourbonnais with the whole of his artillery.

Charolais, with a well-disciplined army, some 25,000 strong, was marching towards Paris, announcing that he came, not to make war on the King, but for the good of the people. He hoped to find the other nobles at Saint-Denis ; but they were not there. He appeared before Paris. But the town, though somewhat shaken, held out for Louis—32,000 men, well accoutred and armed, kept watch on the ramparts and at the gates, ready to fire their arrows, cannon and culverins at the Burgundians. But Charolais did not attempt to enter Paris. He returned to Saint-Denis and waited for Berri and Brittany on the other side of the Seine, at Saint-Cloud.

Louis, in Bourbonnais, heard that most of the peers of the realm had declared against him. But he kept his head. He had public opinion on his side; and he was supported by all those who could see no advantage in changing the King's government for that of the princes of the blood.

Louis, who had begun by attacking the weakest of his enemies, the Duke of Bourbon, captured several of his strongholds and would have taken others, had the Burgundians, led by the Marquis of Rothelin, not arrived.

On the 27th of June, the King was not far from the Rhône valley; and on that date he wrote to Galeazzo, the son of the Duke of Milan, thanking him for sending reinforcements and appointing him Lieutenant in Lyonnais and Dauphiné. On their arrival in Dauphiné, the Italian soldiers had been feasted and hailed as deliverers. The bells had rung, the towns had been decorated in their honour, and the clergy had gone out to meet them.

But Louis understood that the war had to be fought out near Paris; for the fate of the capital would decide that of the rest of France. So he marched northward with all haste; and, finding Charolais at Longjumeau, he established his own vanguard at Montlhéry.

The Count of Maine's army hovered between the two forces, waiting for the Bretons; but it finally rallied to the King.

The so-called Battle of Montlhéry, fought on the 16th of July 1465, was, in reality, little more than a series of skirmishes. Charolais was wounded in the stomach and throat. Louis, charging at the head of his troops, " like a second Cæsar," put courage into the hearts of his followers and succeeded in routing part of the Burgundian army. The engagement lasted for eight hours. Both sides fought furiously, "like mad dogs." But on both sides there were fugitives. And when night fell and fires were lit on the heights of Montlhéry no one knew who had been the victor.

The Burgundians slept round their convoys. Charolais, on his bed of straw, drank, ate and resolved to renew the attack at dawn. At midnight the French camp-fires were seen gleaming only about three bow-lengths away. But Louis was planning to go off to Corbeil; and when day broke, the Burgundians found that their adversaries had disappeared. A carter, who came in from Montlhéry, said they had decamped on the previous evening. Charolais at once became dangerously puffed up with military pride. It was not until after the battle that he was joined by most of the Confederates: Charles of France, Dunois, Dammartin and the Duke of Brittany, with his fine army, consisting largely of nobles.

From Corbeil Louis sent his own account of the battle to the citizens of Lyons. "God in His mercy," he wrote, "hath given us the victory. Thrice did the Count of Charolais take flight with most of his followers. . . . The rebels lost ten killed to one of ours : 1400 to 1500 of them slain, 200 to 300 taken prisoners." Then he announced what was absolutely untrue, viz. : that the Bastard of Burgundy had been killed. "We remained on the field till sunset," he concluded. "Give thanks to God."

Louis reached Paris on the 17th of July, with a part of his army. The remainder he had left to rest in the villages.

Charolais also was bent on entering Paris. He crossed the Seine on a bridge hastily improvised out of wine-casks, and encamped close to the capital, while his followers skirmished at the gates of the city.

Louis brought in the fugitives by offering ten francs a lance. The Parisians entreated him not to fight Burgundy, but to leave them to conduct negotiations. The King was impatiently awaiting the arrival of Galeazzo's Italians. Meanwhile he confirmed the privileges of the

University, reduced the number of his secretaries, suppressed all the offices he had created since his accession and the taxes he had levied, and reappointed Louis Raguier, Bishop of Troyes, President of La Chambre des Aides.

But Louis had to leave Paris to go and recruit soldiers in Normandy. He needed 60,000 men, and money also. If he failed, he would take refuge in Dauphiné, with Galeazzo.

During the King's absence from Paris, the Confederates, having failed to enter the city by surprise, held a conference with certain representative citizens at la Beauté. The Parisians were tired of the devastations committed by this great army ; but they refused to surrender the capital to the Burgundians and Bretons.

Louis, hearing of the conference, returned in all haste to Paris, with the fruits of his recruiting in Normandy—2000 men-at-arms, nobles and bowmen. At Paris he found Galeazzo's reinforcements, which he estimated as being equal to 800 French lances.

After having banished such of the Parisians as had favoured the Confederates, he determined to try and cut off the rebel army from its supplies, but without risking a battle. He preferred negotiation because it was less costly. Rouen had just surrendered to the rebels, and with it went Normandy.

The two armies were encamped on opposite banks of the Seine. The King's people concealed their artillery behind earthworks extending from Charenton to opposite the Hôtel de Conflans, where Charolais had his quarters. One of the King's cannon-balls traversed the room in which the Count was dining, and drove him to take shelter in the cellar. But the bombardment, which continued for three or four days, produced no very tangible result.

It succeeded, however, in alarming the Burgundians. They were deciding to build a bridge of boats, and to go over and attack the King's army, when, one night, they heard Louis' people crying: "Good-bye, neighbours, good-bye!" The royal troops were firing their tents and withdrawing their artillery.

All this was a mere feint on Louis' part. His plan was still to negotiate, and to avoid staking the fate of a great and submissive kingdom like France on the uncertain issue of a pitched battle.

Parleys and conferences ensued; agents passed to and fro across the trenches; there was spying and dissimulation, in all of which Louis excelled. He was always on his guard. For he did not trust the Parisians. One evening he discovered that the gate of the Bastille leading to the open country had been unlocked. The Confederates on their side were nervous, and ready to mistake a field of thistles for an army advancing in the darkness. Strict watch was kept on the ramparts of Paris. Cannon boomed now and again. But all the while negotiations were proceeding. The Confederate demands were exorbitant: Normandy for the Duke of Berri, the Somme towns for Charolais.

Then the King himself crossed the water and entered the Burgundian camp: "My friend," said Louis to Charolais, "will you guarantee my safety?" And the Count replied: "Yea, my Lord." "My brother," began the King, "I know you to be a nobleman of the House of France." Then Louis, with an ingratiating manner and smiling face, reminded him of their friendship and of the services they had rendered one another. But Charolais would not desist from demanding the Duchy of Normandy and the towns of the Somme. All the King would offer was the office of Constable for Saint-Pol. They parted apparently on good terms. Louis returned to his boat and crossed over to Paris. The King's brother, Charles, was prepared to cede Berri in return for Normandy, since that province demanded a lord who would reside in it, and Rouen had already taken the oath of allegiance to him. On some such terms Louis and Charles might possibly come to an agreement.

So the King sent word to Charolais that he would like to confer with him again at Conflans. They talked to one another affectionately. Charolais was at the end of his supplies, having neither victuals nor money for his army. The King sent him clothes and shoes. The nobles were forsaking him. Nothing remained but to come to terms with the King. Louis knew how to gain time. Conversing familiarly, they found themselves in the trenches on the Paris road. Charolais had to be escorted back to his army. And everyone praised the King for his good faith.

Charolais gave the King the names of those who remained with him, and of those whom he had lost. Louis arrived unexpectedly, with thirty to forty horse. He would give Charolais Vincennes as a pledge. And at Vincennes the King and the princes of the blood met on the following day. Charles of France did homage for Normandy, Charolais for the Picard towns. Louis of Luxembourg, Count of Saint-Pol, who had led Charolais' vanguard, became Constable of France and took the oath of allegiance. Later, at Paris, in the great hall of the Palais, in front of the marble table, he received the Constable's sword from the King's hand ; and they kissed one another on the lips, which can hardly have been pleasant. Burgundians and Bretons entered Paris, but in order and disarmed.

There was no concealing the fact that on most counts the King had been worsted. He could not seriously maintain that by surrendering the Picard towns he was paying an old debt of gratitude and the expenses of his coronation. The Duke of Brittany had won in the Nantes affair, and had, moreover, gained the right to coin gold money. Jean d'Anjou was relieved of homage for his lands in Lorraine.

The King accompanied Charolais on his march back to Flanders. They were friendly, but circumspect in their talk. Louis was on his guard ; and Charolais slept fully armed, surrounded by the escort with which the

King had provided him. The people on the Somme did homage to the Count, who took possession of those towns which King Louis had bought back only nine months before, at the cost of 400,000 gold crowns. That was certainly a win for Charolais. But Louis, on his side, had rid himself of a formidable coalition, and kept his army. That was one for him. And he went about muttering : *Sapiens nihil invitus facit.* They had wanted to impose on him a council of thirty-six reformers. No, he would not admit any restriction of the rights of the crown. Thirty-six reformers, forsooth ! When thirty had been enough to endanger the State of Athens ! The storm would blow over, just as that downpour of rain had done when they were signing the treaty at Vincennes.

Charles of France had won Normandy. He had made his entry into Rouen as Duke ; but he was already quarrelling over his booty with the Duke of Brittany. Louis made a treaty with Brittany, and perceived that he would before long be able to recover Normandy. Another win for Louis : by his brother's cession of Berri he had recovered his cherished central dominions. Charles was about to go to the aid of the town of Liége, which was rebelling against Burgundy. Louis resolved to take Burgundy's side. He rode on horseback to review the troops which might have captured him. Now, as in the Genappe days, he fêted Charolais. They might have been two brothers : " one heart in two bodies." The King announced the marriage of his eldest daughter, Anne of France, with Charolais.

CHAPTER XXIII

THE KING AT PERONNE

1468

Louis recovers Normandy.—Day-dreams.—Death of Duke Philip.—His
magnificent Funeral.—Louis observes everything from the Loire,
organises his Kingdom, negotiates with the King of England.—
Military Measures designed to protect his Subjects.—End of the
Truce with Burgundy.—Louis promises to support the rebel Town
of Liége.—Attempts to come to terms with Burgundy.—Invades
Brittany.—Duke Charles advances towards Péronne.—Louis makes
peace with the Dukes of Brittany and Normandy.—Having failed to
come to terms with Burgundy, visits him at Péronne.—News of the
Revolt of Liége.—Charles's Fury.—Louis in danger of Imprison-
ment.—Mediation of Philippe de Commynes.—The Treaty of
Péronne.—Undoing of all Louis' Work.—Louis at the sack of
Liége.—His return to France.

THERE was one province, Normandy, which Louis was
determined to recover without delay.

The Duke of Brittany had accompanied Charles of
France on his entrance into his recently acquired appanage.
The Normans complained that Francis was organising the
duchy for his own advantage and that of his followers;
and, on the 25th of November 1465, they seized Charles
and carried him off to Rouen.

Louis saw his opportunity: " I think I shall have to
take back my Duchy of Normandy," he said, " and go to
the help of my brother." In two months all the fortresses
of the province were in Louis' hands; and his brother
was compelled to accept Roussillon as his appanage in
place of Normandy. .

A year after Montlhéry, the Milanese ambassador
could write that the King had nothing more to fear from

the nobles of his kingdom, who had all been completely subjugated. Louis began once more to indulge in the day-dreams of his youth. He would make peace with his brother, with the Duke of Brittany, with Charolais, and then in the spring he would besiege Metz. With the help of Galeazzo's troops, what might he not do? The conquest of the whole Metz valley would be mere child's play. He had already sent six hundred lances into Champagne. He was learning new methods of warfare from the Italians : the best way to pitch a camp, allowing one tent for every two men-at-arms, the King providing the cloth. After capturing Metz he would win the support of the German League, and push on to clip the wings of the allies of that Duke of Burgundy who had so gravely offended him. Then Louis would suddenly grow very serious, he would seem to peer into the distance. What did he see beyond Metz? The Rhine of his youth? What honours would he not heap on Galeazzo, to compensate him for the crown he had failed to place on the head of his father, Francesco! But then the King paused : there was Charolais. What was to be done with him? Was he to be an ally or an enemy?

Meanwhile the hare-brained Charolais was trying to seduce the frontier towns in order to checkmate Louis. But Louis' agents had renewed his alliance with Liége. The city was in a state of perpetual revolt against its Duke. Charolais had punished Dinant most barbarously. And now it was the turn of Liége. He drew up his army in battle array. The citizens entreated him to have pity. There was a brief truce, during which it was announced that Duke Philip was dead.

He had died on the 15th of June 1467, at the age of sixty-one. For two years he had been in his second childhood, shut up in a little room, where he spent his time tempering old sword-blades and collecting fragments of painted window-glass. In the midst of these childish occupations the full-blooded, choleric old Duke succumbed to an apoplectic stroke. Charolais, surveying the blades and the fragments of glass, thought he might play a different game with them.

He had been considered hard-hearted and hostile to the old Duke. But he mourned for his father, wept bitterly and wrung his hands. Then he discovered Duke Philip's immense wealth, his rich treasures of jewels and trinkets. Sixteen hundred torches flared in the magnificent funeral at Bruges, the pall was of cloth of gold ; and no fewer than fifteen hundred black sheets had to be cut up to provide his household with mourning.

Louis, from the marches of Touraine, kept his eye on everything. He observed Charles's difficulties with the towns. Ghent and Malines were clamouring for privileges. Charles had now become definitely anglophile. He was planning to marry Edward IV's sister, Margaret. Louis determined to prevent the marriage. He, too, was negotiating with England. Charles, he heard, was mobilising his troops. Louis and his Queen reviewed their army at Paris : 30,000 well equipped soldiers, drawn up between the Saint-Antoine and Charenton Gates.

But after all, Louis was a man of peace. So he returned to the banks of the smiling Loire ; and, in the Queen's chamber, married his natural daughter, Jeanne, to the Bastard of Bourbon, Admiral of France. The room was so full that the Milanese ambassador could not enter. What a pity that Galeazzo himself was not there !

Then Louis occupied himself with ordering his kingdom. Learning by experience, he did excellent work, coming to terms with the Pope, permitting his subjects to receive benefices from Rome, regulating the coining of money, establishing a Court of Aids at Montpellier, but most important of all, decreeing the appointment for life of royal officials (Paris, 21st October 1467) ; for stability was one of the essential conditions of good government.

Warwick had just landed at Rouen, despatched by King Edward to propose terms of an alliance. Louis fêted the English ambassador royally for twelve days and sent him back to England with tempting offers to his Sovereign.

Louis desired the peace and tranquillity of his subjects above everything. Nevertheless he was preparing for war, putting Amboise in a state of defence against the Bretons, who had entered Normandy and had to be kept in check, commanding the nobles of the neighbourhood to assemble at Senlis, buying equipments for war, and instructing the Duke of Bourbon to keep his people in readiness.

At this time he made a series of important regulations designed to protect his subjects against military violence and disorder. The troops were to be regularly paid and comfortably lodged in places where there was a market and where justice was administered. Every lancer's company—consisting of six men and six horses—was entitled to a room with a fireplace, three beds, three blankets, two pewter pots, one brass stove, a stable for the six horses, and a place where provisions could be kept. No soldiers were to be billeted on a householder against his will. The civil magistrates were to judge all crimes, except those that were purely military. When the troops were on the march, not more than one night—with the exception of Sundays and the eve of feast-days—was to be passed in the same place. Soldiers must pay the market price for everything, except straw, wood and lodging. But these things they were only to receive from their host. They were always, when possible, to be lodged in inns, rather than in private houses. No horses or mares were to be requisitioned for the carrying of baggage. All captains were required to undertake to observe these rules, swearing the following oath : " I promise and swear to God and Our Lady, on pain of their turning to nought all my affairs and business, that I will do justice and see it done by all over whom I have charge, and that I will suffer no pillage, and that I will punish all under my charge whom I shall find guilty, without sparing anyone. . . . "

These peaceful ordinances were more to Louis' taste than those projects of war he was now compelled to make in order to keep his promise to God that he would uphold the honour of his crown. The Truce was about to terminate. " It looks more like war than anything," wrote Louis to the Admiral at the end of July. And the King had promised his aid to the Duke's enemy, the town of Liége.

Charolais, now Duke Charles the Bold, was encamped before Liége. Louis sent two ambassadors to him: his new Constable, the Count of Saint-Pol, and Cardinal Balue. The latter was a Poitevin of humble origin, who had a veritable genius for intrigue. He had been the protégé of Jacques Jouvenel des Ursins, Bishop of Poitiers. Louis had appointed him his chaplain, and then raised him to be Bishop of Evreux. Now the Pope had invested Balue with the Cardinal's hat as a reward for his services in persuading Louis to abrogate the Pragmatic Sanction. The embassy failed to attain its object, which was to induce Charles to leave Louis a free hand in Brittany, in return for which Louis would not interfere with Charles at Liége.

The Duke refused to enter into any such undertaking. Consequently the two princes went their separate ways. Charles, having defeated the people of Liége at Saint-Trond, entered the city, where, on the death of Philip, little waxen figures representing him had been thrown into braziers at the street corners. Charles razed the walls of the city to the ground and imposed a heavy fine on the citizens.

Louis meanwhile marched into Brittany, and captured Champtocé and Ancenis. The Dukes of Normandy and Brittany appealed for help to Duke Charles, who wrote to the King, telling him to desist from making war on the Duke's allies, who had been included in the truce. Receiving no satisfactory reply, Charles advanced towards Péronne, one of the Somme towns, which he had recently recovered (August to September 1468).

While Louis' army was fighting in Brittany, he himself was at Compiègne. Cardinal Jean Balue appeared in the Burgundian camp. The King's main object was to separate the Dukes of Burgundy and Brittany. He had sent Calabria to his brother Charles, entrusting him with full powers to negotiate ; and at Noyon, on the 15th of September, Louis was able to tell the Duke of Milan that peace had been concluded with the Dukes of Brittany and Normandy. The King might have overcome them with force ; he preferred peaceful measures.

And Louis knelt before the image of the Annunciation in the ancient cathedral of Noyon, where he founded a chantry for the saying of a *salve regina* and other prayers for ten years. Remembering that the church had been founded by his predecessor, " the late Saint Charlemagne," he asked for a prayer to be offered for the " salvation and prosperity of himself and of his kingdom."

Louis' ambassador was honourably received at the Burgundian court, and sent back with fair words : Duke Charles had not taken the field in order to injure the King, but rather to assist his allies. Then the Breton herald arrived, bringing letters from the Dukes of Normandy and Brittany, announcing that they had made peace with the King and renounced their alliances, including, they might have added, their alliance with him. Charles of France declared himself prepared to exchange Normandy for another appanage, which should be agreed upon, and for an income of 60,000 livres.

The Duke of Burgundy realised that he had been tricked ; but he concealed his surprise.

Louis had yet another card to play—at least he thought so. He would try and buy off Burgundy ; for he refused to believe the Duke inexorable ; and he had no idea of the bitterness of Charles' resentment at finding himself duped. Consequently, instead of following the advice of his captains and attacking the Burgundian army, which was not very formidable at that time, Louis instructed his ambassadors, Balue and Tanguy du Chastel, to accompany the Duke to

Péronne. But at Péronne all they could obtain from Charles was the announcement that the people of Liége seemed about to revolt, and that Louis might come to Péronne if he liked ; indeed, the Duke wrote the letter of safe conduct with his own hand.

The King was determined to make some kind of an agreement at all costs, and he resolved to carry on the negotiations in person. This was his way. Suddenly he decided to go to the Duke. Louis would return chivalry for chivalry. But for once the fox was to find himself in the jaws of the wolf.

King Louis went to Ham, where the Constable had a strongly fortified château. One fine morning, making as if he would go out hunting, and with only fifty horsemen, he galloped across the plain to Péronne, and confided his person to the care of the Duke's archers, commanded by the Lord of Esquerdes. Charles came out to meet him. The castle not being habitable, he installed his royal guest near by, in the tax-collector's house, which was very beautiful. But when Louis saw the Burgundian army, bearing the cross of St Andrew, and commanded by captains who were his enemies, coming into the town, he began to regret having confided himself to Burgundy, and asked to be lodged in the castle.

The King had forgotten one important matter : that he had despatched two of his ambassadors to Liége, to stir up the townsfolk against Duke Charles. The citizens, whom the Duke had banished, had returned, bearing the white cross of France, and crying : " Long live the King and our liberties ! " The craftsmen had welcomed them as deliverers, and had captured the town of Tongres, the residence of the Bishop of Liége, some of whose servants they murdered.

When Charles heard of all this his wrath knew no bounds. He accused Louis of having come to Péronne with the set purpose of deceiving him. He had all the gates of the town and castle closed, under the pretext of

having lost a casket containing rings and jewels. The
King was confined in the smaller castle, a gloomy place,
the gates of which were guarded by bowmen. Louis was
afraid. He knew his history of France ; he knew that he
was lodged close to a great tower where one of his predecessors (Charles the Bald) had been murdered by
a Count of Vermandois.

Philippe de Commynes was at this time a young squire,
who had followed Charles in his wars ; and who now
served him as chamberlain. The Duke, who knew
Commynes to be shrewd and prudent, gave him full
liberty to come and go in his house. Now Charles
summoned him and a few others, among them Charles de
Visen of Dijon, the Keeper of the Duke's jewels, to come
to his room. Having carefully shut the door, the Duke
declared that the King had come to Péronne on purpose
to betray him, that the Burgundian troops had entered
the town without the Duke's orders, and that his people
were being massacred at Liége—doubtless at the King's
instigation. Charles was wild with rage, and hurled
threats at Louis. Had one of his counsellors given him
bad advice, the Duke would certainly have treated the
King as his prisoner and shut him up in the great tower.

Charles de Visen was a good man and calm. He and
Commynes endeavoured to appease the Duke. But
Charles's words were being reported. They reached the
King and seriously alarmed him. For several days Louis
was kept almost in solitary confinement. The Duke of
Burgundy stayed away from him ; and he saw only a few
of his own men, who entered the tower by the little door
in the great gate. On the second day, Charles's rage had
somewhat abated. Louis, for his part, was by no means
at the end of his resources. He offered great rewards to
all whom he thought likely to help him ; and he ordered
Balue to distribute a sum of 15,000 crowns, to part of
which the Cardinal helped himself.

Charles's counsellors were divided ; most of them
thought that Louis' safe conduct ought to be observed,

seeing that he was willing to make peace on the terms which had been agreed in writing. But others advised that he should be made a prisoner and that his brother should be summoned. The King himself took the first step by offering to make peace and to give compensation for the action of Liége, provided he were allowed to return to Compiègne. He also proposed to leave hostages with the Duke.

During the third night Charles never undressed, but walked up and down his room in a state of terrible agitation ; only two or three times did he throw himself on to his bed. In the morning, the Duke was more irritable than ever and threatened all manner of violence. Finally he declared that he would pardon the King, if he would swear to make peace and consent to go with him to Liége, to make the Bishop, the Duke's kinsman, take vengeance on the town. Then suddenly, Charles went to the King's lodging to tell him all that was in his heart.

But Louis had a discreet friend who had kept him informed of everything that was going on : Philippe de Commynes had told him of Charles's designs. Consequently Louis was fully aware of the danger of his situation; and he had resolved to be submissive in the presence of his infuriated host. Gesticulating wildly, and in a voice trembling with wrath, Charles demanded to know whether the King would swear to a treaty of peace. The King consented. Then the Duke inquired whether Louis would come with him to take revenge on the people of Liége, for whose treason he held him responsible. The King answered that he would come and bring with him a following, large or small, as the Duke should think fit. Charles was surprised and delighted. The treaty of peace was taken out of the Duke's safe, and with it the true cross that Charlemagne wore, which was called the cross of victory. Louis took the oath. The bells pealed merrily and the people rejoiced. The King was grateful to his friend Philippe de Commynes who had saved him.

Then Louis sat down to his desk and signed a heap of amazing documents, " given at the aforesaid place, Péronne, on the fourteenth day of October, in the year of grace Fourteen hundred and sixty-eight, the eighth year of our reign."

Where was Louis' sovereignty now ? Could he still be called King ? For, as one after the other, these parchments were presented for his signature, he saw they meant the undoing of all his work, the destruction of that great national unity, to the achievement of which he had devoted his life. Nevertheless, Louis signed. He signed every document that was given him : he signed away for eight years the right of the Paris Parlement to determine the frontiers of Flanders. He might as well, as he wrote afterwards, in his heart's bitterness, have made Flanders a completely independent state. Still he went on signing : now it was an order to arrest the prosecution of certain Burgundians who had acted for Charles, now the exemption of the Duke's servants, vassals and subjects from personal service in defence of the kingdom, now the recognition of the jurisdiction of the Duke and of his Council, and of his right to receive the homage of certain vassals without the intervention of royal officials.

All these renunciations, wrote Louis, had been required of him because of the Duke's marriage with Margaret of York.

The next day King Louis and Duke Charles went out of the little postern gate of the castle and took the road past Cambrai and Namur to Liége. Louis wrote to the Grand Master of his kingdom that he went of his own free will, and that as soon as Liége was taken, he would return. To the Lord of Rochefoucauld, Seneschal of Périgord, he wrote announcing the Peace with Burgundy, but also telling him to beware of the English and to prepare to resist them in Guyenne, which he knew they intended to invade.

Winter was setting in, and the weather was bad. The King had his Scottish guard with him, and a few men-at-arms. Duke Charles commanded one part of his army, the Marshal of Burgundy the other.

The Marshal marched straight on the city, without waiting either for the King or the Duke. His one thought was of plunder. During the night of chaos that ensued, the townsfolk took heart, for they had succeeded in massacring part of the Burgundian vanguard. When Charles heard of it, he said nothing to the King, but tried to give courage to his troops, who were beginning to take flight. Louis, who did not remain long in ignorance, had to put on a good face. The King's quarters were in a little house in the suburbs close to the Duke's. In a barn near by were three hundred men-at-arms, who had been charged to see that the King did not try to escape or enter the city with his followers. This "fête" lasted for a week, at the end of which, on a Sunday, the 30th of October 1468, Liége was taken.

The city had neither walls, nor gates, nor moats, nor artillery. It depended for its defence on a few brave soldiers, who, on the eve of its capture, had made holes in the walls of the houses where the King and Duke lodged, and were on the point of taking them prisoners.

Louis was compelled to take part in the storming of the town, if such a term can be applied to the entrance of the Burgundians into a dismantled city.

It was, as we have said, a Sunday. The people were at table, when they had suddenly to flee and take refuge in the churches. Louis strolled in a leisurely manner through the streets and silenced those who cried out "Long live the King." Charles conducted him to the Palace. The churches were being pillaged like the rest of the city. Louis sat down to table with Charles. He tried to show a satisfaction which he was far from feeling, and he went so far as to praise the Duke's courage, somewhat ironically, seeing that all Charles had done had been to kill a man at the door of the Palace with his own hand. In truth Louis' one desire was to return to his kingdom as quickly as possible. The Duke was mad with rage against the town. The poor people, dying of cold and hunger, and dropping with fatigue, were driven out into the Ardennes—a lamentable exodus of women and children, fleeing from the flames of the city, which was to burn for seven weeks.

On the morrow the King left Liége, and conversed calmly with Charles. There was nothing more to be done ; and Louis wanted to go to Paris as soon as possible to get the treaty ratified by the Parlement, seeing that this was the custom in France. In this way he could serve the Duke. In the summer they would meet again ; and Louis would spend a month with him in Burgundy, where they would make good cheer.

Duke Charles had to admit the force of the King's argument, though somewhat reluctantly. But before Louis went, Charles had the treaty brought to him, and re-read it. He wished to insert some additional clauses in favour of certain of his followers. This displeased the King, who proposed to insert others in favour of some of his own supporters, Nevers and Croy. Charles, who detested them, withdrew his demand.

They took their leave of one another ; and the King departed under the escort of three Burgundian nobles.

The *Te Deum*, postponed by Charles's order, was now sung. Bonfires and bell-ringing answered to the flames of Liége ; and throughout Flanders the Peace signed at Péronne was hailed with rejoicing.

CHAPTER XXIV

FROM PÉRONNE TO BEAUVAIS

1468–1472

Submission of Charles of France.—Imprisonment of Cardinal Balue.—
Charles of France receives Guyenne as Appanage.—Alliance between
Burgundians and Yorkists.—Louis supports the Lancastrians.—His
Attempts to recover the Somme Towns.—Burgundy summoned to
appear before the Paris Parlement.—Preparations for War.—The
French enter Amiens.—A Three Months' Truce with Burgundy.—
Death of Charles of France.—Louis takes Possession of Guyenne.—
Pierre Doriole Chancellor.—Burgundy resumes War.—The Siege of
Beauvais.—Burgundy invades Normandy.—Defection of Philippe
de Commynes.—His Reception by Louis.—Truces with Brittany
and Burgundy.

ALTHOUGH King Louis endeavoured to put a good face
on his discomfiture at Péronne, he felt his humiliation
bitterly, and determined to avenge himself on the Duke
of Burgundy.

His first step was to come to terms with his brother,
Charles of France, in whose name the Confederates of
1465 had raised their rebellion.

On the 19th of August 1469, Louis despatched his
Secretary, Bourré, to Angers to fetch the cross of Saint-
Laud. Certain death within a year was the fate of
anyone who broke an oath sworn on this holy relic. The
cross was taken to Saintes; and there, in the presence
of Bourré, Charles swore that he would neither kill his
brother nor cause him to be killed. He also renounced
all thought of marriage with Mary of Burgundy, the Duke's
heiress and only child.

Charles of France, who had no intelligence of his own,
depended entirely on that of others. The Duke advised
him not to accept the province of Guyenne, which his

201

brother was offering him as an appanage, but to demand
Champagne. It was natural that Duke Charles should
wish to see the impressionable heir to the French crown
installed in a province which Burgundy had long coveted.

Louis was perfectly aware of the Duke's designs. He
had also discovered that they were being furthered by the
treacherous Cardinal Balue, who owed him everything.
Balue was imprisoned in the Château of Onzain. But
the story that he was shut up in an iron cage is mere
legend. Charles was so worked upon by Louis' emissaries
that he consented to accept the appanage of Guyenne
instead of Champagne.

In order still further to circumvent Burgundy, and to
attach the quondam rebel, Charles of France, to his
brother's cause, Louis founded the Order of St Michael,
which was intended to rival the Burgundian Order of the
Golden Fleece, and of which he made his brother
" premier chevalier."

The reconciliation between the brothers seemed
perfect. On the 7th of September 1469, the King wrote
a description of their interview, which had taken place
at Port-Braud, on the left bank of the Sèvre. Charles
had asked for the formidable barriers erected between
himself and his brother to be removed. At six in the
evening he had sworn his complete obedience. This was
nothing short of a miracle. And the sailors noticed that
on that evening the tide had begun to ebb four hours
earlier than usual. " We will forget the past," wrote the
King. " Our brother has promised to be a good brother
to his King and his sovereign lord. We will keep him in
touch with affairs of state. He will live near us in
Touraine."

But, at the same time, the King was instructing the
Norman Chancellor of the Exchequer to break the ring,
with which Charles had wedded the Duchy of Normandy,
and which Thomas Basin had put on his finger, in the
Cathedral of Rouen, in 1465.

The King's far-seeing eye led him to oppose the

marriage of Ferdinand and Isabella and to demand the hand of the Queen of Castille for his brother.

Louis was treading warily in those days. For the country needed rest from war. Everywhere, however, Louis found the Duke of Burgundy conspiring against him.

When the King went to pray in the church of Saint-Lô, at Mont-Saint-Michel, sailors told him that the Burgundians were constantly on the coast, harassing fishermen, burning cargo boats, killing the inhabitants or taking them prisoners. The Burgundians were expecting the English to come in great force to help them to fight against the French.

Louis seized the opportunity of averting this danger, when, in April 1470, the Earl of Warwick, now Edward IV's declared enemy, arrived at Honfleur. Louis took him to Angers, where he reconciled him to Margaret of Anjou, and then sent him back to England with an expedition which ultimately succeeded in driving Edward IV from his kingdom and temporarily restoring Henry VI, who had been a prisoner in the Tower.

Louis meanwhile was endeavouring to win back the towns on the Somme, alleging that as Charles had broken the Treaty of Péronne, the King was relieved from any obligation to observe it. But Louis proceeded with great secrecy, anxious not to put himself in the position of being the first to resume war.

All those who had any grievance against the Duke were gathering round King Louis : the King of Sicily, the Duke of Bourbon, the Marquis du Pont. Charles of France seemed inclined to help his brother with men-at-arms. To the Estates of the Realm assembled at Tours the King complained of Burgundy's conduct. " We have tolerated all these outrages," he said, " because we will not act, save after the mature deliberation of our Council."

It required no " mature deliberation of the Council," however, to prompt Louis to a deed which incensed the proud Duke of Burgundy far more than any declaration of war would have done. One day, when Charles was in his town of Ghent on his way to Mass, he suddenly found himself confronted by an usher of the Parlement of Paris, who, in the King's name, summoned him to appear before that court. The Duke was so furious that he detained the usher for several days.

Charles was not ready for war. Louis was.

On the 4th of January 1471, the King openly denounced Charles, " the so-called Duke of Burgundy," as an enemy of the public weal and an ally of Edward, " the so-called King of England," whose object was to destroy the House of France. Louis asked the religious houses for a loan. The people of Lyons sent him what artillery they had, and prepared to cast more. Bourré was despatched to Paris to get money wherever he could.

Charles realised that things were going badly. He returned in all haste from Holland, and with no more than four or five hundred horse, proceeded to Amiens to prevent that town from going over to Louis. For the King had ordered Antoine de Chabannes, with a great company of archers and men-at-arms, to enter Amiens. The aldermen met them at the Beauvais Gate. Chabannes told them that he had come in the King's name to receive the submission of the city to its sovereign and natural lord, and that if such submission were refused, the city would be utterly destroyed. The next day the French entered Amiens. The people sang the *Te Deum* in the cathedral, cried " Noël," and took the oath of allegiance to the King.

After hesitating for some time, taking up his quarters first at Péronne, and then at Arras, the Duke finally marched towards Amiens, and remained encamped outside the city for six weeks.

The King was at Beauvais, and seemed in no hurry to join battle. He was averse to running so great a risk. But in Burgundy proper, near Macon, his troops inflicted a serious defeat on the Duke's army, with the result that a truce of three months was signed between the combatants.

Louis was well pleased with the issue of the campaign.

Already he was preparing to return to Touraine, and sending his falconer on in advance to moult his birds. He left Flanders in July 1471.

In Touraine—at Tours, Montils and Plessis—he waited on events, occupied the while with the organisation and working of the gold, silver and copper mines in Dauphiné and other parts of his kingdom. Their yield was unsatisfactory, largely owing to the lack of efficient miners. There was no reason why they should not produce as much as those of Germany, Hungary, Bohemia, Poland, England and elsewhere. So Louis brought in foreign workmen.

He was still anxious about his brother's loyalty. Was he planning a marriage with Mary of Burgundy ? Was he intriguing with the Count of Armagnac ? But the King's mind was soon to be set at rest. For he began to receive news that Charles was ill. He had been carried in a litter to the frontier of the County of Foix. He was suffering from a quartan fever. One of his chaplains, a spy in the King's service, reported that the Duke of Guyenne had barely a fortnight to live. On the 18th of May the King announced prematurely that his brother was dead, and informed the citizens of Bayonne that he was about to take them under his protection. Charles did not actually die until six days later. Jean, Comte de Foix, advanced the money for his funeral.

The King lost no time in taking possession of his brother's appanage. Before the month was out he was in Guyenne, making his activity felt throughout the whole province, conferring new privileges on certain towns, confirming the existing privileges of others, restoring to Bordeaux the Parlement he had removed to Poitiers, compensating those who had suffered—especially the victims of the English devastations.

On the 18th of June, the King was at Notre-Dame-de-Béhuard in Anjou; for from that place he wrote the letter appointing his Treasurer, Pierre Doriole, Chancellor of France.

Doriole—the son, as we have seen, of a mayor of La Rochelle—was a man of acute intelligence. He had faithfully served Charles VII as his steward. Louis had sent him on embassies to Castille, and had employed him as judge in the Bishop of Nantes affair. He had acted as counsellor to the King's sister, Yolande, Duchess of Savoy, and had helped to collect money for the recovery of the Somme towns. He had betrayed the King in 1465, when he had been for a short time financial minister to Charles of France, and had gone over to the Breton court. This was the man whom Louis now appointed to succeed Guillaume Jouvenel des Ursins. Doriole's conduct may have commended him to Louis as one whom he might at any time—should it prove convenient—arrest as a traitor. It was Doriole who collected evidence for the trial of Balue—and for the trials of several other state prisoners. He afterwards appropriated Balue's library.

The Duke of Burgundy had reorganised his army. Between the 22nd of June and the 19th of July, he published manifestos, accusing the King of having compassed his brother's death " by means of poisons, malpractices, enchantments and invocations of the Devil." On the 4th of June, without waiting for the expiration of the truce, he had opened hostilities. On his march to Nesles, he began, for the first time, to put everything to fire and sword. Nesles was taken on the 10th. Its defenders were either hanged or had both their hands cut off to the wrists. Thus did Charles take vengeance for the loss of Amiens. Louis was furious. " If you can do likewise in his country," he wrote to Dammartin, " then do not hesitate, and whenever it is possible, spare nothing." Louis ordered the dismantling of Noyon and the occupation of Compiègne by a strong force. He was surprised that the garrisons of Amiens and Saint Quentin had not taken the field to harass the Burgundians.

Charles arrived before Beauvais. Louis ordered the Constable to protect the surrounding country, and the

Bishop of Beauvais, with the assistance of the townsfolk, to defend the city until the King's arrival—which would be shortly.

Louis, after organising his artillery at Angers, had entered Brittany and was besieging Ancenis. Thence he wrote encouraging the defenders of Beauvais and sending them wine of Orléans vintage. But Charles had captured the suburbs of Beauvais ; and his artillery had effected a breach in one of the gates. The only defenders of the city were a company of reserves commanded by Louis de Balagny. They threw flaming faggots in the faces of the besiegers. One of the gates caught fire. But the King's Marshal, Joachim Rouault, forced an entrance into the town with a hundred artillery lances. He had the breaches repaired, while Burgundian fire was raking the city. Charles's attempt to storm the city had failed. Beauvais stood firm.

Louis wrote to the townsfolk that by holding out against the Burgundians for three weeks, by sparing nothing, neither their lives nor their goods, their wives nor their children, they had " won great praise from God and the King, and that they would ever stand *en très singulière recommandation* with him and his successors."

But in a document dated Roche-au-Duc, the 14th of July, Louis rewarded Beauvais with more than words : he created it a municipality, and exempted the city from the obligation to pay taxes and from military service, both active and in the reserves (*ban* and *arrière ban*). Moreover, Louis decreed that every year on Saint Agadesme's day, the anniversary of Charles's attempt to storm the city, there should be a procession, mass, and a sermon. For at the request of the women of Beauvais, the reliquary of Saint Agadesme had been carried round the city during the siege, while prayers had been offered to the Saint and to Our Lord. But the brave women of Beauvais had done more than pray. They had gone out on to the ramparts and defended the town side by side with their men. So they were to walk in front of their men-folk and immediately after the clergy in the procession. To the leader of the women, Jeanne Laisné, who had captured the Burgundian standard, Louis gave a husband, Colin Pillon; and he exempted them both from the obligation to pay *taille*.[1] Moreover, the King gave permission to all the women of Beauvais to dress as they pleased; for there had been quarrels in the city because certain women had worn clothes which were considered unsuitable to their rank. The King now decreed that on high days and holidays, at weddings and other festivals, the women of Beauvais might wear any clothes they liked and deck themselves with as many jewels and ornaments as they pleased.

Louis was as pleased as the women. For now he had the laugh at his enemy, Charles the Bold, repulsed by women and townsfolk!

The King was still in Brittany, where Ancenis had fallen.

The infuriated Charles marched into Normandy, captured Eu and Saint-Valéry, and encamped before Rouen. His army was starving; for the barbarous invaders had destroyed everything; and his followers were disgusted. One of them, Philippe de Commynes, went to King Louis at Ponts-de-Cé, to offer him his services. Louis received, with no lack of cordiality, the man who had saved his life. Commynes, having done homage, was granted lands and a pension.

Louis was so short of money as to be reduced to borrowing one hundred crowns from the Seigneur du Lude. At the same time, however, we find him dedicating the model of a town in silver to Notre-Dame-de-Cléry, sending three offerings to Puy-Notre-Dame, two to Saint Martin of Tours, and two to Saint Florent. He thought of his dogs also, and gave votive offerings to Saint Hubert for each of them, as well as the wax model of the last stag he had hunted. Meanwhile this mystic with one eye fixed on heaven, had another for the affairs of

[1] From this incident was derived the legend of Jeanne Hachette.

PHILIPPE DE COMMYNES, LORD OF ARGENTON
(*From the Arras Collection*)

this world ; and he did not scruple to intercept and read letters from the Duke of Brittany to Charles of Burgundy. The Bretons, he learned, were beginning to go home. Their Duke was prepared to renounce his alliance with Burgundy and the English. This was all Louis wanted.

A truce with Brittany was signed on the 15th of October 1472 ; with Burgundy in the following November.

Two years earlier, kind fortune had delivered Louis from one of his most troublesome barons in the south— Jean V, Count of Armagnac. This incestuous prince, who had lived with his sister and tried to persuade the Pope to legitimise their children, had, among other numerous malpractices, been intriguing with Edward IV. Jean had been so ill advised as to employ as his emissary an Englishman, one John Boon, who had once acted for the King of France. Boon fell into Louis' hands and revealed the plot. At least, so Louis said. But some maintained that the whole affair was one of the King's inventions. And it may have been so. Louis was quite capable of fabricating such an incident to serve as a pretext for sending an army against the Count. Jean's stronghold of Lectoure was captured, and he himself fled into Spain. The Parlement of Paris decreed his arrest and the confiscation of his property. But a year later, the rebellious Count was back again at Lectoure. While he was negotiating with the King, a brawl broke out between two noblemen under his palace windows. Jean went down to inquire into the affair, and fell, struck dead by a free-bowman, Pierre le Gorgias.

Jean's no less turbulent younger brother and successor, Charles d'Armagnac, held out against the King in his mountain fortress of Causse-Noir. But a little company of Louis' men seized the fortress and took Charles prisoner. He was tried by the Parlement of Paris, and, in 1472, sentenced to imprisonment and the confiscation of his goods. He remained in the Bastille until the eve of Louis' death. The King undertook the government of his province.

CHAPTER XXV

THE ENGLISH INVASION

1474–1475

Louis' Fabian Policy.—His Attitude towards the English.—Edward IV prepares to invade France.—Louis' Preparations for Resistance.— The Siege of Neuss by Charles the Bold, 1474-75.—Louis' Attempts to make sure of Paris.—Alliances and Counter-Alliances.—Landing of the English.—Their Disappointments.—Edward's Letter of Defiance to Louis.—Treachery of Saint-Pol.—Olivier Mérichon's Mission.—Peace Negotiations.—Revelation of Saint-Pol's Treachery. —A Screen Episode.—Stormy Interviews between the Duke of Burgundy and King Edward.—The English at Amiens.—Meeting of Louis and Edward at Picquigny.—Signing of the Treaty.— Departure of the English.—Execution of Saint-Pol.

LOUIS knew that his great rival, Charles the Bold, was a romantic prince, moving in an imaginary world, the world of King Arthur and *les chansons de gestes*—that Charles was the kind of person, who, if left alone, would inevitably work out his own ruin. This knowledge strengthened the King's determination to avoid any decisive engagement, and to sign truce after truce. But all the while he took care to guard and fortify his towns, especially those on the frontiers of Picardy, Lorraine and Champagne, confirming them in their loyalty to the crown by an impartial administration of justice, and by well-timed honours and rewards.

In January 1474, Louis won Creil and visited Beauvais, holding his council in the Bishop's palace and ordering the moats to be cleared ; for the Duke of Burgundy had declared his intention of besieging the city.

But while Louis gained the affection of the towns through these measures, his Fabian policy annoyed the barons, who longed for the excitement and the opportunities of plunder offered by the battles, which the King had resolved to avoid. His policy was to let the Burgundians advance into a country denuded of supplies, where they would be reduced to make long and fruitless sieges, to suffer famine and the hardships of winter—to destroy themselves, in short—while the King would run no risks. A sound, common-sense policy this seemed to Commynes, with whom the King talked frequently.

Louis never failed to realise that his most formidable enemies were the English. After the short-lived triumph of the French King's protégés, Warwick and the Lancastrians, the fugitive Edward IV had returned to England and inflicted two crushing defeats on the Lancastrian party. At Barnet, on the 14th of April 1471, Warwick had been killed. At Tewkesbury, in the following month, Margaret had been taken prisoner and her son, the Prince of Wales, slain. A few days later her husband, Henry VI, had died mysteriously.

Now that the victory of the Yorkists was assured, Edward IV was at liberty to turn his attention to England's hereditary enemy, France, and to plan an invasion of that country.

The English King declared his intention of commanding his army in person. And Louis realised the magnitude of his design, which was nothing short of the conquest of France by a formidable English army, acting in collaboration with that of Burgundy. But Louis and Commynes both knew that the English Parliament would be in no hurry to vote the necessary supplies, and that consequently the French would be able to gain time. Louis made haste to impose a tax on the provinces, to equip a fleet, to raise troops and to arm the towns of Guyenne, Poitou and Normandy.

Closely observing Charles, Louis saw that he had nothing to fear in that quarter. The Duke, puffed up with military pride and eager for adventure, had his eye on the Empire. Louis, also, in his youth, had suffered from a similar obsession, and he knew what it led to. So he encouraged Charles by renewing his truce with him and leaving him a free hand. The world marvelled at what seemed to them the obtuseness of the French King. But Louis knew what he was about. He made alliances with the Hanse Towns, who were the sworn foes of the English, with the people of Berne, and with the Emperor, Frederick III.

Events turned out just as Louis had expected. Charles found himself involved in one dispute after another. The Archbishop of Cologne, Robert of Bavaria, was quarrelling with his Chapter. Charles took his part, and in June 1474, laid siege to the impregnable town of Neuss, situated on an island in the Rhine.

Here, within but the space of a bow-shot from the town, the Duke assembled all his most formidable engines of war. He himself with his household occupied a luxurious movable palace. The whole heraldic college of the Golden Fleece was lodged in a neighbouring abbey; and the monks' dormitory became a veritable temple of Mars.

Encircled with trenches, with a branch of the Rhine dammed up and drained, Neuss was besieged by land and water. Culverins and cannon, rockets, cranes, and a tower on wheels—every possible engine of war that had ever been invented from Vegetius onwards bombarded it perpetually. But the townsfolk made light of the flaming missiles these machines discharged, and crafty peasants laid in wait for the Burgundian foragers to slay them. Whole forests were cut down to provide wood for the bastions and lodgings for the soldiers. Charles seemed to have established himself in front of the city for ever. He had built a veritable town at its gates, with streets and trenches, a market where the wares of Ghent and Bruges were sold and where justice was administered, two hundred tents, gorgeous pavilions, casemates containing halls, kitchens and brick chimneys; ovens, mills, baths, brewhouses, and a gallows. Weddings and christenings were celebrated. Minstrels sang songs and funeral dirges. Bagpipes, drums and flutes played constantly ; and from the Duke's quarters arose a music so heavenly as to entrance the chaste and abstemious Charles. Amidst such gorgeous surroundings, in tents of cloth of gold, Duke Charles received the Kings of Denmark and Norway.

To the frugal Louis all this magnificent display seemed mere childishness. While the King of France was making serviceable alliances, the Duke of Burgundy was wearing himself out and exhausting his resources in this second siege of Troy, from which, at the end of a year, nothing but the intervention of the Pope's legate could induce him to desist. Commynes told the King that he thought Charles mad and believed that God had confused his mind.

Louis meanwhile, was at Paris. He stayed there from December 1474 to April 1475, trying by various measures to propitiate and make sure of that doubtful and rebellious city. With this object, he endowed a scholarship at the College of Navarre for a chorister of Notre Dame de Paris when his voice was breaking. He endeavoured to please the people by regulations concerning the free-bowmen, a regiment instituted by Charles VII, which had become very unpopular. All manner of charges were brought against them : they were perpetually bugling ; they were thieves ; they were constantly spoiling their clothes and demanding new ones from the townsfolk. Louis made arrangements for the mending of their old clothes : they were only to be given new ones when they went to reviews. They were to be paid regularly and reviewed regularly. Carts were to be provided to carry them to battle ; but under penalty of death they were not to make war without their captain's consent.

In those days of intrigue there was no depending on anyone. Louis suddenly found his old ally, Galeazzo Maria Sforza, Duke of Milan, forsaking him, and, on the 30th of January 1475, entering into an alliance with

Charles the Bold. Louis replied by an alliance with
Ferdinand and Isabella and a promise to marry his son,
the Dauphin Charles, who had been born in 1470, to the
Infanta of Castille. Louis' intervention in the complicated
politics of the Spanish peninsula had met with no signal
success ; he had been compelled to spend vast sums for
the recovery of Perpignan and other towns occupied by
the King of Aragon. But at length one piece of good
fortune came to him : one of the Duke of Burgundy's
most powerful allies, the Prince of Orange, was taken
prisoner.

At this juncture, the blow fell which Louis had long
been expecting ; on the 4th of July, the English, with
a formidable army, landed in France ; and Edward IV
himself disembarked at Calais. For three weeks previously,
five hundred Dutch flat-bottomed boats had been trans-
ferring the English troops. Such a catastrophe might
have been prevented had Louis paid as much attention
to naval as he did to land affairs. Now all he could do
was to write to his Grand Master, instructing him to lay
waste the whole of Picardy, in order to starve out the
English.

It was horrible : from Hesdin to the Somme, everything was in flames. Now the English might invade
Picardy if they liked : they would find nothing.

But the invaders hesitated to advance. Edward was
disappointed in his allies : Brittany did not move ; the
Duke of Burgundy, threatened by the Emperor, who was
marching on Metz, was compelled to divide his forces into
three, only one of which he could send to help the English.
Edward's army consisted of 1500 men-at-arms and 14,000
archers with their servers ; 3000 of these the King was to
send into Brittany. Louis knew everything ; for he had
bought letters addressed to the English Secretary of State.
Louis cannot have been ignorant of Charles the Bold's
proposal—that instead of attacking Normandy, which was
well defended, the English should march on Reims,
passing through Burgundian territory and endeavouring

to induce the Constable Saint-Pol to surrender Saint Quentin.

Louis, having heard that the King of England intended to be crowned King of France at Reims, sent word to the city that if it were not promptly put into a state of defence, he would destroy it. Meanwhile Louis was ingeniously stirring up all manner of difficulties for Duke Charles—in Switzerland, Lorraine and Alsace.

On his landing in France King Edward had sent Louis a letter of defiance, demanding the kingdom of France as his lawful possession, in order that he might restore to the church, the nobles, and the people the liberties that were their due.

Edward, by thus posing as the deliverer of the French from the King who was oppressing them, showed his ignorance of the French and of their King. Louis was much more shrewd. Having read the letter, he retired into his closet, and summoned the English herald, who had brought the despatch. The King, in a friendly way, explained to the Englishman that he knew Edward had not invaded France of his own free will, but that he had been constrained by the ambitious Duke of Burgundy and by the Commons of England, for whom war with France meant business. Louis explained further that the Duke of Burgundy had been ruined by the siege of Neuss, that the Constable Saint-Pol, who had entered into relations with the King of England, whose niece he had married, was a deceiver, that he sought nothing but his own advantage, and that Louis did not like war. The English herald could now return to his King and explain the situation. Louis gave him 300 crowns down and promised him 1000 more if he succeeded in inducing his master to make peace.

After the herald had left the King, Louis sent him a fine piece of crimson velvet, thirty ells long. The people outside in the hall would have liked to know the subject of their conversation. But the King remained inscrutable. He called Commynes, and told him to accompany the Englishman. Then he gave Edward's letter to his people to read. He was obviously not in the least alarmed, but very pleased with his conversation with the herald.

The King of England had just left Calais with the Duke of Burgundy, who had joined him at last. They had passed through Boulogne to Péronne; and there Charles the Bold had received a letter from the Constable of France, Saint-Pol, whom he had long known for a traitor. The Constable excused himself for having failed to deliver up Saint Quentin, and promised to serve the Duke in the future. Charles showed King Edward the letter, exaggerating its importance. Edward believed what he was told. These English who had come away from their own country and had suddenly discovered France, were simple folk, at once choleric and cold. They never would understand the French, who were much more versatile and many-sided, loving moderation before all things. Philippe de Commynes realised all this and knew that the French and the English would never understand one another. So here for a while we may leave King Edward rejoicing over the news the herald had brought him. We may leave him in the company of Duke Charles, who was daily becoming more and more involved in the affairs of Bar and Lorraine.

Louis, having settled the affairs of Normandy, proceeded to Beauvais, which he found ravaged by an epidemic. His doctor, Jacques Coitier, writing to announce the King's arrival, had sent instructions that all the sick should be kept indoors and that fires should be lit in the streets, especially those in which people lay ill. The King arrived on the 26th of July, and immediately took measures for the defence and revictualling of the city.

Meanwhile the English had appeared before Saint Quentin. Having been welcomed by a bombardment when they had expected bell-ringing and rejoicing, they began to realise that the Constable was really a traitor. Then, on the next day, Edward heard the astounding news that Duke Charles was leaving him and going to join his troops in Bar. The invaders felt betrayed on every hand. Winter was coming on; and their hearts were more inclined to peace than to war.

Louis was soon informed of their state of mind. For the English had taken prisoner the valet of one of the King's gentlemen. Edward had set him free, telling him to go back to the French and to commend him to the good grace of King Louis. The liberated valet joined the French army, which was then encamped near Compiègne. At first he was taken for a spy and put in irons. But the next morning the King talked to him. And before sitting down to table Louis considered as to whether it would not be advisable to send someone to the English. He drew Commynes aside and conferred with him in whispers. This was King Louis' favourite way of consulting people. Then the King invited Commynes to join him at table and to bring with him one of the King's valets, Olivier Mérichon. Commynes was to inquire of Mérichon whether he would be willing to disguise himself as a herald and venture into the English ranks.

Mérichon was dumbfounded; he fell on his knees and thought he was ruined; for the King had never even spoken to him before, except on one occasion. Commynes reassured him, however, and told him he was being sent on an important mission, for which he would be handsomely paid. He was ushered into the King's presence. Louis was pleased with him and ordered his equerry to go and get a trumpeter's banner, out of which he would have a tabard made for Mérichon. This was the best that could be done, for Louis was not one of those princes who went about with a complete college of heralds and tents of cloth of gold. On to this improvised herald's coat was sewn a small enamelled plaque which the King's equerry had borrowed from a little herald in the Admiral's service. Thus attired, Mérichon was set upon a horse and sent secretly to the invading army.

Edward was at dinner when the herald-valet was

217

brought into his tent. Mérichon, on being asked his business, replied that he came on behalf of the King of France to announce that his master had long desired friendship with the King of England, so that the two countries might live at peace, that Louis had never harboured any design against England, and that if Louis had welcomed Warwick, it was merely to annoy the Duke of Burgundy. Duke Charles had persuaded the King of England to come to France entirely to serve his own ends. The King of France knew that it was only the English nobles and merchants who wanted war. It would be to King Edward's advantage to treat with the King of France. He had only to send his ambassadors to King Louis. Or why should not the two monarchs meet in some village half-way between the two armies ?

Mérichon proved an excellent negotiator. For on the next day French and English emissaries found themselves face to face at Lihons-en-Santerre.

Louis had understood. He sent for the great seal. All that he needed now was money, piles of money.

The following day, in a village near Amiens, the French and English met for a second time ; and with the invaders was King Edward.

The English, as usual, demanded the crown of France, or at least Normandy and Guyenne. But that was a mere matter of form.

The negotiations proceeded satisfactorily ; and the terms which the French ambassadors brought to Louis at the close of the day pleased him well ; 72,000 crowns to be paid to the invaders ; a promise of marriage between King Edward's daughter, Elizabeth, and Louis' son, the Dauphin ; the province of Guyenne as the bride's dowry ; and various commercial arrangements. The peace was to be for nine years, and to include all the allies on both sides—among those of England, Burgundy and Brittany were specially mentioned. King Edward offered to supply Louis with the names of those who were betraying France. Some of Louis' subjects thought these terms humiliating. But the more serious realised that the King did right to accept them. Terrible misfortunes might have resulted from the English invasion. Louis had many reasons for anxiety, especially in the direction of Brittany. He urged his Chancellor to send to Amiens on the following day the great seal and the money for which he asked.

The King summoned his council. Some held the opinion that the English were not sincere in their offers. Louis differed from them on the ground of Edward's annoyance at the trick the Duke of Burgundy had played him. Louis was certain that the treacherous Constable was too well watched by French spies to deliver up any fortress to the English. Moreover, Louis knew his man : Edward cared for ease and pleasure more than for anything.

Provided he had not to surrender territory to the English, Louis was prepared to buy them off at any price. Consequently he set about raising money in every direction.

The Constable was wild. He persisted in sending messengers to the King, among others a gentleman of his household, Louis de Sainville, and his secretary, Jean Richer. Louis had with him at that time one of the Duke's followers, the aged Seigneur de Contay, who was a prisoner on parole. The King arranged a scene for Contay's edification. The old Burgundian nobleman and Philippe de Commynes were stationed behind a screen, in the room in which the King was about to converse with the Constable's messengers. Louis sat down on a stool near the screen. Louis de Sainville and his companion appeared before him and told how the Constable had sent them to the Duke of Burgundy to try and persuade him to abandon his alliance with the English. They had found him furious with his allies, storming against them. Then de Sainville imitated the Duke stamping with wrath, swearing by St George that he would have the better of Blayburgh—as he called King Edward, referring to the rumour that the King of England was a bastard, the son of a bowman, Blayburgh. At this Louis laughed heartily, and bade the emissaries speak more loudly, as he was deaf. Contay, behind the screen, was amazed ; his one concern was to escape from the French and to go and tell the Duke everything.

That was precisely what Louis desired.

As the result of all this bargaining, it was decided that King Edward should receive his 72,000 crowns, and return to England, after having sworn to keep the peace ; that his followers, too, should receive their rewards ; the Chancellor 2000 crowns, smaller sums to my Lords Howard, Saint-Léger and Montgomery, plate for others.

Himself frugal and economical, King Louis always believed in paying generously.

No one was more surprised at the news of the truce than the Duke of Burgundy. He left Luxembourg at once, and in all haste arrived at Edward's camp with no more than sixteen horsemen.

Edward was no less annoyed than surprised by this sudden visit. And it was not long before the Duke perceived that the King was in a bad temper. But the impetuous Charles insisted on talking to him at once, it mattered not whether in public or in private. " Was it true," he asked the King, " that he had made peace with the French ? " Edward answered that he had made a truce for nine years, and that the Dukes of Burgundy and Brittany had only themselves to thank if they were not included in it. Charles was furious ; he began to speak in English, hoping thereby to make a stronger appeal to the King. Recalling the noble deeds of Edward's predecessors who had invaded France, he denounced the truce, alleging that his only design in persuading the English to cross the Straits had been to help them to recover their lawful dominions. Never would he sign the agreement. These words made an unfavourable impression on the King of England ; and he felt no regret at Charles's departure. Edward then took up his quarters half a league from Amiens.

King Louis was awaiting him at the gates of the city. He saw the English coming on in their usual slovenly

array ; and it occurred to him that he would send King
Edward three hundred tuns of his best wine : the convoy
was almost as long as their army. Louis knew the English.

Taking advantage of the truce, they entered the town
armed and wandered about, regardless of discipline and of
the King's presence. Louis had had two huge tables laid
at the gates : one laden with salt beef, the other with
wine, and, waiting behind them were five or six stout and
stalwart men of noble family. As soon as the English
arrived they were invited to break a lance, and then taken
to the tables. Thence they passed on to the taverns,
where they were given as much food and drink as they
wanted. After this lavish entertainment, the drunken-
ness and disorderliness of his subjects made King Edward
so ashamed that he ordered them to leave the city.

The strongly fortified château of Picquigny, partly
burned down by the Duke of Burgundy, had been chosen
as the meeting-place of the two kings. It was three
leagues out of Amiens, on the River Somme, which was
not fordable at that point. The place was well chosen ;
for it offered no opportunity for a surprise. The murder
on the bridge at Montereau [1] had not yet been forgotten.
Another bridge had now been hastily constructed over the
rapid winding river. A grille had been erected half-way
across, with spaces between the bars large enough to admit
a man's arm. It had a roof overhead broad enough to
shelter twelve men. The only boat on the river would
carry no more than two passengers. The kings met on
the 29th of August 1475.

King Louis was the first to arrive. He had eight
hundred men with him. On the opposite bank of the
river the whole English army could be seen in battle array.
Louis, on his side of the grille, accompanied by Jean
de Bourbon and his brother, the Cardinal, awaited King
Edward. At Louis' side was Commynes, whom Louis
had taken the precaution to have dressed exactly like

---

[1] The assassination of Jean Sans Peur, Duke of Burgundy, by the
partisans of the Dauphin (afterwards Charles VII) in 1419.

himself : they both wore flat velvet tam-o'-shanters adorned with jewels and a large fleurs-de-lys. When Edward approached, Louis uncovered and bowed. The King of England made a royal salute ; and the sovereigns kissed one another through the bars. Then Louis began graciously : " My Lord Cousin, you are welcome. You of all the world have I most desired to see ; and I praise God for bringing us together."

Edward replied in good French. Then the Lord Chancellor spoke, announcing one of those prophecies, which the English have always been so clever at discovering. Its trend was that a great treaty between France and England would one day be made at Picquigny. The text of the treaty was unfolded. A missal was brought ; and on the cross it bore, each of the Kings placed first one hand then the other, swearing to keep the peace for seven years.[1] The King of France undertook to pay a war indemnity of 75,000 crowns and an annuity of 50,000. The Dauphin Charles was to marry Princess Elizabeth.

Louis was in the best of tempers, gay and jocular. Seeing Edward to be a handsome man and fond of ladies, he invited him to come to Paris, where he would find many a fair one who would make him wish to revisit the capital. Edward's face glowed. Then Louis became serious. He asked to be left alone with the King of England, though he kept Commynes, whom the English King had known at Calais, close at hand. The two monarchs discussed various problems, including the question of that madman, Charles of Burgundy. If it were true that he refused to be included in the peace, Louis would have a free hand. The Duke of Brittany's position was also discussed. He was the friend of the King of England ; and Edward insisted that he should not be proceeded against. Finally, with genial words of farewell from Louis to each and all, they took their leave. Edward rejoined his army ; Louis returned to Amiens.

---

[1] The truce as finally concluded was for seven years with England, nine with Burgundy (Trans.).

The King rode with Commynes, to whom he confided
that he hoped Edward would not take him at his word
and come to Paris. The English had been too much in
Paris and in Normandy. But it was well to be friends
with them, especially when they kept to their own side
of the Channel.

On his return to Amiens, Louis invited the English
nobles, who had helped to make the treaty, to supper. He
talked in whispers to Lord Howard, who told him that
he would devise means for bringing Edward to Paris, to
which remark the King made no reply, but washed his
hands and barely concealed a grimace. It was a happy
day. For now the English were going; and those
enemies, who but recently had wrought such havoc in
France, had become our friends.

Above all things that traitor of a Constable, Saint-Pol,
with his promises to surrender Eu and Saint-Valéry—
which, by the way, Louis had taken the precaution to
burn down—had been well tricked. Now Charles the
Bold sent to Louis proposing to set upon the English
during their return journey. Louis refused to listen to
any such evil proposal. So the King of England and his
money reached Calais in safety, and thence they crossed
quickly to Merrie England—for his good commons did
not care for sleeping in tents. On his return home
Edward counted up the crowns he had received from
France and those he had extorted from his Parliament.

Louis had his seven years' truce announced at Notre-
Dame-de-la-Victoire, near Senlis; and he gave thanks to
the glorious and blessed Mother of God, who had turned
the King of England and his army out of France. Was
there anything humiliating in the treaty? On the
contrary, it contained one clause, which was quite honourable: Edward, at the King's request, and in return for
a ransom of 50,000 crowns, had surrendered his prisoner,
Margaret of Anjou.

Louis now had in mind a further convention, which

was to secure to France and England the monopoly of the trade between the two countries.

A treaty of alliance with the Duke of Brittany, who was appointed Lieutenant-General of France, was also confirmed at Notre-Dame-de-la-Victoire.

On the 13th of September, Louis concluded a nine years' truce with Charles of Burgundy, at Souleure in Luxembourg. There also the two allies agreed on the ruin of the traitor Saint-Pol, who had taken refuge with the Duke. Charles violated the safe conduct he had given the Constable, betrayed the traitor and delivered him up to Louis, who had him beheaded at Paris, on the 19th of December.

CHAPTER XXVI

THE END OF CHARLES THE BOLD

1476–1477

Louis leaves Charles to work out his own Destruction.—Granson.—
Morat.—Nancy.—Uncertainty of the Duke's Fate.—Announce-
ment of his Death.—Identification of the Body.—The Quarry.—
Burgundy goes into Liquidation.

IT was only against his will that Charles the Bold had
allowed himself to be included in the truce with England.
Louis did not expect him to keep his word. Consequently
the King observed him closely, but continued his policy
of leaving the Duke to work out his own destruction.

Charles had completed his conquest of Lorraine and
was now proceeding against the Swiss. He captured the
town of Granson, and treated its defenders with extreme
brutality, leaving their mutilated bodies to hang from
the trees. The Swiss took their revenge. On the 1st of
March 1476, they rushed down from their mountains in
great force and with the cry of " Granson, Granson ! "
threw themselves on the Duke's army and scattered it.
Then they pillaged his camp, and carried off all his jewels,
lace and cloth of gold.

Louis was at Lyons. He had his spies everywhere.
Commynes was sending him message after message. The
King heard of the battle and rejoiced heartily. Not
waiting for the compliments and congratulations of the
Chapter of the cathedral, he dressed as an ordinary
pilgrim and went to give thanks and to place a generous
gift on the altar of the Virgin. He kissed the little golden
image of Our Lady, which had been given him for the
Queen, and had it sewn on to his hat. But all the while

225

he was taking precautions, deepening the moat at Beauvais, reconciling King René and the Duke of Calabria, so as to leave himself a free hand in Lorraine.

The Duke of Burgundy was now encamped before Morat, a fortified town on the lake of that name. Assault after assault was being repulsed. The Confederates threw themselves on the Burgundian forces and almost exterminated them (22nd June 1476). Charles was compelled to flee with twelve of his followers. René of Lorraine that evening slept in the tent of his adversary.

The King heard with rejoicing that Charles had been put to flight and had lost his camp. Louis sent congratulations to the Swiss, confirming his alliance with them.

Charles was at Salins, asking his Estates for more money and a new army, letting his beard grow, giving way to melancholy. Then, like a mad bull, blind with rage, he threw himself upon Nancy.

King Louis was not in the least anxious. Absorbed in his spider-like work, he was rounding off his domains, settling the remuneration to be given to his ambassadors, whose number was constantly increasing, and preparing for the defence of Amiens.

To those who threatened him at home he showed no mercy. The Duke of Nemours was in the Bastille, under the watch and ward of one Philippe Luillier, to whom the King recommended special vigilance.

Then there was the arrogant Duke of Brittany. " As he is so fond of poisoners," wrote Louis, " I will try to find Master Ithier Marchant, and send him to the Duke."

So all through the winter, which was to witness the last of Charles the Bold's sieges, Louis remained on the watch. He knew that the end of Charles's great adventure was approaching. Louis' spies were alert, for they were well paid. The news they sent was not always pleasing : for example, Galeazzo Sforza had been assassinated in one of the churches in Milan.

Charles the Bold had just heard that his army, encamped before Nancy, had surrendered the town to Duke René II. The Duke of Burgundy reached Toul on the 11th of October. He had received reinforcements led by the Count of Chimay and Campo Basso. These encouraged him to open the bombardment of Nancy. The weather was cold and Campo Basso was treacherous. Charles owed him money, which King Louis paid. The King had also sent money to the Duke of Lorraine, who was bringing up 12,000 Swiss. Charles's troops were barely 2000. The battle was joined on the 5th of January 1477. Charles's army was routed. What became of Charles himself ? No one knows. The Count of Chimay and Olivier de la Marche were taken prisoners.

It was Monseigneur du Lude who brought the good news to King Louis. He had had it from a horseman whom he had met by chance. At break of day, Du Lude was heard knocking at the King's gate. It was opened : " Charles the Bold is dead ! " he cried. But it was not yet quite certain ; for some said that he was a fugitive.

Du Lude was right however. Charles was really dead. His body had been recognised as it lay, half-eaten by wolves, among other corpses, on the ice of a frozen pond. There lay the Duke, with two deadly wounds on his naked body : a halberd wound which had split his head open down to the teeth, and a pike wound through the loins.

Louis was so filled with joy and amazement that he hardly knew how to behave. He lost no time, however, in writing to the Seigneur de Craon : " If it be true that the Duke of Burgundy is dead, occupy the country forthwith." And he demanded the hand of the Duke's daughter in the marriage which had been arranged between her and the Dauphin. Louis reminded the people of Dijon that they were the subjects of the crown, that Charles's daughter was his kinswoman, and that Louis intended to protect her rights. At the same time he ordered a procession at Poitiers and offered a silver screen to St Martin.

The King had already determined to treat the northern

provinces belonging to Burgundy as if they were appanages of the crown and could be granted to members of his own family. He needed money, vast sums of money. He would borrow it from the towns.

There was now no doubt about the death of Charles the Bold : his doctors had identified his body by his broken teeth, the wound he had received at Montlhéry, and his long nails.

This was the end of the great adventure, the end of the comrade of King Louis' youth, who had dreamed of being a second god Mars. This was the end of the House of Burgundy and of its magnificence. The fox had strangled the lion.

And now for the quarry. The King intended to have his share. The Count of Brienne and Lord Craon seemed inclined to forget this : so Louis wrote to them ironically : " I have received your letters, my lords, and thank you for permitting me the honour of sharing the booty. I am content you should have half the money found, but I ask you to keep the rest for me and to use it for the repair of fortresses on the German frontier. As to the wine in the Duke of Burgundy's cellars, I am willing for you to have it. . . ."

On the 23rd of January 1477, a letter was read publicly at Ghent, as from Mary of Burgundy, asserting that never at any time had the Duchy of Burgundy formed part of the domain of the crown of France.

Nevertheless the King wrote to his officers : " Prepare to keep the country in subjection to me and defend the most important towns and fortresses."

It was not long before Louis' activity was electrifying the Low Countries : Ham, Saint-Quentin and Péronne surrendered. The King's Lieutenant, Jean d'Estouteville, occupied Abbeville. His barber, Olivier le Daim, was despatched on an embassy to Ghent, with instructions to the little Mary of Burgundy, to whom the King had decided to act as guardian and counsellor. But the barber, being a native of the country, was received with no great honour and met with no signal success. All he could do was to get a French garrison into Tournai. The Flemings were defeated close to the city walls.

Louis himself was at Péronne in February, at Arras in March. Artois having failed to do him homage, he had resolved to lay hands on the province. The keys of Arras were brought to him by the elders of the city, whom the King received cordially. They might send their representatives, he said, to the provincial Estates about to assemble; and if they promised him obedience, he would pardon every one. Let them all return to their work in peace. Then Louis distributed Charles the Bold's furniture and plate among his followers.

The House of Burgundy had gone into liquidation.

CHAPTER XXVII

A PORTRAIT OF KING LOUIS

His Land Hunger.—A strange blend of mysticism and common sense.—
The typical Frenchman of his Day.—His resolve to unify France.
—Work his only Pleasure.—Louis' exceptional Cruelty a Legend.—
His consideration for the Poor and Unfortunate.—His essentially
Latin Intelligence.—His admiration of Italy.—Francesco Sforza his
Hero.—His Scholarship, Diplomacy, Realism.—His astounding
Industry and Loquacity.—The embodiment of Caution.—Louis'
Game of Chess.—His Revenue as compared with that of Charles VII.
—His Care for the People.—His simplicity in Dress.—The Chase
his favourite Pastime.—Fondness for Animals.—Louis and Women.
—His Piety.—The Independence of his Attitude towards the
Pope.—Louis orders a Statue for his Tomb in Notre Dame de
Cléry.—His Personal Appearance.

Now that the lion is dead, let us sketch the physiognomy
of the fox.

King Louis was a man moulded by experience. As
Dauphin he had been a rebel ; but he was learning all the
time, and when he became King, he played the part of
a King. Though revenge may have been his guiding
motive through the opening years of his reign, it very soon
gave place to that passion for organisation and conciliation
which animated his government until the end.

He reacted easily to all the vicissitudes of life. We
have seen him in his youth laughing, loving, conspiring, and
now that he has attained to middle age, we see him as
a prosperous proprietor of a domain called France. Seated
at his fireside like a peasant, his elbows on the table, he
meditates and talks ; he has considered everything. He is
fifty-four. When any allusion is made to fat lands with
which he may enlarge his domain, *dilater* his kingdom, to
use his own word, his hands tremble feverishly, his eyes
gleam, his face glows, and he can hardly contain himself.

230

King Louis was a curious blend of mysticism and common sense. He had sworn an oath at his coronation, which he was resolved to keep. He had undertaken to unify his territory and to add to it all the domains which had ever belonged to the crown.

Consequently the great object of his life was to round off his inheritance, that fine inheritance he was to leave to his son. For Louis was essentially a father. He was also that symbolical figure of the age—the shepherd, the shepherd of his flock, the shepherd whose knowledge embraces the stars in their courses, the fruits of the earth, the diseases and the destiny of man. Louis, as the shepherd, was the typical Frenchman of his day. To one thing and one thing only Louis was devoted. He lived for his kingdom : and in his opinion the kingdom and the crown were identical. His mission was to guard it, care for it, enlarge it. To this end he worked and laboured incessantly, wearing out mind and body, employing every device craft and cunning could suggest. This work was almost his only pleasure. With regard to himself he was miserly ; with regard to his kingdom generous : the good coins of the realm must remain in it : he would not have the pious sending them to Rome or traders paying them to Geneva. A fine army he must possess, and powerful artillery, to be used as little as possible. In cases of necessity England must be bought off, and the Duke of Milan. Indeed there was nothing, not even heaven and its saints, that Louis was not prepared to buy. Though he kept no written accounts, he had them all in his head, all his gains and losses. In a preamble to one of his ordinances, he declared his chief concern to be the administration of justice and the organisation of finance.

Louis was severe both to himself and to others. He rarely admitted that he was pleased. Once you had understood his will, you were at liberty to carry it out any way you liked, provided you acted rapidly. Rapidity he always demanded. He established posts throughout the kingdom : couriers and horsemen, riding swift little horses, galloping along the roads with the King's despatches, relay after relay, well equipped, well controlled and well paid.

King Louis' exceptional cruelty, which is so often asserted, is mere legend—a legend we may leave to the guides who take tourists over the Château of Loches and show them its *oubliettes*, its iron cages and the dungeon of Jean Balue. There are other legends that he poisoned his brother and that he invented iron cages. The age was cruel : one had to protect oneself. The use of torture in the examination of an accused person was the common method of procedure. The King had to defend himself against those who sought to take his life. A terrible example was made of one, Jean Hardy, who tried to poison Louis. Hardy was beheaded in the Place de Grève, his head stuck on a lance and exhibited, while the four quarters of his body were distributed, one to each of the four extremities of the kingdom. Louis punished well and paid well. To those like Jean Balue, who owed him everything, received his confidence and then sold it, he was pitiless. There were iron cages for political prisoners, because in those days that was the only way of preventing their escape. But while Louis was pitiless to the great, he was benevolent to the poor and humble. He sent assistance to the inhabitants of Languedoc when the province was laid waste by hailstorms and to those of the Loire valley during the inundations. After the suppression of a riot at Bourges the King gave instructions that only the great should be punished, because the poor had merely acted at their instigation. For the townsfolk he was always especially solicitous. Amiens sent a deputation to him at Amboise shortly after the city had become French. Louis assembled the delegates in a gallery of his château and, after he had dismissed the members of his Council, he addressed the deputation, and said : " I wish to speak with my good friends from Amiens, not as ambassadors but as friends." Then he encouraged the mayor of the city to discuss all the interests of the town frankly, adding that he knew Amiens had become French not because it had been conquered, but of its own free will.

The secret of Louis' power lay in his intelligence—the lucid intelligence of a Latin. Francesco Sforza was his hero, the model he had tried to copy ever since he was a child. The King adored Italy, a country he had never seen—he adored the Italian people, who vied with him in subtlety. He liked their coolness, their arms, and their language, which he was proud to speak well. Sforza presented him with a war-horse and a suit of armour. Louis was delighted. He put on the armour at once. It would have taken days to repeat to the Duke of Milan the interminable questions the King asked about it. When he heard of Sforza's death, Louis became speechless with sorrow and insisted on being left alone with his grief.

Louis differed from the majority of the potentates of his day in his personal knowledge of the affairs of his kingdom.

The King was well educated—he knew Latin and Italian. Commynes described him as *assez lettré*. We must not take Louis seriously when he says : " I have no Latin." He was heard to quote Lucan. The ambassador Cagnola wrote of him in 1479 : " Sometimes he studies and cites the best authorities." Louis could read the Duke of Milan's letters as easily as an Italian. He would take off his hat to a letter from Sforza. The King sometimes wrote his own despatches. But on the whole his was the learning of a prince rather than of a scholar. His favourite subject, and the one he knew best, was the history of France.

Louis was great at asking questions and at acquiring information by the way. " No one was ever so ready to lend an ear to the people, or to inquire about so many things," wrote Commynes. The Seneschal de Brézé said he bore " his whole council " in his head. In short, Louis was richly endowed with that common sense which stood him in better stead than any mere knowledge. He used books mainly to remind him of the past.

Louis could not be ignorant of European affairs after having interrogated so many foreigners. He was not only Commynes' friend, but his disciple. The King received his ambassadors in person, often booted and spurred. He could be eloquent ; he could discuss and persuade, threaten and coax by turns. One day, at a joust, he was seen looking out of a window, and—to everyone's amazement—leaning familiarly on the shoulder of the ambassador from Milan, while he talked to him. The King would carry on his diplomacy while at table, or hunting, or out for a walk. Frenchmen in general were not inclined to like Italians ; but Louis so imposed his own taste on his subjects that they soon came to swear by no one else. During those animated discussions with the Milanese ambassadors, what witticisms sparkled, what home truths were uttered on both sides ! The King might grow angry ; but when his wrath had abated he would embrace the Italian, not as a sovereign but as one gentleman embracing another. With Alberic Malleta, he remained alone for two whole hours, shut up in his closet, while his horse was at the gate, saddled for the chase, pawing the ground.

In the agelong dispute of the schools between Nominalists and Realists, Louis posed as a Realist. But, in spite of his decree against the Nominalists in 1474, he was no philosopher. It pleased him to play the umpire in that great scholastic quarrel, in imitation of his hero, Charlemagne. But of all the Realists—Albertus Magnus, St Thomas of Aquinas, Ægidius of Rome, Alexander of Hales, Duns Scotus and Bonaventura—Ægidius was probably the only one he knew anything about, and that because he had written a book on the education of princes which had become a classic. Nevertheless the University registered the King's decree, and made a search for books on the other side in order to suppress them.

Far from being a philosopher, Louis lived from day to day, but always for France. He was constantly changing, adopting one course of action one day, then altering it on the morrow, mistrusting his own impetuosity and the flow of words which poured too easily from his lips. The King was an adaptable person. He saw that he had made a mistake when he had dismissed his father's ministers, and that he had made others when he reformed the Court of Aids, abolished the Pragmatic Sanction, and increased the number of officers in the Châtelet law court.

Louis was one of those rare persons who are capable of envisaging at once the parts and the whole. His people marvelled at his attention to detail. His fellow-workers had immense confidence in him. They were spellbound by his intelligence. His memory was astounding. He never forgot anything. Wherever he went, he seemed to know everyone; and he never underestimated the personal factor. This King really seemed to be " better qualified to govern a world than a kingdom."

Was Louis ever, at any time in his life, addicted to pleasure ? No doubt he found his chief delight in work. He knew the value of time. He knew that a king's life is no easy career. He said he would not live to be more than sixty—because that was the tale of years allotted to French Kings—and at sixty he died. Four folio volumes of Louis' ordinances and thousands of his letters, all marked with the personal note, prove him to have been an indefatigable worker. He read his correspondence himself, and, as we have seen, dictated his letters, which abound in characteristic words and phrases.

There was a certain regularity about his life, both in war and in peace. His winters, spent at Plessis-du-Parc, Tours, Thouars and Cléry, were devoted to home affairs and to foreign relations. His summers, spent with his troops in Artois or Burgundy, to military matters. But neither in summer nor in winter was the King's mind ever at rest. His messengers and spies were constantly reporting rumours and delivering despatches. The King would receive them at any hour. Not infrequently he heard of an event almost directly after it had occurred. Sometimes his counsellors, eager to curry favour with the King, would intercept a messenger and seize his despatch in order to present it themselves. No sooner had he taken cognizance of one situation, perceiving in a flash all its implications, than he passed on to the next.

His companions were never in doubt as to his real sentiments. Expressions of joy or grief were allowed to play freely over his countenance.

He held no regular meetings of his Council. But when he needed advice, he would discuss the matter at table, sometimes in whispers, as we have seen. He insisted on concision in the replies made to his questions. " Be brief," he would say.

But he did not practise what he preached. He was addicted to thinking aloud—a defect of which he was well aware. " I know that my tongue has done me great hurt," he would say, " but at other times it may have done me good. At any rate it is a fault I must amend."

Louis had the gift of correcting his mistakes and of extricating himself from an awkward situation. He was never so good as in adversity. He would give or promise anything to those who would serve him at such times. If he saw it to be to his advantage, he would take back into his service those with whom he had disagreed, like Pierre de Brézé, who died for him at Montlhéry, and Antoine de Chabannes, who became his most faithful and devoted general.

Though Louis devised many a great adventure, he did not like taking risks. His principle was never to engage in anything in which he was likely to be worsted. He did not lack courage. As Dauphin, he had led the spirited storming of Dieppe ; at the siege of Dambach an arrow piercing his thigh and saddle had nailed him to his horse. As King, he had fought at Montlhéry with a valour that had fired the whole army. But he had no desire for the hazard of battle : he preferred to negotiate ; and in the art of negotiation he was unequalled.

Diplomacy was his favourite weapon—not that he

invented it—for the Italians were already past-masters of this art—but he did invent a special kind of diplomacy—a process of bargaining, carried on in person, generally by word of mouth, or in some cases by the most meagre written instructions; they might be given to a valet or a barber; they were always imbued with a profound knowledge of the character of his adversary, of the difficulties of his situation, or of the situation in which the King intended to place him. It was a game of chess, often a double game, in which Louis seldom made a false move; but when he did lose, he was surprised and furious. Once he had attained his object, he became as conventional as any lawyer, and set down the results of his dealing in documents, carefully drawn up and registered according to legal formalities. Not content with such legal precautions, he would send to Angers for the famous fragment of the true cross, known as " the Cross of St Laud," and seal the undertaking with the most solemn oath of the day, the breaker of which would inevitably die within the year. The Cross of St Laud, mounted in gold, set with precious stones of divers colours, had come down from Foulques of Anjou, King of Jerusalem. Wondrous tales were told of the fate that had overtaken perjurers : the hair of one had turned white while he was taking the oath : the arm of another had stiffened as he raised it to swear, and he had died before the year was out.

In this game of his, Louis knew all the pieces—the nations and the princes of his time—better than any of his contemporaries. Had he not been brought up in the House of Burgundy and bred with his most inveterate foe !

Some there are who condemn this royal diplomacy as spasmodic and confused. But it should be estimated by its fruits ; and they are astounding. No one can deny, however, that Louis enjoyed exceptional good luck, and that in more than one instance his good fortune was due to the timely death of an adversary.

Money ranked next to intelligence in Louis' estimation. As we have seen, he himself needed and succeeded

in procuring vast sums. Charles VII had a revenue of
1,800,000 francs, Louis of 4,700,000. This revenue was
not raised without difficulty. One tax-gatherer wrote to
Bourré : " My Lord, it is piteous . . . the people have
been stripped of everything, and try as I may, I can get
nothing more out of them."

Though, according to the chroniclers, Louis was not
popular, he lived among, or at least very near to, his people.
One New Year's Day a young girl presented him with
a rose. The King gave *les filles de joye*, who followed the
court, wherewith to celebrate their May Festival. He
protected the minstrels and the recorders of popular songs,
regarding them as wandering propagandists. He was not
ashamed to drink wine with an innkeeper and his wife. He
supported his nurse, Clémence Sillonne. He gave money
to the drummer of Amboise for accompanying the dancing
round the bonfires on Midsummer Eve. He was generous
in giving alms to the poor. He never cared for the great,
preferring to associate with those of humble rank. He
would talk familiarly to his guides, to passers-by, and to the
hosts of houses where he lodged. A poor woman one day
brought him grapes and peaches. Once, as he was about
to leave Orléans, a poor man held up a baby to him, asking
the King to hold it over the font ; Louis consented to
stand sponsor to the child. He had a goodwife's fancy for
burning candles in front of the images of saints after mass.
He frequently dressed like one of the common people,
saying that princes ruined their subjects by spending too
much money on clothes.

The King's simplicity of attire struck all his contemporaries. We have seen how the people of Hesdin failed
to distinguish him from his retainers when he rode into
their town. And if on certain great occasions he had to
dress more sumptuously, he would, as on the bridge at
Picquigny, have one of his servants attired like himself.
His customary garb was a traveller's, often a pilgrim's.

He never followed fashion, but always—even when
long robes were in vogue—wore short garments after the

manner of the Italians, whose clever devices in sartorial, as well as in other matters, he admired. Thus, when he felt Alberic Malleta's wet cloak, and found it to be lined with cloth, he exclaimed on the ingeniousness of the Lombards, displaying his own undergarment, which was a petticoat of wool-backed satin, in imitation of Sforza's, who, like most warriors, wore the same clothes summer and winter.

The King's accounts show that he affected dark colours and cheap materials, robes of Rouenese fustian, and black or brown serge breeches for hot weather. But he accepted a length of black velvet and stockings of gold and silk as a present from the Duke of Milan. Red and white were the colours of a king ; but Louis preferred black, grey and a brownish tan. One seldom finds him wearing furs. His linen, the fine Dutch linen of his shirts—was always scrupulously clean. His military outfit was poor : he would have his coats of mail enlarged, his helmet repaired and his spurs regilded.

The King became bald early. To keep his head warm he wore black or scarlet hoods and big felt hats, protecting his shoulders from the rain like a roof. They were trimmed with little leaden figures, *souvenirs* of his pilgrimages, strung together on a silken thread. He wore no other ornaments, only two enamelled rings, each set with a diamond. He had one little gilded cane engraved with a motto and the image of a chamois. He also possessed a gold chain of twenty-five links, valued at 171 *livres*. Dye was bought for the colouring of his gloves. He had his buttons regilded. Tailors found him a poor customer ; and sometimes they had difficulty in getting paid. He gave away his old clothes. His only luxury was a little silver-gilt dressing-case, used by his barber, Olivier le Daim. He paid great attention to personal cleanliness and to hygiene, using rose-water for his toilet.

The King's favourite pastime was the chase—falconry, but more especially stag and boar-hunting. The latter he would pursue in all weathers, rising in the early morning, returning late at night, worn out and generally angry with someone; or he might not return till the next day, having spent the night in some humble cottage in a distant village. For the pleasure of spearing a boar of unusual size, hard worker as he was, he would abandon even affairs of state. One day, in the Forest of Mortagne, a wounded boar threw himself on to the King's horse, endangering his life. But it was only beasts of prey that Louis allowed to be killed. Certain kinds of birds he protected, and he reserved hunting rights for himself and his friends.

Louis adored dogs of all kinds. He describes them like a true connoisseur. They must have large heads and big ears, he writes to Milan. He bought dogs wherever he went. He received them as gifts : five bulldogs from the English ambassador, Thomas Langton, five greyhounds from the King of Scotland, a big watch-dog from Lorenzo di Medici. In one marriage-contract the King inserted a clause stipulating that he should be sent one greyhound annually. In another case he exchanged a prisoner for a dog. He called his dogs by name—" Chier Amy," " Paris," " Artus." He had them combed and brushed, and carefully tended when they were ill. He gave offerings for them to St Hubert in the hope that he would protect them. The King dressed his dogs far better than himself. They slept on raised bedsteads. They had collars studded with gold and buckled with silver. " Chier Amy's " collar was set with ten rubies and twenty pearls. Louis felt the death of one of his dogs keenly. When he lost his big greyhound one Christmas in the Marmoutier woods, he ordered the Mayor of Tours to announce it at midnight mass. It is true that big dogs were rare in those days. Jean Bourré offered the King in return for a cession of houses and gardens at Angers, an annual tribute of " a fine light-coloured spaniel, a beautiful white greyhound, a hawk or two harriers." Louis, like every other prince of his day, had aviaries—at Plessis, at Montils ; they contained white peacocks, eagles, ostriches, aigrettes, quails, goldfinches, owls, hundreds of canaries and flocks of pigeons. For talking-birds, jackdaws and magpies, he had a great liking ; and a certain Perdriel was sent to Paris in 1468, to fetch him birds which said : " Thief, whoremonger, harlot's son, get you gone," or " Perette, give me to drink," and such like phrases. Louis had also a menagerie : in his youth it contained a favourite lioness and a leopard, which were joined later by an elephant, two dromedaries, lions, boars, wolves and monkeys. On one occasion, when he was playing with a bear at the Saint-Vaast Abbey, and his dog was afraid, the King went into the bear's cage and let him eat out of his hand.

Louis cared little for women, and he did not like to be dominated. He detested Agnes because she domineered over his father. He had had affairs with middle-class women in Dauphiné, as we have seen. He knew the wiles of Parisian women, for had he not played the dandy with Guillaume de Bische, in Paris streets soon after his accession ! His wife, Charlotte of Savoy, was an excellent woman. And Commynes, during all the years that he knew the King, never once detected him philandering. In 1472, Louis lost a one-year-old son, François. The news was brought to him when he was hunting in the Forest of Loches. In the rage of his grief he had half the forest cut down ; and he made a vow that henceforth he would know no woman but the Queen. Commynes, who was a witness to the oath, says that though by taking the vow, Louis was merely doing his duty according to the Church, yet in the keeping of it, considering the unattractiveness of his wife, he acquired great merit.

The King was as pious as the age in which he lived. He heard mass every day, and afterwards remained for a while wrapt in meditation, which no one was allowed to interrupt. He told his beads and abstained from meat on Wednesday. He confessed once a week, and, on Maundy Thursday, followed his predecessors' example and washed the feet of thirteen poor people. No one was allowed to speak to him during his frequent pilgrimages—generally undertaken in order to keep some vow—or while he was at prayer.

Though in the matter of relics Louis shared the credulity of his age, he did not like the idea of being duped. Consequently he had inquiries made into the history of relics, even into that of the famous Cross of St Laud. Once he was convinced, the King would prostrate himself before these objects of veneration : he had the bones of St Bernardius brought from Italy, he shed tears when he beheld the painting in the Cathedral of Cambrai which was attributed to St Luke. But with all his veneration for and generosity to the saints—a generosity which, contrary to prevalent opinion, was rare in those days, Louis took care to see how the money he gave was spent. He sent his confessor, Jean Bochard, Bishop of Avranches, to Tours to inquire into the employment of the 1200 crowns the King had dedicated to the church of St Martin, in gratitude for the capture of Perpignan, on St Martin's Eve. Bochard reported that the money had been used for the building of a vestry and that he had seen the glass window painted with the picture of the King presenting the edifice to St Martin, and bearing an inscription describing the miracle.

Not satisfied with this inquiry, the King, in order to justify the interest he took in the saint and the donations he had made to his church, ordered researches to be made into his lineage. Ambroise de Cambrai, the King's counsellor and steward, was commissioned to draw up St Martin's genealogical tree. The genealogist discovered the saint to have been not merely the kinsman of certain Roman senators and of Flavius, King of Hungary, but heir to the Emperor Julian, in which capacity the holy Martin had renounced his earthly for his heavenly inheritance.

When undertaking the reparation of the church of St Eutropius at Saintes, Louis asked for an estimate of the cost. "Workmen always try to make as much as they can," he wrote, "especially when they are dealing with someone whom they believe to possess a long purse."

Louis shared the common predilection for shrines and holy places. But at the same time he was well aware that such places were a source of wealth for France. His religion was as utilitarian as his politics ; and his liberality laid the foundation of French influence at the Vatican.

But Louis, as we have seen, always assumed an independent attitude towards the Pope. When Sixtus IV threatened him with excommunication, the King replied that he regretted he had not had a vote in the conclave, for he would never have voted for anyone so vicious as the Pope. Louis was the servant of the Church but not of the Holy Father. He admonished the Pope to leave Lorenzo di Medici alone for fear of endangering the peace of Christendom, threatened by the Turk. The King cannot have been a bigot or he would not have ordered the Grenoble Parlement to leave the Vaudois heretics in peace. But there is no question of his lavish liberality to the Church ; for in one year—1479—he endowed it with no less than 13,046 *livres.* Many of his gifts, like the silver grille round the relics of St Martin at Tours, still rank among the great ecclesiastical treasures of France.

The patron saint of Louis, as of France, was Our Lady. She had saved him from drowning, she had helped him in the storming of Dieppe ; and when, with great reluctance, Louis brought himself to consider the unpleasant subject of his own death, it was the sanctuary of Our Lady of Cléry that he chose for his last resting-place. He had built two houses at Cléry—one of brick, the other of wood. They were to have long galleries, a garden planted with trees and surrounded with a trellis-work of vines, an oven for the baking of his bread, offices and a stable for his mules. He had transformed the modest oratory of Notre Dame de Cléry, partly destroyed by fire in 1470, into a vast and majestic collegiate church, endowed with the same privileges as la Sainte Chapelle in Paris. To this church the King sent silver ships, *ex-votos* in memory of Arques and Dieppe. In this church was buried his little son, François, and here, under the protection of Our Lady, close to his vines and his little houses, he himself desired to rest. He had no wish to join the solemn assemblage of his ancestors in the golden gloom of Saint-Denis. He had too little in common with them.

Jean Bourré was instructed to order Colin of Amiens to draw a portrait of the King from which the goldsmith, Conrad of Cologne, and the King's gunner, Master Laurens Wrine of Tours, were to cast a bronze statue—a life-size figure, to be placed at one end of the stone tomb, opposite the image of Our Lady. Bourré indicated certain points which were to be carried out in the sketch : the King was to be represented kneeling on a pavement, his dog at his side, his hands clasped, holding his hat ; he was to be dressed as a hunter, with his horn hanging down his back, showing both ends : he was to be made as handsome as possible, young-looking, not bald, his hair rather long at the back, his nose long, slightly arched.

The King was obviously not without a certain personal vanity. But it must be admitted that those who knew him did not consider him physically attractive. Undersized and spindle-legged, he had grown stout in middle age and suffered from varicose veins. His bearing was undignified. His eyes were sunk deeply in his head, his nose long, his lips thick, his chin prominent, and before he became bald, he wore his hair short, not long, as in Bourré's instructions to the artist.

Of Jean Fouquet's famous portrait of the King we have only copies, made long after the execution of the original. They represent him in profile, wearing a cap, and over it a little leather hat ornamented with a medallion. He is close-shaven, with a very long nose, thickening at the tip, thin lips, a heavy chin, prominent jaws, and big, slanting eyes : a grave, unattractive face. He wears the cross of the Order of St Michael on his scarlet doublet, and white breeches. The expressive medal by Francesco Laurana in the Bibliothèque Nationale would appear to be much more life-like.

It is natural that a man so utterly lacking in self-consciousness as Louis should have left no image of himself, just as he has left no history of his reign. His true portrait is to be found in his words and deeds.

So now, let us leave him, as he would have wished, to his prayers and meditations, with his gaze turned to the little statue of Our Lady of Cléry.

CHAPTER XXVIII

THE HOUSEHOLDS OF THE KING AND QUEEN

The Protean Louis.—The Ordering of his Household.—Simon Coffin's Contract.—The King and his Doctors.—His own ideas on Health.—Character and Appearance of the Queen.—Constitution of her Household.—Her Amusements.—Library.—The Royal Children.—Birth of the Dauphin Charles, 1470.—Louis' Collaborators.—Olivier le Daim.—Philippe de Commynes.

THE King's household was royal in every respect : the household of a King of France, the greatest European sovereign of his day.

But Louis was a veritable Proteus. At times he would appear in all the majesty of a monarch ; at others, when it suited his purpose, in the garb and humility of a pilgrim. At no time had he a properly constituted court, any more than a properly constituted council of ministers.

At Paris, after Montlhéry, he appeared as a royal knight : he dressed his retainers in red and crimson ; he commanded artists to paint him war-standards and banners with golden suns, bearing the images of St Michael of St Denis and of Our Lady of Aix. He ordered from the drapers green hose, black velvet cloaks, doublets of violet damask, velvet hoods and black caps for his pages, for he thought their scarves, embroidered with silver foliage, were not rich enough. He also ordered handsome carpets of fleurs-de-lys design. He had fine horses. His Scottish guard, commanded by William Stuyers (or Stuyer), was very imposing in its plumed helmets and short cloth coats, red, green and white. Louis himself wore a plume and, when he entered his good towns, cut a very fine figure, girt with his handsome sword, *la bien aimée*, wearing a white and red doublet over his armour in the Italian fashion, and a cloak embroidered with a winged stag in gold.

When the King presided over the first assembly of his newly constituted Order of St Michael, he appeared in a blue robe, embroidered with fleurs-de-lys, and a fine cloak of white silk, with a high black cap showing his hair, before it had begun to grow thin.

Louis was indeed a versatile monarch, able to adapt him-self to any circumstances. Burgundian chroniclers, intent on glorifying their Dukes at the King's expense, would have us regard him as an insignificant person who was for ever trying to hide himself in the crowd. But far from that, Louis was every inch a King ; and his accounts show him to have been capable of magnificence, to have dressed, as we have seen, not always in black, but sometimes in colours, usually red and white.

The King's household resembled that of his father : he had as many chamberlains, stewards, cup-bearers, pantlers, squires of the kitchen, valets, clerks, confessors, barbers, doctors, guards, and a stable of as many horses as Charles VII. It was only at les Montils that Louis appeared as an ordinary huntsman, master of his own hounds. We are surprised to find the expenses of the royal household constantly on the increase, notwithstanding that the most striking features in its ordering were always strict attention to detail and avoidance of waste.

A royal ordinance of 1464 throws light on Louis' house-hold management. It provides that henceforth the Queen, my Lords the King's children, and their suites shall take their meals in court. And for this purpose the King makes a contract with one, Simon Coffin, merchant, for 13,000 francs a year. Louis requires his table to be furnished with all the commodities of the neighbourhood then in season, at the rate of eight francs per day for four dishes. The King, the Queen and their guests are to sit at the high table and to be waited on by three gentlemen and seven pages. At the second table are to sit the ten chamberlains, at the third the ladies and maids in waiting to the number of eighteen. The number of dishes served at the different tables is carefully regulated according to the rank of the participants. Certain retainers have their meals in the closet, others in their own rooms. A knight of the kitchen is stationed in the great hall to gather up the fragments of the repast in order that nothing shall be wasted. Broth is served at every table except the King's. Those who had waited sat down in the great hall after their superiors had finished. Coffin was required to supply extra food if it was needed. He also had to furnish all the royal apartments with wood and candles, and to provide *le vin de congé*, *i.e.*, the wine brought to the King as a signal that it was time for everyone to go to bed. Coffin, too, at his own expense was required to equip the royal household with plate and linen, to pay the servants' wages, and to provide the King with the spices and spiced wine he took on fast-days. All this the excellent Coffin had to deliver a month in advance of payment. He was, moreover, given to understand that his contract would end if the King were to receive a more advantageous tender.

Coffin does not seem to have made a very good bargain.

The wine at Louis' table was good, the same that he sent as a diplomatic gift to King Edward IV. Louis' butler, Pierre de Castello, used to make the round of all the vineyards in order to procure the most delicious vintages—those of La Faye and Montjau were the King's favourites.

Though Louis did not like doctors, we know that he always had several in attendance. He preferred the protection of his patron saints to medical prescriptions, and he had a weakness for the astrologers who were so clever in prophesying good fortune for himself and bad for his enemies.

But Louis had his own ideas on matters of health ; and among the books that went with him on his progresses were always certain medical treatises. We find the King writing about his nieces : " I am no physician ; but I do not think they ought to be kept from drinking when they are thirsty. Let them water their wine well and abstain from *le petit vin de Touraine.* Do not give them anything bitter or meat that is spiced, but broth and tender meat. With the exception of very ripe grapes, they should not eat fruit. Though I have heard that apples are good, provided they be not acid, which causes wind in the stomach."

Louis had chosen his wife, Charlotte of Savoy, against his father's wish, for the sake of her large dowry and the support an alliance with Savoy would give him in Dauphiné. But if we may believe Commynes, and also the admirable drawing of the Queen in the Cabinet des Estampes at Paris, Charlotte was extremely unattractive : her eyes were large, gentle and sad, her glance timid and constrained ; in the towering hennin and the heraldic robe of this portrait, she looks like a peasantess wearing a crown.

Charlotte was indeed a sweet, pious woman, who spent a great deal of money on charities.

On the 16th of January 1464, when, being pregnant, she arrived at Amiens in her litter, she was received with high honour. The people cried " Noël," and all the clergy awaited her in front of the cathedral. They escorted her into Notre-Dame, where she knelt at prayer while the great organ played. Afterwards, at her residence, in the house of the King's Councillor, Jean Vilain, she herself read all the letters addressed to her by the aldermen of the city, and she recommended a certain barber for attendance on the sick in the Hôtel Dieu. Charlotte was always kind to everyone, and always ready to help her servants ; she brought up two children at her own expense. But, shy and retiring, she was totally without influence. On one occasion, when the mayor of Tours refused to allow her escort to enter the town at night, she was waiting patiently at the gate when he came to ask her pardon. Her complaint of the bad smells from the tanneries at Amboise seems to have been disregarded. The Queen loved her husband; but Louis, though he kept his vow of fidelity to Charlotte, which he had taken after the death of his child, regarded her rather as a mother than a wife. Nevertheless, he often separated her from her son, the Dauphin.

Occasionally she was allowed to figure at feasts and court ceremonies, but generally very simply dressed, like her husband. She seems to have possessed few jewels and sumptuous gowns. Black or brown satin was her usual attire. Her plate was of no great value. She had some money at her disposal; for in 1470, she received 32,125 *livres* for the upkeep of her stables and of her household, comprising forty-two retainers. When she went to town or to church, it was with two leather chariots and twelve cavaliers. She had only six horses in her stables: four for the cart which carried her luggage, her coffers and her two camp-beds, one hackney, caparisoned in cloth of gold, for her to ride, and a horse with a saddle-cloth of black velvet for her pillion. Her favourite amusements were embroidery, cards and backgammon. But the hours marked by the escutcheoned timepiece outside her room must have passed somewhat monotonously.

Charlotte possessed books; for we find her buying illuminated breviaries and works of devotion. She seems to have admired one Guillaume Danicot, a cultured person on whom she asked the Pope, Paul II, to bestow a secular benefice, in order that he might devote himself to the preaching, for which he showed so great an aptitude. She gave orders to the artists of Tours, assisted struggling illuminators of manuscripts, and took an interest in the education of the poor. Everyone loved her.

Charlotte bore Louis six children: Joachim, the Duke of Burgundy's godson, who lived only a few months; Louise, who died in 1460, before she was a year old. The third child, Anne, was her father's favourite. Shrewd and intelligent, she resembled him in every way. Anne and her husband, Pierre de Beaujeu, son of the Duc de Bourbon, of whom Louis had a high opinion, were the confidants of his later years and the recipients of his

Photo : A. Giraudon

CHARLOTTE OF SAVOY, SECOND WIFE OF LOUIS XI

(*From the Arras Collection*)

generosity. Louis' third daughter, Jeanne, was that poor little, sickly, deformed creature whom, for dynastic reasons, he compelled Louis of Orléans to marry.[1]

Charles, the long expected and fondly cherished son, for whom the King had so earnestly prayed to the Virgin, was born on the 30th of June 1470. He was dedicated to Our Lady of Puy in Anjou. His image was placed on the tabernacle in Chartres Cathedral. The new-born infant was made a member of the Order of the Holy Spirit. He was carefully guarded in the Château of Amboise. Every attention was paid to his health and upbringing. No detail, neither his teething nor his colds in the head, was too insignificant for the King to take an interest in. Louis had already lost one son, the little François, who had died of the plague. And his constant fear was that Charles would succumb to the same malady. So when, in 1473, Charles fell ill with a feverish cold, the King trembled for the permanence of his family and for the heir to that patrimony, to the organisation and augmentation of which his life was devoted.

In this all-absorbing task, Louis was now ably seconded by a band of invaluable helpers : Georges de la Trémoille, Lord of Craon, whom the King addressed as *mon ami* and who served as his Lieutenant-General in Champagne ; the Grand Master, Antoine de Chabannes, the most striking military figure of his day, who, as we have seen, had served Charles VII and had fallen into disgrace in the beginning of Louis' reign, but had been restored to his favour in 1467 ; Tristan l'Hermite, Provost of Merchants, resolute and far-seeing, a brave and faithful soldier, who had likewise served Charles VII ; the Chancellor, Pierre Doriole, superintendent of finance, the mayor's son, who conducted the great political trials of Balue, Saint-Pol and Nemours ; Jean Bourré, Monseigneur du Plessis, in whom

---

[1] The forcing of this marriage on Louis of Orléans, afterwards Louis XII, was one of Louis XI's most discreditable actions. His object was to prevent Louis of Orléans, who was heir-presumptive to the throne, from having legitimate children. (Trans.)

the King placed absolute confidence and who superintended his building enterprises; the Scotsman, William Moneypenny, Seigneur de Concressault, a specialist in English affairs; Commynes, of course, who knew everything.

The most remarkable and the most famous of the band was the King's barber, Olivier le Mauvais, Olivier le Daim, who came from the neighbourhood of Courtrai. Louis made him his confidant, and entrusted him with all manner of missions, sending him on embassies to foreign lands, employing him in the negotiations with Ghent, despatching him on one occasion from Amboise to Paris to arrest certain persons of whom he had been given the charge, on another to fetch magpies for the royal aviary. During the royal progresses it was to Olivier's care that the crates of distilled waters for the King's use were committed. He even advanced money out of his own pocket to his royal master. The barbers of those days were also surgeons. They shaved and they bled; and while exercising these avocations they culled much valuable information. Olivier passed his on to the King. It was through Olivier's influence that the French barbers obtained their royal charter; he himself drew up its articles: they are a protest against the ignorance of the day, for they prescribe cleanliness and other measures of public health, and suggest the advisability of some knowledge of the anatomy of blood-vessels. Olivier, who had the courage to be frank with his master, seems to have inspired him with a wholesome dread, at any rate during his illnesses.

But of all those who served Louis, Philippe de Commynes was, without doubt, the most intelligent and the one who most closely resembled his master.

The Fleming, Commynes, was a handsome man. His fine and dignified literary style delighted Montaigne. Commynes must have been born at Renescure, the lordship of his father, Colard. The Lord of Renescure was a Knight of the Golden Fleece and Sovereign Bailiff of

Flanders, one of Philip the Good's most highly favoured servants. The young Commynes himself became a squire in the service of Philip's son, the Comte de Charolais, at whose side we have seen him fighting at the Battle of Montlhéry. But the squire was too shrewd to follow his headstrong master to the end. After he had been dubbed a knight at the age of twenty-two, Philippe helped Charolais to escape from the hands of the people of Ghent, just as later, at Péronne, he was to help Louis to escape from the hands of Charolais, then Duke Charles the Bold. Philippe admired Louis' astuteness. He had earned eighteen sous a day in the Duke's service ; and the King of France had but to increase Commynes' wages for the Duke's confidential secretary to transfer his service ; and as the shrewd Fleming had at the same time perceived that Louis stood for intelligence and the future, he lost no time in joining his new master. It was, as we have seen, in 1472, in Normandy, that Commynes forsook the Burgundian camp and came to Louis at Ponts-de-Cé. He, who was the personification of naturalness and of reason, could no longer stand the Duke's absurd violence and pomposity. Of course he lost his Flemish estate, which the Duke confiscated. But adequate compensation awaited him in France. Louis and Commynes were kindred spirit, both devotees of reason : both keen to see on which side their bread was buttered. The King bestowed on his new vassal a pension of 6000 *livres*, a rich wife from Poitou, and the unjustly confiscated lands of Louis d'Amboise, Vicomte de Thouars.

So now the obscure Seigneur de Renescure is Monseigneur d'Argenton, Seneschal of Poitou, Captain of Poitiers, and above all, confidential adviser of the King of France, who has at length found his equal.

Commynes soon became the universal inquirer, making himself a master of every situation, not only of English and Burgundian affairs, but of those of Savoy, Milan, Florence and of the whole of Italy. In the matter of the Burgundian succession, Philippe urged moderation on his master ; for he was always more intent on striking home than on striking hard. In the opinion of Lorenzo di Medici, there was no one like Commynes—" the true pupil of your Majesty," he wrote to Louis, " and the best administrator of your will." It was for Commynes that Louis called during his first seizure. It was Commynes who was with the King at the last. Louis was his master, his benefactor, " the Prince of most excellent memory," to whom he owed the truth.

It was in order to preserve the august memory of having served and aided the King, and at the request of another of Louis' servants, that philosopher and physician, the Archbishop of Vienne, Angelo Cato, that Commynes wrote his " Mémoires."

CHAPTER XXIX

LOUIS AT ORLÉANS AND AT TOURS

Louis strengthens the Fortifications of Orléans.—Builds himself a Palace.—
The town celebrates the Dauphin's Birth.—Louis' excellent relations
with Tours on his Accession.—The Town created a Municipality.—
The King virtually Mayor of Tours.—Opposition of the Clergy.—
Louis establishes Order, promotes Cleanliness, Hygiene, founds a
School, encourages Trade and Industry.—Disadvantages of the
Proximity of the King's Residence.—Benefits conferred on the
Town by the King.—*Le Pouvre de St Martin.*—Prosperity of Tours
in Louis' Reign.—A letter from Francesco Florio.

KING LOUIS, as we have said, spent his summers in military
expeditions or royal progresses. It was only in the winter
that he occupied any fixed abode ; and that was generally
in one of the towns on the Loire : in the early years of his
reign at Amboise or at Tours, with occasional hunting
expeditions at Montrichard or in the Chinon Forest.
Later, in 1465 and 1466, Orléans, Meung-sur-Loire,
Montargis and La Motte d'Egry were his favourite
residences.

At Orléans, he was not in his own domain, but in that
of the Duchess of Orléans. But the town, as a holy city,
which had miraculously withstood all the onslaughts of
the enemies of France, made a special appeal to King Louis.
For that reason he granted the townsfolk the privilege of
acquiring fiefs and rising to the ranks of peers of the realm.

The English had set fire to the suburbs of the city and
to all their beautiful churches. These Louis undertook
to restore. He also determined to make Orléans a vast
military camp and an arsenal of war. He erected new
fortifications, enclosing the churches of St Aignan and St
Euverte ; and he insisted on the work being carried out
with the utmost rapidity. As this newly enclosed part

of the town was uninhabited, the King granted drapers, weavers and cutlers the right to set up their booths there. The adequate defence of the city was one of his chief concerns : he placed it under a strong guard, and had its fortifications constantly inspected. He levied a duty on wine and salt for their upkeep. The city aldermen and the canons of Ste Croix, St Pierre, Eupoint and St Aignan protested against the new fortifications, which involved the destruction of some of their property. The King summoned a meeting of the townsfolk in the market. The objections were overruled. So the work began.

Louis showed special favour to the church of St Aignan —no doubt because it was the church that had suffered most at the hands of the English. He was received as its abbot and canon. When, on the 17th of February 1466, he made his entry into the church, he was presented with an amice, a purse and a surplice, which last he put on. Orléans was then the only place in France where the memory of the Maid was still honoured and cherished. At Orléans alone was celebrated the anniversary of her deliverance of the city.

While Louis was in residence at Orléans, order reigned. Thieves and other malefactors were hanged.

In the shadow of the apse of St Aignan, Louis built himself a house, or rather a palace in miniature, bright and cheerful, with facings of stone and brick, dormer-windows ornamented with carved bosses and a low arched doorway on which were carved syrens, winged beasts and chimeras. Beneath the high chancel walls the King laid out a terrace and gardens. From the towers at the end of the terrace he could see the wide sweep of the Loire, spanned by its great bridge, with shelving beaches, and willows growing on its banks—a flat, bare landscape, but restful, and eminently appropriate for the abode of a king who was at once mystic and clear-minded.

In 1470, Louis rejoiced to announce to the people of Orléans the advent of his son, the future Charles VIII, who came into the world on the 30th of June, shortly after

midnight. On the 1st of July, as soon as the canons
received the letter which announced the event, they
formed a procession of the townsfolk. The notables
assembled in the chapterhouse of Ste Croix, whence they
proceeded to a banquet in the Town Hall. The following
Sunday, Monday and Tuesday, bonfires blazed in the
squares. The streets were decorated. Everyone made
merry. There was morris dancing and music in all
quarters of the town. Wine circulated. Pasties, called
" Dauphins," were eaten. No one was forgotten, neither
the paupers in the Hôtel Dieu nor the lepers in the lazar-
house outside the town.

Cléry was not far from Orléans; and Cléry, as we have
seen, was one of Louis' favourite residences at this time.
To Cléry he came in 1471, to give thanks to the Virgin for
the Dauphin's birth.

But it was at Tours that Louis spent most of the time
during which he had any fixed abode. Just outside the
town was his hunting-lodge of les Montils, surrounded by
woods and bordered by two rivers, the Cher and the
Loire. Tours, like Bourges, had been the capital of
France during part of Charles VII's reign. In the chapel
of the fortified château which commanded the bridge
Louis had wedded Margaret of Scotland. His parents
also had been married at Tours.

The people of the town had been among the first to
swear allegiance to King Louis after his accession. They
sent to him in Brabant declaring that they placed great
hopes in their new lord, who came, so they heard, to save
his people. Louis was as well disposed to the people of
Tours as they were to him. On the 8th of December
1461, he sent to ask them what privileges they desired for
the town. They deliberated, and replied that they
desired, among other things, exemption from the *taille*
and the right to levy a tax on the retail sale of wine, the
proceeds of which would be used for the upkeep of the
town, which had suffered sadly during the English and the

Civil Wars. They would also like their city to be created a municipality with a mayor. That was precisely what Louis himself wanted. They should receive, he replied, privileges identical with those of La Rochelle.

The townsfolk on inquiry discovered that those privileges included a mayor and aldermen, in return for which the King received 500 crowns. The clergy made certain reservations. But the people won the day. The King was benevolence itself. To the mayor, elected annually, and to the aldermen, he granted patents of nobility. He encouraged trade, and himself did not disdain to dabble in commerce, for he sold wine at Amboise. In gratitude for Louis' protection, the town of Tours sent a silver ship to Amboise for the Queen.

The King and his good town of Tours were not always on these excellent terms. There came a time—in January 1467—when Louis, threatened by the Duke of Brittany, wished to strengthen the fortifications of the city, and ordered its citizens to widen their moat. The clergy refused to take part in this work, and the laity followed their example. But the mayor intervened and settled the matter by discovering a precedent in 1425. The mayor was, in reality, the King's man of straw. Louis, from his hunting-lodge at les Montils, kept a vigilant eye on municipal affairs, controlling the mayoral elections, putting in his own nominee, and acting virtually as mayor of the city. On the 4th of October 1468, we find the docile mayor announcing to the assembled townsfolk that the King is about to take up his residence at Tours, that he will keep watch and ward over the town, that he will not permit any man to injure his neighbour, that if any citizen resort to the use of force he shall be proceeded against by force, and that all delinquents shall be arrested and imprisoned. Any varlet going out after nine at night or carrying a dagger or truncheon in the streets will be liable to arrest.

This policing of the town was rigorous, but also just. Thus on the 3rd of November 1469 we find the King at

Montils, consenting to listen to complaints against the action of his own Provost of Merchants, in the case of a certain gentleman from Germany.

Louis infused his own energy into the municipality. He practically re-made the town : he founded one common school for all the citizens ; he engaged a teacher from Paris ; he improved the navigation of the Loire ; he tried to establish the silk manufacture by introducing weavers from other towns ; but the citizens of Tours treated these new-comers so badly that the King was obliged to place them under the protection of his Provost of Merchants.

With matters of public health Louis was always concerned. The death of his little son, François, of the plague had given him a horror of infectious diseases. Hot weather and the ensuing epidemics filled him with anxiety. While an epidemic was raging in the neighbouring town of Châteaurenault he had the gates of Tours closed against all incomers. He insisted on the streets being kept clean and free from the geese and pigs which had been allowed to wander through the town.

While Tours benefited from this personal supervision of the King, the royal proximity was not an unmixed blessing. For the city groaned under the contributions which Louis continually demanded for his wars, and under his constant requisitioning of horses and victuals.

There were other burdens, too : the butchers complained of having to provide meat for the royal aviaries. The King's petty officials and the pages of ambassadors, who lodged in the city, seem to have made themselves a nuisance to the townsfolk ; and, in 1472, during the King's residence at Plessis, we find the municipality offering twelve hogsheads of oats to the King's foragers, in the hope that they might behave with less brutality when billeting the King's retainers on the citizens. Louis also had a way of committing his most dangerous prisoners to the care of the townsfolk, who were often expected to keep them at their own expense and even to take turns in guarding them. One Canto, an Armagnac, was given in charge to the mayor, at whose house he fell seriously ill. Another famous prisoner, Simon de Quingey, who had been the Duke of Burgundy's cup-bearer, was imposed on the mayor, who was charged to imprison him in an iron cage. Both Quingey's guardian and the citizens of Tours took pity on his misfortunes. They covered his cage with cloth to protect it from the draughts of the mayor's cellar, in which it had been erected; and they gave Quingey a feather-bed to lie on. When the chafing of his irons produced sores on his feet and legs, the King's stewards ordered the iron-founder, Master Laurens Wrine, who kept the key of the chains, to unlock them, and Quingey was examined to see whether he had not contracted some disease which might aggravate his sufferings. Then Quingey and his cage were, by royal command, removed to Plessis, but only with great difficulty: for a wall in the mayor's house had to be broken down and carpenters employed to place the cage on rollers and hoist it into a cart. At Plessis the cage was set up in the house of the Commune. There Quingey was allowed to see his wife, and to confess to a chaplain on Easter Day. His torn doublet was mended and had new sleeves put to it. He was given two new shirts, because those he possessed had rotted.

About the same time, the much-tried mayor of Tours was relieved of another prisoner, an Aragonese, who was conveyed to Poitiers. He was given a horse, shoes and a cloth cloak. The King seems to have paid the mayor for this prisoner's board.

But Louis knew his people well; and if some of his actions were unpopular others went straight to the hearts of his subjects. He was always good to the poor. His religious endowments were, as we have seen, munificent. Through his liberality the magnificence of the services at St Martin's outshone that of the Roman basilicas. In connection with St Martin, and as a perpetuation of the ancient legend, which was portrayed on the church door, of St Martin's gift of half his cloak to a beggar, the King instituted a curious foundation, dedicated to the support of one poor man. The recipient of the charity was to be stationed in front of the statue of St Martin, or on fête days by the holy-water stoup, with a tablet close by describing him as *le pouvre du mondit sieur saint Martin;* he was to wear a red-and-white robe. The charge of choosing *le pouvre* was committed to the canons, who were empowered to substitute another *pouvre* for him should he turn out to be incorrigible or dissolute.

Another of the King's popular actions was to exempt from taxation those excellent, skilled craftsmen, the lock-makers, who worked so conscientiously that they took a whole fortnight to produce a lock.

Indeed, Louis showed a perfect comprehension of the interests of all classes at Tours, not forgetting his own. He had found the ancient commercial city almost in ruins. He had fired it with his own energy and imbued it with his own ideas. We must not allow the town records to mislead us when they describe the people as impoverished and downtrodden; the citizens were richer than they admitted. The fine buildings they erected leave no manner of doubt on this subject. But we possess other evidence which dates from the year 1477. This is a Latin letter written by Francesco Florio to a friend in Rome. Florio was a Florentine, a humanist, and, we must admit, somewhat addicted to hyperbole. It was sixteen years since he had left his native Tuscany. He hoped to end his days in France, in peace and tranquillity. He was now living at Tours, in the house of François Thomas, Canon of St Gatien, where he was completing a story of the Loves of Camillus and Æmilia, modelled on the Loves of Lucretius and the " Euryalus " of Æneas Sylvius.

Florio calls Touraine " the orchard of France." The city of Tours, with its noble circle of fortifications, its wide, handsome gates, its well-kept streets, bustling with animation, seemed to him to surpass the most famous cities in greatness. He admires the handiwork of its craftsmen, its high, spacious houses, its fine ecclesiastical foundations—St Gatien, St Martin, St Julien—and its castle, built on the tomb of Turnus, with its chapel royal, in which the most gifted musicians of the kingdom, conducted by the famous Okeghem, sang vespers and matins daily.

Florio also describes les Montils, a royal residence well adapted to the tastes of a King who was fond of tranquillity and the pleasures of the chase. Louis in the midst of his court appeared to Florio as a second Augustus, ruling the world by law, moderation, wisdom and prudence. Tours was a second Rome, and its citizen, Fouquet, the greatest artist of his day. Florio loved everything in Touraine, its fruit—its *bon chrétien* pears— and its climate.

All this Louis loved also ; and to a great extent it was his work.

CHAPTER XXX

THE DESTRUCTION OF ARRAS, 1477.

The King's Violence.—Commynes in Disgrace.—The Question of Mary of Burgundy's Marriage.—The Politics of Arras.—Vacillation of the Townsfolk.—Louis enters Arras.—Prepares to treat the citizens with moderation.—A Burgundian attack on the City.—Treachery and Revolt.—Bombardment by the King's Artillery.—Destruction of the Fortifications and Ruin of the City.—Louis intrigues with Ghent on the subject of Mary's Marriage.—Execution of Mary's Counsellors.—The laying waste of Flanders.—Trial, Condemnation and Execution of the Duc de Nemours.

Louis, who had shown such moderation and caution in adversity, was now to lend an ear to those who counselled violence. The delays of diplomacy began to irk him. He banished his friend Commynes to Poitou. In the avidity of his greed for land, his former shrewdness and dexterity forsook him : his negotiations with Ghent, entrusted to Olivier le Daim, failed, so also did his attempt to capture Mary of Burgundy in order to marry her to the Dauphin ; and Louis descended so low as to spread a false report that it was the English who were plotting to lay hands on the Duchess, having landed at Calais for that purpose.

The King was intriguing with the former servants of the late Duke Charles, with that Guillaume de Bische, whom the Duke had raised from obscurity and who now occupied Péronne for the King, with the Duke's Chancellor, Guillaume Hugonet and with the Seigneur de Humbercourt, who were all ready to come over to Louis, once he had succeeded in marrying the Burgundian heiress to his son.

The situation was very involved. The citizens of Arras could not believe that the Duke was really dead. They had always vacillated in their allegiance. In January 1464, they had received King Louis and delivered up to him the keys of the town : but on the 10th of July 1467, they had also received Charles the Bold, and had raised troops for the reduction of Liége. This, however, did not mean that the townsfolk of Arras were Burgundians. They were simply merchants harassed by a war which had put an end to their trade with Lille, and had ruined their town and the surrounding country. They did not know which side to take. They desired enlightenment as to the position of Mary of Burgundy ; and in order to obtain it, they despatched envoys to the Estates at Ghent. At the same time they sent their sergeant, Jean du Flos, to discuss the affairs of their town with King Louis.

Louis was on good terms with the general in command at Arras, the Seigneur d'Esquerdes, who was prepared to deliver the town into the King's hands. Louis entered the citadel on the 4th of March 1477. Monseigneur d'Esquerdes, after taking the oath of allegiance to the King, withdrew, leaving his followers to join which side they pleased.

Louis at that time had no intention of taking revenge on the soldiers of Nancy, who had sought refuge in Arras, nor on those who had grossly insulted him, calling him " a coward King," on his entry into the city. Neither did he wish to establish a garrison there, unless it were the will of the inhabitants.

Then he went off to besiege Hesdin, one of the Bur-gundian strongholds, which had declared for Mary. After a few hours' bombardment, Hesdin surrendered, and Boulogne-sur-Mer followed suit on the 28th of April. Meanwhile the Burgundians, under the leadership of the Seigneur de Vergy, made an attempt to enter Arras. Their leaders were taken and hanged. Louis brought his artillery up to the walls of the town ; and Arras came to terms, agreeing to pay 60,000 crowns. Among those who had betrayed the King was a certain Oudard de Bussy, Procurator-General of the town, whom Louis had appointed to an office in the Paris Parlement. The King sentenced him to be executed and his head to be displayed in the market-place of Hesdin. " In order that there shall be no difficulty in recognising him," declared Louis, " the head shall wear its accustomed handsome fur cap." So there it was, and by it on a pole Bussy's scarlet hood and a scroll, bearing the words : " This is the head of Master Oudard de Bussy, counsellor of the King in the court of the King's Parlement at Paris." While Louis' executioner was busy cutting off heads, the King's treasurer was pocketing crowns. Louis had demanded 12,000.

Louis had entered the citadel on the 25th of April, the city on the 4th of May. He had ridden in on horseback, through a breach in the walls. Addressing the people, who had assembled in the Place du Petit Marché, he said : " You have not treated me well. But I forgive you. If you will be good subjects, I will be a good lord." All the same, he beheaded one of the town's captains, Pierchon du Chastel, and a bowman who had shot at him from the ramparts.

In March, the King had issued a letter of amnesty and had confirmed the customs of the town.

Now Arras was ruined : its walls had been shattered by the royal artillery. The city was condemned to pay a fine of 40,000 crowns, its gold plate was taken to Paris. Louis had resolved to include Arras in the royal domain.

Mary of Burgundy was then at Ghent, in the midst of one of those popular revolutions which were frequent in that town. The King sent ambassadors to confer with the delegates from the Estates. The latter decided to agree to the French marriage. But it was now Louis who hesitated : he felt certain of Flanders and Artois ; he knew that the people of Ghent always hated the overlords of their town ; and he resolved to sow dissension between the Duchess and the townsfolk ; so he showed them the letters in which Mary had consented to deliver herself up to four persons appointed by the King. The townsfolk were furious ; they seized her counsellors, Hugonet and Humbercourt, and condemned them to death, ignoring their appeal to the Parlement of Paris. Mary appeared before the people assembled on the market-place and implored them to spare her counsellors : there was a difference of opinion, blows were exchanged ; but Hugonet and Humbercourt were beheaded.

Louis was furious ; his rage knew no bounds. He called up all the forces of Flanders ; he suppressed a rebellion at Péronne ; he marched on Cambrai, storming Quesnoy-le-Comte and Avesnes by the way. At Cambrai he had the defenders massacred and the walls of the town razed as an example to other towns in revolt. He ordered his Grand Master to bring Valenciennes to terms ; and for that purpose sent him three or four thousand harvesters to destroy the crops—*faire le gast*, he called it. " Set them to work," he wrote, " and spare not five or six pipes of wine to make them drunk, so that they may do their work the better, and that I may hear of it. I assure you, my lord, that there is no better way of bringing the folk of Valenciennes to say the word."

Thus did Louis wage war on the crops, on the oats when they were yet green. Thus did he transform lances into reaping-hooks.

Meanwhile, he was demanding lusty pioneers for the destruction of the walls of Arras. The Flemings, in full retreat from Pont-aux-Pierres to Oudenarde and Bruges, were setting fire to everything. The people's sufferings were more than they could bear ; and even the King's officers superintending the fortification works at Reims were molested. Free-lances were deserting and going home ; when caught they were accused of high treason and dealt with accordingly. The President of Burgundy was murdered at Dijon.

Louis had also to contend with enemies nearer home. It was high time that Jacques d'Armagnac, Duc de Nemours, should be brought to trial. He was tried at Noyon, where the Parlement was in session. The King, who had determined that the Duke should be condemned,

and with the greatest possible publicity, had summoned
" grave clerks to Noyon from divers cities of the realm."

Jacques de Nemours was a traitor, like his friend, the
Constable St. Pol. Nemours had been the comrade of
the Dauphin's youth, but he had always intrigued, though
his amiability had prepossessed people in his favour. In
1474, he had endeavoured to form a second Ligue du Bien
Public. He had rejoiced at the coming of the English.
Louis knew all this, and insisted on his surrendering without
terms. He had been imprisoned first in Pierre Seize, the
Bastille of Lyons, where his hair had turned white and his
poor weak brain had begun to grow confused, and then he
had been removed to the Bastille at Paris. The King
hoped that the trial would reveal important secrets. No
method of inquiry by torture and otherwise was neglected.
The Duke's letters were intercepted ; he was surrounded
by spies ; he offered rewards to his guards who betrayed
him ; and when he asked for ropes by means of which he
intended to escape up the chimney, there was nothing for
him but the iron cage and torture. Shivering with cold,
the Duke wept and asked whether the scaffold was being
erected. He entreated the King to pardon him ; and he,
who had been a traitor all his life, pathetically promised to
be loyal. His wife, too, who was pregnant, vainly implored
the King to pardon her husband. She died in childbed.
No pardon was possible for one who had conspired against
the King and the Dauphin. Nemours was guilty of high
treason, and must be beheaded. This was the verdict at
Noyon. At Paris, in the Palais, Pierre Doriole read the sentence, which condemned the Duke to have his head cut off.
He was brought out of the Bastille, white and trembling;
on a horse draped in black he was taken to the Fish Market,
which smelt of vinegar on that day. While the King's
officers drank white wine, Nemours confessed, then placed
his head on the block, which was lined with silk. The
crowds of onlookers shuddered ; for it was Armagnac blood
that was shed that day. When night fell, the grey friars
bore the body into their church by torchlight.

The King proclaimed his law against high treason. He had horrified the Parisians, who mourned for a prince whom they believed to be innocent and who had asked to be buried in the Franciscan habit.

Louis' rage knew no abatement. He was harrying Flanders and distressing the loyal towns by his requisitions and forced labour. Tristan, the Provost of Merchants, went everywhere demanding sheep, horses and carts. Though it cannot be denied that he was hard and rough, legend has exaggerated his cruelty. It was not difficult to come to terms with him. He acknowledged, for example, that the people of Orléans were not liable for military service. When he overstepped the bounds of his duty, complaints were made to the King, who did not always take his side.

The tide was still flowing in the King's favour. The Burgundian Prince of Orange had been defeated at Gy. News of the Duke of Brittany's final submission had been brought to Louis, when he was encamped outside Arras. The Archduke Maximilian had sent ambassadors to demand a truce. And now the King's men-at-arms were able to go into winter quarters on the Flemish frontier and in other regions, which owed allegiance to Mary, while Louis himself went off to Plessis, where he spent part of the winter.

CHAPTER XXXI

THE CONQUEST OF BURGUNDY

Louis and Dijon.—He poses as the Protector of Mary of Burgundy.—
Organises the Government of the Province.—Georges de La
Trémoille appointed Governor.—Resistance of Franche Comté.—
Defeat of La Trémoille.—Charles d'Amboise appointed Governor.—
The dead Duke convicted of High Treason.—Louis enters Dijon.

FROM his camp outside Arras, the infuriated Louis was
carrying on the conquest of Burgundy. His was the haste
and skill of the sovereign who had quoted Lucan to the
English ambassadors : *Tolle moras saepe nocuit differre
paratas*, which, in English, amounts to saying that if
matters ripe for action are not dealt with at once they are
likely to become harmful.

From his friend, the Burgundian Philippe Pot, the
King learned that the people of that province were more
like those of France than the heavy, pugnacious Flemings,
and that the Burgundians cultivated vines like the
inhabitants of Touraine. Consequently the King treated
Philippe Pot's compatriots with kindness and amiability.

On the 9th of January 1477, he wrote to the citizens of
Dijon announcing the death of Charles the Bold, a misfortune " over which we grieve," and reminding them that
they belonged to the crown and were part of the kingdom
of France.

The King gave himself out to be the protector of
his god-daughter, Mary, whose rights it would be his duty
to safeguard. Let the citizens of Dijon say whether they
would do likewise.

This royal communication created consternation in the
city. Could it be that the Duke was really dead ? The
matter must be inquired into.

Louis made every effort to win Burgundian support. The precise attitude of the people of Dijon towards him is not clear from the official documents we possess. There is no doubt that the King had a considerable following in the city; and it is equally certain that Charles the Bold was held in no high esteem. Dijon had of late seen little of its dukes. Except when they came for their sumptuous burying in the chapel of the Charter-House, they had neglected their Burgundian capital. All their wealth and energy had been concentrated in Flanders. The only part the Burgundians had taken in the mad adventures of Charles the Bold had been to pay the wages of his German mercenaries and the cost of his artillery wagons. Charles might be rich. But the citizens of Dijon were poor.

They seem to have given a fairly good reception to the King's general, Georges de La Trémoille, Seigneur de Craon. The Provincial Estates met on the 25th of January 1477. The Dijon citizens were too cautious to attend in large numbers, and none of the nobles came. But the majority declared for Louis; and all that the Prince of Orange, Mary's representative, could obtain was a grant of twelve torches, weighing three pounds each, and eight casks of the best wine. Why could not the King of France be trusted to protect his god-daughter ? The Estates tendered him their submission, but only on condition that he would keep Burgundy until Mary's marriage, and that he would restore his possessions to Charles the Bold, should he return, for the Estates could not believe him to be dead.

The King delegated the government of Burgundy to a group of four—the Seigneur de Craon, Charles d'Amboise, Seigneur de Chaumont, Monseigneur d'Albi and the Prince of Orange. He appointed a receiver-general to act in his name. He granted pensions to certain Burgundians. He bestowed gifts on the churches. He set up a council of state at Dijon. None of these measures met with any opposition except in the county, la Franche

Comté, as it was called, a wild, mountainous region, inhabited by a rough, independent race.

Louis' first occupation of Burgundy was not oppressive. The King's garrisons were small—imprudently small, perhaps. Little heed was taken of Mary's somewhat tardy proclamation that Burgundy never belonged to the crown of France. The King, on his side, was endeavouring to obtain legal justification for his claims, and having a search made in the archives for anything which could either confirm or invalidate his position. But already a Dijon goldsmith was engraving the King's seal; and M de Craon, who had been appointed governor of the province, was demanding an inventory of the late Duke's jewels. The Prince of Orange, disappointed in his hope of the governorship, made every effort to foment discontent in Franche Comté. Several towns revolted. The French army was put to flight. An insurrection, promptly quelled, broke out in Dijon itself. The King was furious. He ordered the arrest of the Prince of Orange. This being impracticable, he was burnt in effigy. His estates were confiscated, his mansion razed to the ground. But the sins of Franche Comté were not visited on Dijon. The King confirmed all the privileges Duke Charles had granted the city, and took various measures for the encouragement of trade in the province.

But a serious blow was struck at the King's authority when, in September, an ex-freebooter, Guillaume de Vaudrey et Salazar, took possession of the one fortress in the county, which Louis had occupied, destroying La Trémoille's artillery, and leaving, so it was said, three thousand slain on the battlefield. La Trémoille, who had been loyal, but rather too careful of his own interest, was superseded by Charles d'Amboise, who was instructed to call up the militia, to destroy all fortresses which could not be held, and to show no mercy to deserters. The King distributed Burgundian fiefs among his officers. But he did not abandon his work of organisation. The Paris Parlement received instructions to refer all suits in which

Burgundians were concerned to the Burgundian Parlement. The Burgundian chancellery was established on an equal footing with that of France. Louis had allowed Charles the Bold to ruin himself. The King was now going to kill him definitely and legally, viz. : by convicting him of high treason, an offence which involved the confiscation of his territory. With this object Louis published a circular, which was nothing more or less than a page of history, written by the King for the benefit of his people, setting forth all the crimes of Duke Charles and of his daughter, *notre cousine*, crimes which constituted high treason, an offence which must be tried by the Parlement at Paris. The King adjured his lawyers to act with all diligence—Louis, like a true peasant, was going to have his lawsuit.

Meanwhile the King's general, Charles d'Amboise, had been doing good work in Franche Comté. Charolais, Morvan, Auxois, Châtillonnais were the King's. Dijon had sent him mustard and wine ; and even the keys of the city had not been refused when asked for by the King's officers.

Louis made his triumphal entry into Dijon on the 31st of July. He had been expected for two months ; and a grand welcome awaited him. While the grapes of Burgundy were ripening in the scorching sun, the King and his nobles were regaled with wine, and the clergy brought relics for him to kiss. Louis entered the city on horseback, beneath a canopy of cloth of gold held over his head by the notables and aldermen. In the Abbey of St Bénigne the King was presented with a symbolical ring as a sign of his alliance with Burgundy. Then, preceded by minstrels, drummers and trumpeters, he entered the palace of the Dukes. On its painted windows the royal arms now figured in the place of the arms of Burgundy. Louis displayed his usual generosity. But he required those who held the lands of fugitives to pay taxes. He also left with the people of Dijon a monument, for which they were not grateful, viz. the fortified castle, which he built near the Porte Guillaume.

CHAPTER XXXII

MARY OF BURGUNDY AND THE HOUSE OF AUSTRIA

1477–1481

Mary's Suitors.—Question of an English Marriage.—Relations between England and France, 1477-1481.—The Suit of Maximilian.—His Marriage with Mary.—Louis' Attitude towards the Marriage.—His Dealings with the Swiss.—The King begins to show signs of Exhaustion.—Alters his mode of Life.—Withdraws from his People.—A change comes over the House of Burgundy.—The War in Picardy.—Attempt on the King's Life.—A Year's Truce with Maximilian.—The English "Tribute."—Negotiations with the Papacy.—The Battle of Guinegate.

DURING the months which followed the death of Charles the Bold, the intrigues, jealousies, and ambitions of north-western Europe revolved round the hand of Mary of Burgundy. Among her suitors were the Dauphin Charles—but he was too young—and Anthony Scales, Lord Rivers, the Queen of England's brother—but he was too old, and not wealthy enough for so rich an heiress.

King Louis does not seem to have had any objection to an English marriage, provided it allowed of the dismemberment of Flanders. But it was the King of England himself who hesitated. He was not eager to involve himself in the complications of the Low Countries, which might entail a war as prolonged as that with France. Edward would prefer to hold Boulogne and to continue to receive from Louis that pension of 50,000 crowns which the English called "tribute." Louis also wished to hold Boulogne; for that reason he had placed the town under the protection of Notre-Dame, and bestowed upon it a virgin's heart in fine gold.

In reality, for six years, from 1475 till 1481, England

273

and France settled their differences by negotiation. The King saw that the English were paid regularly, sending over the 50,000 gold crowns in two ships, *Le Volant* and *le Dauphin de Dieppe*. In the year 1479, we find Guillaume Restout specially appointed to take over from Dieppe the crowns due to the King of England. Thus, while Louis was conquering Arras and Burgundy, the two kings on opposite sides of the Channel were playing a cautious game, tricking and dissembling. The King of France was giving pensions to Edward's counsellors. The King of England was reminding Louis of the clause in the Treaty of Picquigny, which had stipulated for a marriage between the Dauphin and Edward's daughter.

Meanwhile Mme de Hallwin, Commynes' cousin and Mary's chief lady-in-waiting, had her own ideas on the subject of her young lady's marriage. In her opinion there was no doubt of the Dauphin being too young : he was seven, while Mary was of marriageable age. She must have a man for husband : it might be my Lord of Angoulême ; the Duke of Clèves had hoped it would be his son. A letter was produced, which Duke Charles had dictated to his daughter when he was thinking of marrying her to Maximilian, King of the Romans and Archduke of Austria. Maximilian had once received a diamond ring from Mary. During one of her visits to Ghent, Mary's step-mother, the Dowager Duchess Margaret, had done all she could to promote this union. The Emperor's ambassadors had appeared in the town. Mary had received them graciously, had acknowledged the letter and the ring, and had said that her decision must depend on the deliberations of her council. Maximilian went to Cologne, where the Duchess' representatives preceded him. He was a poor creature, with a long nose and the Habsburg jaw, rough and penurious, as headstrong as Duke Charles, and equally ambitious.

Having been escorted to Ghent, he made his entry into the city on the 18th of August 1477, with between seven and eight hundred horse. The ladies kissed him on his arrival; and, according to an ancient custom, Mary hid a carnation in her bodice, which Maximilian was to find, and when he failed to discover it, Mary, at the suggestion of the Bishop of Trèves, undid her bodice. The marriage was celebrated in the Hotel of Ten Walle, at five o'clock in the morning. The bridegroom was nineteen, the bride twenty. Though Maximilian was penniless, Mary was rich enough for two. Neither of them knew anything about public affairs.

While Louis was capturing fortresses in Artois, Commynes, now restored to favour, was reflecting that had women possessed the right to inherit the French crown, the kingdom would have long ago passed into foreign hands.

Louis regarded Mary's marriage with a certain apprehension. But he had so many other things on his hands that he made no protest, replying in his usual soothing way to the letter in which Maximilian announced his marriage and complained of Louis' conquests and violence, which were contrary to the truce he had signed with Duke Charles nine years previously.

In the first year of her marriage, Mary gave birth to a son, who was to be the Archduke Philip, known as Philip the Handsome, in the second to a daughter, Margaret of Austria, in the third to another son, Francis, whose godfather was that ancient enemy of France, the Duke of Brittany.

The King's conquest of Burgundy made it necessary for him to conciliate the Swiss. They made him pay dearly for their non-intervention. But Louis knew what he was about. He realised the importance of having their mercenaries at his disposal, though he preferred to take towns by negotiation; for he always—whenever it was possible—chose peace rather than war, knowing war to be a great adventure. Louis bought penurious Germans as well as Swiss. He pensioned the Cantons, and granted 20,000 *livres* to four towns, Berne, Lucerne, Zurich and Fribourg. The Swiss engaged to furnish him with

6000 men, at a wage of four and a half florins a month. Louis wanted them to regard him as their ally, one of themselves.

There was no end to the King's preoccupations. At the end of March 1478, he was obliged to return to the north. His health was beginning to give way. Commynes observed certain symptoms of disease. But Louis refused to spare himself or to follow any treatment. He had no faith in doctors. He was suffering from overwork. He had laboured hard all his life : he had known neither childhood nor youth. Now he, whom we have seen mixing freely with his people, giving alms to beggars by the roadside, drinking wine with tavern-keepers, began to isolate himself, to hunt alone, to erect high walls round his parks, to surround himself, on his progresses, with a numerous guard, to take with him a vast retinue and mountains of baggage, borne on huge drays, whole wooden houses, with chimneys and glass windows.

Louis was growing more and more exacting. When a grey friar at Paris made a stir by calling the justice of the King's government in question, maintaining that he was surrounded by traitors, who would ruin him, Louis had him silenced by his Provost of Merchants.

The war in Picardy was giving him serious trouble, especially when the Archduke put himself at the head of the Flemings and besieged Thérouanne. A change was coming over the House of Burgundy ; and Louis was keen enough to detect it. Burgundy was still French ; but it was also beginning to be foreign. Everyone noticed the change. The King's men tore down the imperial eagles and trampled them underfoot.

In the spring of 1478, the King reached Arras, then he went on to Cambrai. He was busy, as we have seen, collecting all the documents which could serve as proofs of Charles's treason, and he was instructing the Paris Parlement to circulate the announcement of the confiscation of his territory. He was revictualling Condé, sending it supplies of munitions, strengthening its artillery.

Another attempt was made to poison him ; this time it was instigated by Jean de Châlon. The King was accustomed, when mass was over, to kiss the ground at the four corners of the altar. The would-be murderer tried to impregnate the earth with a virulent poison. But God, Our Lady and St Martin saved the King's life.

All parties were exhausted ; and in July, a year's truce was signed at Arras. Everyone was to give up the fortresses they had occupied unlawfully, those held by the King of France in Burgundy and Hainault included. Nobles with twelve horsemen were forbidden to enter towns. But merchants were allowed to travel freely without let or hindrance. The truce included all the allies. The English had waged the Hundred Years' War with France. Now Louis made the Hundred Years' Truce. For the next hundred years the English were to receive their 50,000 gold crowns. Such a price was Louis willing to pay for peace.

Now once more the King was able to pass the summer in France. Once again he visited the shrine of La Vierge de la Victoire at Senlis and gave a donation of 2000 francs to be spent on silver lamps for her altar. It was now that he dedicated the great silver *clôture* to St Martin at Tours. The Parisians, hearing that it was to cost 2000 francs, hid their silver plate for fear of its being requisitioned, though Louis was willing to buy it at a reasonable price.

In his negotiations with the papacy in September, Louis continued his work of peace. He laid down certain conditions : that all Christian nations should forget their differences and unite to defend the Catholic Faith against the Turk ; that the Church should put itself in order, thus avoiding scandals and the wars, which were constantly breaking out in Italy ; that the Church of France should no longer suffer from the financial exactions of the Holy Father. Further, Louis inveighed against the Pope's nephew, Count Girolamo, who kept his Papal uncle in his power, and against his conduct towards Lorenzo di Medici.

Let the Holy Father convoke a council in France, at Lyons, for example, in order that peace might be established.

But peace, so greatly desired, was long in coming.

The Seigneur d'Esquerdes, Louis' Lieutenant in Picardy, had assembled all the King's forces on the frontier, and gone to the assistance of Thérouanne with 8000 bowmen. The Archduke had raised the siege and taken up his position at Guinegate, not far from St Omer. His troops numbered 20,000, or more. English and Germans were among them. The French cavalry succeeded in separating the Burgundian men-at-arms from the Picards and in pursuing them at close quarters as far as the River Aire. But the French commanders, with that bad habit which was essentially French, had pursued with all their men. Meanwhile, the Archduke's infantry had stood firm, following the example of two hundred noblemen on foot, who had adopted the English tactics, and who had bared their right arms, as a sign that they made light of their adversaries. The courage of these two hundred inspired their comrades ; and Louis' free-bowmen, who were amusing themselves by plundering the Archduke's baggage carts, were cut down and massacred by the Burgundians. Though the Archduke's losses were heavier than those of the French, the field of battle remained with Maximilian ; and, if he had thought of it, he might have marched on to Arras unhindered.

The conflict had been severe ; the result was a draw, and not that triumph for the Burgundians of which their poet, Jean Molinet, sang.

Philippe de Commynes was with the King when he received news of Guinegate. Louis, accustomed to win, was a bad loser. He believed that when a battle was engaged nothing should be left to chance. Now he made no attempt to conceal his vexation. This check would not have occurred had he been in command. And was it no more than a check ? Had he been told everything ? If a veritable defeat had been inflicted on his forces, then all his work was undone, and the whole Burgundian question would have to be reopened. But the King was reassured. So he gave his orders. Nothing was to be undertaken until he had been consulted. He said he was satisfied with M. d'Esquerdes. But was he really ?

Louis was already thinking of coming to terms with the Archduke, intending to give him so much to do in his own dominions that he would not have the leisure to attack those of France. Moreover, he was thinking of marrying the Dauphin to Maximilian's daughter. If the King were to be given a free hand in Burgundy, the Archduke might have Artois. Arras was now valueless ;[1] the town had been destroyed, and Louis had the citadel. The surrender of Arras would cost him nothing. Meanwhile he was gaining time. Winter was approaching.

[1] Louis' vain attempt to found a new town, *la Franchise*, on the ruins of Arras, a town which was to be inhabited by workmen from various parts of France, is an interesting story. (Trans.)

CHAPTER XXXIII

LOUIS' DECLINING YEARS

1479–1482

The King's first Seizure, March 1479.—Partial recovery.—Begins to be anxious about his Health.—At Plessis in 1480.—Receives the English Ambassadors at Paris.—Double-dealing of Edward IV and Maximilian.—Intervention of Margaret of York.—Cardinal della Rovèra arrives in France.—Received by Olivier le Daim.—Louis' second Seizure, March 1481.—Stages of the King's gradual recovery. —Release of Cardinal Balue and Simon de Quingey.—Reorganisation of the Army.—Louis receives the Papal Nuncios at Plessis.— Maximilian intrigues with the Pope.—The King's third Seizure, September 1481.—He recovers and hunts at Argenton.—Makes a Royal Progress.—Activities of his Ministers.—Death of Mary of Burgundy, 27th March 1482.—Louis intrigues with the Citizens of Ghent for a Marriage between the Dauphin and Margaret of Burgundy.—Louis inherits Maine and Provence.—Organises the French Navy.—Opens up Trade with the East.

In March 1479, Louis was at his little château of Forges, dominating the Chinon Forest, a wonderful hunting district. It was Sunday ; and the King had gone to mass at St Benoît-du-Lac-Mort. During dinner he had a seizure and suddenly lost the power of speech. He had to be taken back to Forges, where he was put near a fire, with all the windows closed, while he was pining for air.

In the following June, the King had recovered so far as to be able to go to Dijon. But on the way the heat overcame him, he could not breathe, and he had hæmorrhage of the stomach. After a few days in the cool woods of Gâtinais, he recovered. He wrote to the people of Lucerne that he had subdued Franche Comté, that the Duke of Brittany had sent in his submission, that he had conquered Picardy and would continue hostilities until the Archduke submitted. But the King was obviously concerned about his health, craving fresh air, inquiring whether there were any epidemics at Dijon. He had ordered a broad-brimmed hat made of long-haired beaver, like the one the Bishop of Valence had brought him from Rome. It was to be worn when he was riding, to serve both as umbrella and sunshade, being broad enough to protect his shoulders and spine.

The greater part of 1480 the King passed at Plessis. He now had his Hundred Years' Truce with the English, for it had been ratified at London in 1479; and he paid his tribute of 50,000 crowns regularly. On the 3rd of June he left Plessis for a short time and went to Paris to receive the English ambassador, Lord Howard, and others. The King escorted them to the Palace at nine o'clock in the morning, and conferred with them in private, with no witnesses save their own retinue. The King's stay in Paris was short. He was soon back in Orléanais. But the English ambassadors had been presented with silver plate on the Pont-au-Change. Charles the Bold's widow, Margaret of York, who lived in retirement in London, had been able to write to Maximilian that Lord Howard had brought back all the tribute owing from last Easter. The King of France had overwhelmed him with gifts and promises, she added, undertaking to act as mediator with the Holy See, if only Edward would keep his promise to marry the Princess Elizabeth to the Dauphin, and more especially if he would dissociate himself from Maximilian and the Duke of Brittany.

Maximilian was sly and pig-headed. He had been playing a double game with Louis and Edward: endeavouring to negotiate a truce with the former, which he was urging the latter to break. Margaret of York, his representative in England, was endeavouring to form a league against France. And the King of England had agreed to place 1500 bowmen at her disposal. On the French side, Admiral Coulon and other sailors attacked Flemish fishing-boats and wrought more havoc at sea than had been experienced for a hundred years or more.

Never had the situation been more involved. At home Jean de Doyat and Jean Avin made an inquiry into the conduct of the King's brother-in-law, Jean II de Bourbon. His intimate friend, Jean Hébert, Bishop of Coutances, was arrested on the charge of practising astrology. On the 4th of September, the Legate of Pope Sixtus IV, Cardinal della Rovèra,[1] was received at Paris. The Pope had endowed him with special powers and had instructed him to bear his crozier everywhere, save in the King's presence. Would the Italian prove an angel of peace, dispelling bitterness and silencing liars ?

The streets of Paris were hung with tapestry as he passed on his way to Notre-Dame. Cardinal Bourbon [2] followed him like his shadow. The King superintended everything from Touraine. His barber, Olivier le Daim, received the Cardinal on the 6th of September, feasted him sumptuously and took him to hunt in the Vincennes Wood. Rovèra officiated at Notre-Dame, gave suppers in the Hotel de Bourbon, saw nobles and ecclesiastics, and visited St Denis. Then he took the road to Flanders to negotiate with the Flemings and to attempt to settle their differences with the King.

Rovèra had written to Maximilian that he had found the King at Vendôme disposed to make peace, and that he had exhorted him to continue the good work. But Maximilian procrastinated. He refused to recognise the legate and even to see him. Edward IV was growing anxious : he reproached the Archduke with making an alliance with Scotland and with negotiating with King Louis on his own account. English troops were ready to cross over into Flanders ; and yet the King of England wrote to Maximilian urging him to make a two years' truce with the King of France. In this event—pending the death of King Louis, which must shortly take place— he would put a force of five thousand at Maximilian's disposal.

[1] The future Julian II.
[2] The Papal Legate whom Rovèra had superseded.

King Louis had a second seizure at Plessis in March 1481. This time his life was in danger; and he lost his memory as well as his power of speech.

Commynes' friend, the Neapolitan Angelo Cato, the famous astrologer, philosopher and physician, to whom Commynes dedicated his " Mémoires," arrived in hot haste. Cato had attended the Duke of Burgundy; now he came to the King of France. He immediately administered an injection, had the windows opened and the room ventilated. The King, who had difficulty in speaking, communicated with him by signs. He had summoned the Official from Tours to hear his confession. He asked for Commynes who was at Argenton. When Philippe arrived, he found Louis at table with Master Adam Fumée, who had been his father's doctor and was now Master of Requests. Another physician, Master Claude, was with him, though Louis had no great faith in doctors.

Commynes observed the King closely. He did not appear to be suffering, but his hearing was bad. Louis looked at his friend, articulated a few words, and indicated by a sign that he wanted him to sleep in his room. This Commynes did for a fortnight, serving his royal master as valet-de-chambre, and proud to be so honoured. Louis liked to have with him the man who had saved his life at Péronne. Moreover, Commynes was quick to comprehend and divine the King's meaning; and Louis had perfect confidence in him. He even confessed in his presence, though he had little to say, having confessed regularly every week.

Then Louis shook off his lethargy, and awoke as if from a bad dream, asking who it was who had held him down, and expelling those unfortunate persons Monseigneur de Segré and Gilbert de Grassay from the house. For he was terrified of losing the power to impose his will and exact obedience. He must have had a bad dream, probably about the false rumour that he had wanted to poison his father. For he imagined that an attempt had been made to poison him at his son's request. And he was determined not to be forcibly fed, as Charles had been.

But gradually this fear vanished ; and Louis began to take an interest in affairs of state. He inquired what despatches had been sent, what resolutions passed by the Council ? Those responsible for them during his illness had been Louis d'Amboise, Bishop of Albi, his brother, Pierre de Rohan, Governor of Burgundy, the Marshal de Gié and the Seigneur du Lude. They had lodged in two small rooms under the King's apartments. Now Louis began to look at the outside of the letters which were constantly arriving. Sometimes he would take them in his hand and make a pretence of reading them. Commynes read him the most important. Louis would utter a few words or make a sign indicating the reply that should be sent. Little was done during that fortnight. For Louis was a master in whose service one had to be very careful.

The King's memory and power of speech returned to him. But he was left in fear of another attack ; and he was anxious to relieve his conscience. He remembered Cardinal Balue, who for eleven years had been wearing out his life in captivity at Tours. Let him go and get himself hanged at Rome, since the Holy Father had been for ever clamouring for him to be set at liberty. The Legate would be pleased. Then Louis sought absolution as if for a crime, for the prolonged imprisonment of the man who had wronged him. He sent one of his own doctors, Chrétien Chastel, to attend him.

It was about this time that Louis liberated Simon de Quingey, then at Plessis, from his iron cage.

At the time of his second seizure Louis had been reorganising his army, on the basis of 20,000 paid infantry, 2500 engineers and 1500 gunners. The King had disbanded the free bowmen, who had disgusted him by their cowardice and lack of discipline. The pikemen were to have their camp on the Somme. The army was to be provided with carts for the soldiers and with those tents that had been found among the booty taken from the Duke of Burgundy.

The condition of foreign affairs rendered these precautions highly necessary ; and all the cutlers of the kingdom were busy manufacturing pikes, halberds and large daggers with broad blades.

The winter had set in late ; but by February all the rivers were frozen ; and when the thaw came, bridges and boats were carried down with the ice. The late frosts of May nipped vines and fruit-trees. Meanwhile the sick King dragged himself from Poitiers to Forges, from Forges to Plessis, and then on to Tours. He thought he was being betrayed on every hand. Every one was lying. No prisoners were being taken on the Flemish front. The hanging of captives is always a bad sign.

Louis had established a camp in the Seine valley. He himself visited his 6000 Swiss mercenaries. Having reached their camp on the 22nd of June, he returned to Plessis on the 10th of July 1481, thus reassuring the English, who imagined that he was at Boulogne, about to besiege Calais.

Though Maximilian had instructed his ambassadors in London to make a league against France, Edward IV persisted in keeping himself free from all entanglements, and he went so far as to advise the Archduke to make a truce with King Louis.

But the breeze of peace was to blow from Rome.

At Plessis, on the 29th of April, at nine o'clock in the morning, the King in great state, surrounded by his counsellors, chamberlains and notaries, received the bulls of Pope Sixtus IV. After listening to Louis, the papal envoys described the formidable advances the Turks were making, even into Italy, and insisted on the importance of a three years' truce between all Christian princes, so that they might unite against the unbeliever. Louis withdrew and deliberated, then he returned to the nuncio and declared that he was prepared to act according to the Pope's recommendation provided that other princes did the same—it would not be right for Louis to keep the peace while his enemies made war on him. The nuncio replied that the Pope would be able to constrain them also to make peace. In the afternoon of that day, the King sent Beaujeu, the Chancellor, and the Bishop of Albi to the legate in the house where he lodged. After compliments had been exchanged, Louis' messengers explained that three matters touched the King very nearly : first, his relations with the English, with whom he had made a truce, which he meant to keep ; second, his relations with the King of Castille, said to be threatening him, but he did not believe it ; third, his dealings with Maximilian and his wife, concerning the Burgundian dominions. In this last matter it was not King Louis who was the aggressor, but the late Duke, who had broken his oath and rebelled against his natural lord. His daughter had followed in his footsteps. And the Emperor, who ought to have been the first to make peace, in order to oppose the common enemy, had stirred up war by marrying his son, Maximilian, to the heiress of Burgundy. If the princes were disposed to make a good peace, the King would resign himself to it, for the glory of God and in order to avoid further bloodshed. The legate thanked the King and congratulated him on his submission to the Holy Father.

From that day Maximilian and Mary redoubled their intrigues at Rome, and did their best to put off any decision as to the rival claims of Mary and Louis to the Burgundian territory. While King Louis took care to seem supple and far-seeing, the violent and procrastinating Maximilian appeared to disadvantage.

The King had a third seizure at Tours, in September. Again he lost the power of speech ; and for two hours, as he lay on a mattress in the long gallery, he was thought to be dead. Then Commynes and the Seigneur du Bouchage made a vow to St Claude : and the King's power of speech returned to him. He was able to walk in the house, though he was still very weak. Soon, however, he was going up and down the country as before, though he was still sick, very sick. He stayed for a month at Argenton, on the fine estate which his friend Commynes' wife, Mme de Chambes, had brought to her husband. The house was beautiful. Philippe had spent a great deal of money on it. The King, as we have seen, was a master who paid well.

Louis now seemed absorbed in the pleasures of the chase. He wrote from Argenton to the Seigneur de Bressuire : " I am returning to hunt and kill boars so as not to lose one season, while waiting for the next, during which I shall hunt and kill the English."

There had come into Louis' possession the Archduke's summons to arms which proved his alliance with the Duke of Brittany. The King sent the document to Paris to be registered by the Parlement, and thence to Angers to be placed side by side with the Duke of Brittany's oath of allegiance sworn on a fragment of the Cross of St Laud.

At Thouars in Poitou, where Louis spent the January and February in 1482, he was far from well. His mind dwelt on the long line of his predecessors, on Clovis, the first Christian King, the perfect friend of God, who defeated Alaric on the Vienne, on Hugh of sainted memory; and he asked for masses to be sung for him, for his beloved consort and for Charles the Dauphin.

The King was mellowing.

He had just been to visit the Dauphin at Amboise. Father and son had seen very little of one another. Louis gave the boy his blessing and left him in the care of his brother-in-law, the Seigneur de Beaujeu, who was the King's Lieutenant-General. From Thouars the King went on to Saint-Claude, Bourges, Nevers, Macon, Tournus, Saint-Laurent-la-Roche. As we have seen, he no longer travelled as an ordinary pilgrim, but with a retinue of eight hundred lances and an army of six thousand men-at-arms to guard his royal person.

It was a bad year. The crops were poor. The people,

ground down by taxation, were dying of hunger. Every one gave what help they could.

Meanwhile, Commynes and the admirable Doyat, Baron de Montréal, were carrying on the government. In Auvergne, Doyat kept the House of Bourbon in check, establishing the royal authority in that mountainous region, taking fortresses, raising money for the King, and capturing mules which were carrying arms to Brittany concealed in bales of silk.

The King sent Commynes to Savoy, where he suspected his nephew of being implicated in a plot against his French tutor.

Though worn to a skeleton, the King seemed full of energy. Then, suddenly, he heard that Mary of Burgundy was dead. She had fallen from her horse at Bruges on the 22nd of March, and had been buried at Notre-Dame.

Louis, himself on the verge of the grave, rejoiced at her death. He told the news to Commynes with great delight.

It was not cruelty, but simply the pleasure of the player who wins the game, a game which Louis had lost when the Duchess had married Maximilian. Her two children, Philip and Margaret, were entrusted to the guardianship of the citizens of Ghent. Louis was not afraid of them. He knew their hostility to the ruling House of Burgundy. He relied on the Seigneur d'Esquerdes to persuade them to favour a marriage between the Dauphin and Margaret. This was the schemer's last great dream. He turned it over in his head during his intervals of lucidity.

Death had recently brought fulfilment to another of King Louis' dreams. His uncle, the good René of Anjou, King of Sicily, had died in 1480, and eighteen months later his heir, Charles of Anjou, died also, having bequeathed the provinces of Maine and Provence to his kinsman, the King of France.

The news was brought to Louis at Thouars on the 19th of December. Ill as he was, this bequest of two of the richest provinces of France, for the possession of which he had schemed and plotted for years, filled him with joy and fired his imagination : in his fevered brain he saw those coasts of Provence, the fine harbours of which had been centres of world trade from antiquity, now taking a new lease of prosperity. He saw them sending forth vessels to sail the high seas, bound for Bordeaux, Paris, Rouen, the ports of England, Scotland, Holland and Germany. The King straightway appointed Michel Gaillart, one of his chief financiers, to reorganise his fleet. He wrote to the King of Tunis demanding the restitution of a shipwrecked vessel, the cargo of which the King's son had seized. For Louis was resolved to make it known that he was the heir of René of Provence and that he would not tolerate piracy. The King commended the royal galleys, *Notre-Dame Sainte-Marie* and *Notre-Dame Saint-Martin*, about to sail to Alexandria, to the protection of the Sultan of Egypt.

The gates of the East stood open to the realm of France.

CHAPTER XXXIV

FATHER AND SON

The King's concern for his Son's health and for his safety.—His Education.
—" Le Rozier des Guerres."—Plots to capture the Dauphin.—
The King visits the Dauphin at Amboise.—Instructs him in his
Royal Duties.

LOUIS' dynastic instinct was too strong for him not to love
his heir. In spite of all that has been written to the
contrary he was a good father.

He chose Amboise as a residence for his son because
that strong fortress, dominating the Loire, was easily
defended against the enemies whom the King suspected
of desiring to kidnap the Dauphin, and also because the
town of Amboise, being little more than a small group of
dwellings clustered at the foot of the fortress, was less
exposed to infectious diseases than the castle of Plessis,
which was close to Tours. Louis had appointed his
secretary Bourré, one of the most reliable of his servants,
to be his son's guardian. Bourré was charged never to
leave the Dauphin. For five years, this aged man, close
on seventy, had been banished from the fine châteaux he
had built in Anjou and from his wife and children. When
he asked for a holiday, the King replied : " Monsieur du
Plessis, I have read what you have written. But you are
not to go home." Equally stringent were Bourré's
instructions to forbid all strangers to enter the château or
even the town. When a visitor arrived, Bourré went down
into Amboise to welcome him, and after dinner took him
up to see the Dauphin for a few minutes. But there would
be no lodging for him in the castle, not even for Bourré's
brother, for fear he should bring in the plague or act as the
emissary of some conspirator. The strictest watch and
ward were kept on the ramparts of the château.

The King was well advised in thus guarding his son. For the execution of traitors like St Pol and Nemours had failed to extinguish the spirit of rebellion, which was now reviving, encouraged by Louis' ill-health : and the malcontents, of whom the Duke of Brittany was the chief, had their eye on Louis' heir.

Bourré was required to keep the King informed of the slightest detail concerning the child's health. Charles was frail and delicate. The King's doctor, Master Adam Fumée, attended him. If he coughed, Louis was anxious, inquiring where and how he had taken cold. " He sleeps well, eats well," wrote Bourré, " and lies on an eider-down quilt. He hunts with his birds, but without getting overheated."

The King was anxious that his son should know the history of France, and also that he should profit by his father's experience. Accordingly he instructed his physician and astrologer, the Norman, Pierre Choisnet, to compile a book of maxims, " le Rozier des Guerres," for the guidance of a prince in peace and war.

Pierre Choisnet had been on several missions for the King. He was a scholar, who was not much good at verse, but who could write strong and concise prose. He prepared himself for the task Louis had imposed upon him by reading Vegetius, Jacques de Cessole's " Jeu des Echecs Moralisé," "the Upbringing of Kings and Princes," by Ægidius of Rome, and especially Aristotle in that translation by Nicole Oresme, which had been the great political treatise of the time of Charles V. But above all, Choisnet had listened to and observed the King, meditating on his example and his principles. A king in this book is represented as an ordinary man, working out his salvation like anyone else, in expectation of death and judgment. He lives for the common good. His main duty should be to keep his kingdom in peace. He should never make war without the consent of his people. For war never profited anyone. The King should not go to battle in person. God having made him the guardian of his realm, he ought to be pious and honour the pastors of the Church.

In addition to this book of maxims, Pierre Choisnet, at the King's bidding, wrote an abridged history of France. The King loved the history of his country. Among the few books he had read and which he took with him in a wooden coffer on his progresses, were books on law and medicine, a Froissart, and the Chronicles of Saint Denis.

We have reason to believe that Louis had read Pierre Choisnet's book, and that he had even annotated it. All the passages in the manuscript which deal with unhappy divisions in the kingdom have been underlined; those relating to the Dukes of Guyenne and to children who conspired against their parents are marked, also the treachery of kings' brothers and the story of Charles the Simple, who was imprisoned at Péronne.

The King sent the book to his son, whom he dearly loved but seldom saw; and he sent with it the following dedication : " As fragrant odours are gratifying to those in love, so are good and virtuous maxims to the wise ; and we, desiring that when, by God's grace, thou shalt have come to govern and reign over this noble kingdom of France, thou shalt know and bear in thy heart that which is suitable and necessary for the government of the said kingdom, send thee this *Rozier* which concerneth the guard and defence of the public weal. And when thou shalt have attained to the estate of complete adolescence, then shalt thou smell a rose every day and find therein more delectation and solace than in any other rose in the world . . . and then shalt thou know which of thy predecessors have done best."

Everyone was talking of the King's approaching death. But from time to time he surprised them all, and recovered. Louis' arch-enemy, the Duke of Brittany, was now taking courage again. He thought himself sure of English support and dreamed of restoring the old days when soldiers ruled in the land. Another of these malcontents was René, Comte du Perche, son of the mad Duke of Alençon, who had twice been convicted of treason. With Breton help, René hoped to recover his lands.

On the 21st of September 1482, Jean Bourré—he was then sixty-eight, tall and bent, grave looking and shrewd, as we see him in his portrait, with his hand on his chest, wearing a black cap, from beneath which strayed locks of grey hair—scrutinised the King closely. Louis had just arrived at Amboise from Saint-Claude. He was better, but still very ill. Assembled in the castle hall, in the presence of the King and Dauphin, were M. de Beaujeu, Marshal of France, the Archbishop of Narbonne, Jean de Doyat, Governor of Auvergne, and other nobles, with Olivier Guérin, the Steward. Louis had summoned them to hear his instructions to his son. They were to be read aloud to him. The child, who was then twelve, listened gravely to the father, whom he had hardly ever seen.

The King began with considerations on the brevity of human life, the short tale of years vouchsafed to us. But God in His grace, he said, had set him to rule over the most remarkable land and nation in the world: that kingdom of France, in which so many of his predecessors had won the title of "Very Christian King" by reason of the wars they had waged against the infidel, by the extirpation of heresy and the maintenance of the liberties of the Church and the Holy See. "And now," he continued, still addressing the Dauphin, " these predecessors of yours are a glorious company, the saints of God in His Paradise. This kingdom your father hath increased on every hand, by dint of his own care and diligence seconded by true and loyal officers of the crown, and in defiance of the treachery of wicked nobles and princes of the blood, whose wars have caused terrible shedding of blood and desolation among the people."

Then the King admonished his son, telling him that he hoped he would be a credit to his father and a blessing to his subjects, advising him to take counsel with those of his own rank, with wise and experienced nobles and captains, and above all with those who had been the good subjects and faithful servants of his father and grandfather. He warned the Dauphin, when the time came for him to ascend the throne, not to follow his father's disastrous example and to dismiss his father's ministers, but to retain them in office.

Then Louis asked his son whether he was prepared to carry out these counsels. And the child replied, thanking his father and promising to obey all his commandments. But that was not enough for Louis. He told the Dauphin to go apart and to discuss his father's admonitions with the nobles there assembled. And the Dauphin, having obeyed, returned to his father to declare that he was prepared to fulfil all the promises he had made to him. Then the King required the boy to swear this, taking an oath of obedience, which he instructed a notary who was present to register in due legal form.

CHAPTER XXXV

The Château a pleasant Country-House, not the grim Fortress of Legend.—Louis' increasing Suspiciousness.—The nature of his Illness.—Was it Leprosy?—His Scheme for the Marriage of Margaret of Burgundy with the Dauphin.—Betrothal of Margaret and the Dauphin at Amboise.—Louis' last Appearance in Public.—He receives Delegates from the Towns at Tours.—Death of Edward IV.—The complete success of Louis' Foreign Policy.—His efforts to prolong his Life.—Brings St Francis of Paola to France.—The Holy Ampulla is brought to Plessis.—The King's last instructions to the Dauphin and to Beaujeu.—Death of King Louis, 31st August 1483.

THE King, as we have seen, had not yet withdrawn to the complete isolation of Plessis-lez-Tours, as some historians would have us believe. In May 1482, he had been in Orléanais. He had spent the summer at Cléry; and it was not until after his meeting with his son at Amboise in September, that he shut himself up at Plessis. By that time his condition was such as to make him refrain from appearing in public for fear he should not be able to maintain his royal dignity. The Italian emissaries, who, though friendly, were practically spies, wrote that it was impossible to see the King or to do business with him, seeing that he refused to delegate his affairs. He had been putting his papers in order. Those who knew him best noticed that he appeared strange, almost as if he were losing his wits.

Sad, suspicious and ill, he wandered up and down his house of Plessis (Plessis-du-Parc or Plessis-lez-Tours), the large manor house, which he had built in the park of Montils, where his father had had his hunting-lodge. As late as 1477, Plessis was still in the workmen's hands. The house had little in common with the grim, dark fortress of legend. It was well lighted and comfortable, composed of a series of small rooms with high chimney-pieces. The main façade looked gay with its red brick facings. From the first story, where the King had his apartments, he could see Tours.

The entrance to the château was over a drawbridge and through a fortified gate, flanked by two round towers with pointed roofs, leading to a kind of drill-ground, surrounded by trenches, and thence to a courtyard. Crossing this obliquely, one came to a well and a horse-trough, and in the corner to a fine spiral staircase. On the right of the gateway, a fence shut off the vegetable garden, on the left ran a beautiful gallery with glass windows, leading to the little St John's Chapel, which stood at right angles to the main block. The façade gave on the park, which had little formal squares of garden. Opposite the entrance, offices and stables abutted on the spiral staircase.

Here, in this pleasant country-house, the King, whose life had been spent on the road or in hunting-lodges, now finally settled down. Here his pack-horses were disburdened of his baths and bed ; here his history books and medical treatises were taken out of their cases, his tapestry hung, his portable striking-clock and a few other articles of furniture set up in his apartments, where he had two billiard-tables and two bowling sets, and where he kept his canaries and other singing-birds, while his favourite dogs slept on cloth cushions.

As Louis' days drew to an end he grew more and more suspicious ; and he refused to lodge even his friends at Plessis. Two merchants of Tours were instructed to surround the château with a trellis-work of strong iron bars. Iron spikes were placed along the walls, and four sentry-boxes were erected at great expense, from which either of the forty bowmen who kept watch all night long might shoot down any stranger approaching the château in the dark.

Here we have the origin of the grim legend of Plessis-lez-Tours.

THE CHÂTEAU OF PLESSIS-LEZ-TOURS

Louis' only servants were a few lackeys who were well aware of the fate which awaited them on the accession of a new King—and this they knew to be imminent. Louis had ceased to take interest in anything which did not bear on the condition and preservation of his kingdom. He was now at peace with every one. He had done his work. He was tired out. His doctor, Jacques Coitier de Poligny, who had been first Clerk then President of the Treasury, was the only human being with whom he cared to converse. And Coitier received 10,000 crowns a month. The King was barely alive. Crushed and worn, he had shrunk into hiding, trying to conceal his condition from his subjects.

What was the nature of these seizures from which the King was suffering ? Were they, as some have maintained, *le haut mal*, epilepsy ? Louis suffered from headaches. He would lie with his head propped up. He had difficulty in breathing ; from time to time he lost the power of speech. He was careful to have his room well ventilated ; it was decorated with flowers and perfumed with sweet scents. Poitevin shepherds came from Saint-Côme and played their pipes under his windows to prevent his sleeping. At least, so it was said in Paris.

It seems probable that Louis XI suffered from congenital arthritis (no one knows exactly what arthritis is, it may be no more than a mere term). He certainly had three attacks of cerebral congestion, accompanied by aphasia and temporary unconsciousness. One of the recognised symptoms of arthritis is herpes, a skin disease, which might very easily have been confused with leprosy. In connection with this symptom reference has been made to the expedition Louis sent to Cape Verd to fetch a certain medicament, and this has prompted the remark that tortoise blood was regarded as a cure for leprosy. Consequently certain scholars, and among them M. Ch. Petit-Dutaillis, have asserted that during the last years of his life Louis was a leper, and that herein lies the explanation of his isolation at Plessis-lez-Tours.

M. Charles Samaran has authenticated the voyage to Cape Verd. The King had two vessels armed and equipped, and despatched them to Cape Verd " to fetch certain things intimately connected with his personal health and well-being." These " certain things " may have been that tortoise blood which was considered a remedy for leprosy and other skin diseases.

But may not the King's so-called leprosy, of which he is accused by the most venomous of his enemies, Thomas Basin, have been some form of eczema ? If we were to represent the King as a leper, we might be giving rise to a new legend worthier of the attention of a romantic poet than of a historian.

Louis loaded his doctors with gifts. Did he, like his father, think he was being poisoned ? True he ordered the experiment of poisoning a dog and the post-mortem of a man who was thought to have died from poisoning. He tried the experiment of the transfusion of blood on himself. One night the citizens of Tours were commanded to go out and take possession of numbers of turkeys which were being taken into Brittany. Two days afterwards, at two o'clock in the morning, the birds were brought to les Montils.

While in his own kingdom he was surrounded by mystery and no one knew whether he was alive or dead, abroad he continued his activities. He sent his ambassadors in all directions. He paid the English their tribute and continued his negotiations for the marriage of the Dauphin to Princess Elizabeth. But all the time he was thinking of another bride for the Dauphin, Margaret of Austria, daughter of Maximilian.

The turbulent citizens of Ghent, who had captured Maximilian's children, clamoured for this marriage, to which Maximilian himself was strongly averse. Louis was growing impatient. He insisted on the wedding-day being fixed without delay. The marriage-contract, which was also a peace treaty, must be signed at once, by the nobles of the blood, by the peers of France, and by the

Three Estates. The day was appointed on which the Princess was to be taken to Hesdin. The treaty was to be signed at Arras, now called *Franchise*, on the 23rd of December 1482. Louis ratified it at Plessis. He ordered bonfires, *Te Deums*, processions and thanksgiving at Notre-Dame for so great a blessing. But all the while the King himself remained invisible.

The people of Ghent, whose one idea was to weaken their Prince, made a treaty which was in Louis' interest. He was to keep the whole of Burgundy and Artois. In May 1483, Mme de Ravenstein took Margaret to Hesdin, where the Seigneur d'Esquerdes received her. The Princess made her entry into Paris on the 2nd of June and met the Dauphin at Amboise on the 22nd. There, in the presence of the representatives of the good towns, whom the King had invited, Margaret's betrothal was solemnly celebrated—her father all the while strongly disapproving—indeed he would have prevented her going into France had he been able.

At Amboise the infant Margaret, who was barely three —to be exact, two years and ten months—was affianced by the Protonotary to the boy Dauphin, who was thirteen. Charles was asked whether he would take Margaret to be his wife. He replied loudly in the affirmative. Margaret to a similar question made the same reply. The Protonotary joined their hands. The Dauphin kissed Mme la Dauphine twice.

This civil ceremony was followed by a religious service in the church of the château, to which M. le Dauphin, wearing a long robe of white damask and escorted by his brother-in-law, M. de Beaujeu, proceeded and waited at the church door for Mme la Dauphine, whom Mme de Segré carried in her arms. The affianced swore the marriage oath to take one another "for worse for better." The Dauphin placed a ring on the finger of Mme la Dauphine. Mass was sung. The people of the good towns thanked the Dauphin for the honour he had done them. The Dauphin replied, thanking them for the trouble thay had taken on his account and adding that he was at their service for anything they desired of him.

In neither of these ceremonies had the King taken any part. But it was the King who had converted them into a festival for the good towns and a celebration of peace.

His Chancellor declared that the King had summoned the delegates from the towns to Amboise in order to assist him in establishing justice in his kingdom, in order to give free circulation to merchandise and, if possible, to institute one system of weights and coinages throughout the realm. Let them all come before the King at Tours and deliberate on the best way of bringing about these reforms.

On Friday, the 26th of June, the delegates appeared at Tours. And there the Chancellor told them the King's pleasure, which was to abolish all duties on goods, except those payable at the frontier, to permit anyone wishing to engage in trade to do so, as in England and Italy, without any derogation of his rank of nobility or other privileges, to allow no one but the local judges to exercise jurisdiction over the merchants. Then the delegates from the towns requested the Chancellor to express their thanks to the King. And, on the following Tuesday, Louis summoned them to his presence at Plessis. There, for the last time, King Louis appeared in public, wearing his robe of crimson velvet, lined with marten, reaching below the knee. The King received the deputies from the good towns, who bowed low before him. The King took off the two scarlet caps he wore, disclosing a bald head, with such hair as remained to him cut short. "Gentlemen, you are welcome. I thank you for having come to see me," he said. "Put on your hats, all of you." The delegates obeyed. But their sire remained bareheaded. Then, holding his caps in his hand, the dying King explained and amplified what the Chancellor had already told them, stressing the point that he desired so to organise justice as to establish identical laws throughout the realm and to cut short those interminable lawsuits which did so much harm and gave opportunities for so much bribery and corruption.

Here we have Louis the man of peace in contradistinction to Maximilian, the man of violence and bad faith.

At times the King displayed his old vigour and severity, as when, in May 1483, he dismissed his Chancellor, Pierre Doriole, who had conducted all the famous trials of the reign.

The news of this revival disquieted the King of England, who feared that Louis was becoming stronger than ever. But again luck was on Louis' side ; for on the 9th of April 1483, Edward succumbed to an attack of apoplexy, and his brother, Gloucester, ascended the throne.

Louis, who had so often betrayed satisfaction when his enemies had been stricken down, forbore to rejoice on hearing of Edward's death. His own was too near. His one thought was of peace. He recommended the inhabitants of Honfleur to avoid hostilities against the English. The King, who had so greatly benefited from internecine strife, sent an ambassador to the Duke of Milan to urge him to promote unity in Italy and with all his might to resist the enemies of the Catholic Faith.

As Commynes remarked, Louis dominated till the end. He had made the marriage he so greatly desired. He had won over the Flemings and the people of Ghent. He held in check both Francis, Duke of Brittany and the King of Spain, the former by means of a large army, encamped on his frontiers, the latter by the occupation of Roussillon and Cerdagne, which Louis had bought from the King of Aragon. Louis was in constant touch with friendly powers in Italy. The Swiss, the King of Scotland and the King of Portugal were all his allies. Pope Sixtus IV sent him relics and the corporal of St Peter. The Sultan Bajazet supplied him with a list of the relics at Constantinople which he held at the King's disposal. Louis' subjects trembled before him, before their invisible King. At no period of his reign had he been stronger.

And yet never had he been more detached from the things of this world. His hope was in God and his saints. He knew that nothing but a miracle could keep him alive.

He tried to find some holy man through whose intercession his miserable days might be prolonged. The names of several were suggested to him. Louis appealed to the Archbishop of Tours, Elie de Bourdeilles, a Franciscan and a cardinal, who replied that it would be better for the King if he removed some of the burdens of taxation from his people and gave less money to churches. But Louis' piety was like his diplomacy, that of a peasant making a bargain. He wanted to buy the support of the saints. So he spent 200,000 francs on a silver screen for St Martin of Tours ; he gave golden chalices to St John of the Lateran at Rome, and a reliquary to St Eutropius at Saintes and to the three kings of Cologne.

He may have dreamed of retiring to Cléry, near his beloved church, for which he had just ordered four new pillars. At any rate he was consulting Bourré about long galleries that he thought of building on the garden side of his house.

At length Louis discovered his holy man. He was Francis of Paola, a simple soul, who ate neither fish nor flesh, eggs nor butter, who drank no milk and lived under a rock in Calabria. Louis sent for him to come to France. On his way through Rome, Francis had a long interview with the Pope, who authorised him to found in France the Order of the Hermits of St Francis, the Minims.

Then the holy man committed himself to the waves and, landing on the French coast, sailed up the Rhône in a boat. Thus he reached Lyons, where the consuls came to meet him and presented him with fruit. For the remainder of his journey Francis travelled in the painted cart, which bore the litter the King had sent for him. At Orléans his arrival was eagerly expected. Men were waiting for him on the bridge. He went down la Rue Sainte Catherine and lodged in the house of a burgher near the Hôtel de Ville. Meanwhile the dying King at Plessis was counting the hours till his arrival. Louis had ordered a hermitage to be prepared for his saintly guest. It was in the courtyard, near the chapel, just across the drawbridge.

When Francis appeared before him, Louis prostrated himself as if the holy man had been the Pope. His joy knew no bounds. Anything Francis desired the King would give him. He must pray to God to prolong the King's life. But Francis, speaking in Italian, through an interpreter, for he knew no French, replied like a prophet. Refusing the oranges, lemons, and muscat pears the King had provided for him, he would take nothing but roots. He slept on a mat of reeds, which he had woven with his own hands. Louis was won by the innocence and simplicity of a saint who refused to accept money. The King became as gentle as a lamb, and began to make restitution to his good towns, and to chastise his poor feeble body.

For the miracle which Francis of Paola had failed to work, Louis now looked to the Holy Ampulla at Reims. The sacred vessel containing the holy oil, with which the Kings of France were anointed at their accession, had never yet been removed from Reims, where it was kept in the Abbey of St Remy. Louis craved and received the Pope's permission to have it brought to Plessis. He desired but one tiny drop of the sacred oil and promised, immediately after he had worshipped it, to send it straight back to Reims. The holy vessel was brought and placed on a sideboard in the King's room between the staff of Moses and the Cross of Victory.

Now at length the King had come to understand the saint's words when he had said that the monarch's one hope lay in God's mercy. So he sent M. de Beaujeu for " the King his son "—as Louis called him. When the Dauphin came, Louis commended his servants to him and expressly charged him not to change any of his father's ministers.

On the 28th of August 1483, he had another seizure, which deprived him of the power of speech. When he recovered it, he was so weak that he could not put his hand to his mouth.

Now all his royal dignity had vanished, and Commynes noticed how his new retainers spoke to him with an audacity and absence of respect, which in other days he would never have tolerated, even from those brought up in his house. The rudest and most grasping, as well as the most learned, was his doctor, Jacques Coitier. He terrorised over the King, and spoke to him as if he were a valet. " It is useless for you to put faith in this holy man or in anything else," he said to Louis, " for it is all over with you, nothing can be done for you, and you had best think of your conscience." Then the King replied humbly : " I trust in God, who will help me. Peradventure I am not so ill as you think."

But Louis knew by the tone of the doctor's voice that the end had come. He summoned Beaujeu, into whose hands he committed the government of the kingdom. Louis asked for them to be left alone together. The injunctions he gave were concise and explicit : any hazardous attempt to regain Calais must be avoided ; the English must be left alone. The kingdom needed peace for five years at least. Contentions with Brittany should also be avoided. Let Duke Francis be left in peace until Charles should be of an age to dispose of things according to his pleasure. Peace—that was Louis' last thought.

Then he sent his Chancellor to the Dauphin to deliver up the seals to him. His guard, his captains, his bowmen, his hunting-train and his falcons the King also sent to Amboise.

As Louis' power of speech returned to him, his brain cleared, he gave orders about everything—not a thought for himself or his sufferings. He gave special charges to Etienne de Vesc, the Dauphin's chief valet-de-chambre, who had been with him from his early childhood.

At the foot of the bed stood Francis of Paola and a few other ecclesiastics muttering prayers for the dying. A murmur came from the King : he was invoking the Virgin of Embrun : *Ma bonne maîtresse, aidez-moi.* Then he repeated the words of the Psalmist which he had had painted in his room : *In te, Domine, speravi, non confundar in aeternum : misericordias Domini in aeternum cantabo.*

Louis died at eight o'clock in the evening, on the 31st of August 1483. And Commynes turned to look at the Holy Ampulla as it stood there on the sideboard in the King's room.

For four days grave anxiety had reigned at Tours. M. de Beaujeu had ordered the mayor to garrison the town and the château and to have good watch kept on the ramparts. Every evening the mayor and the townsfolk, who had been chosen for the purpose, were there with their torches. The watch were going up to the De la Riche and Hugon Gates at the very moment of Louis' death. Wax candles were lit. A message was sent to Guyot Pot, Governor of Amboise. Ought not the people of Tours be the first to go to Amboise ? For now Charles is King.

The bells of St Martin at Tours tolled for three days. Then the canons came with great pomp to bear the body of their King and Abbot to their church, where the funeral rites were performed ; and afterwards, by Louis' wish, his body was conveyed to Cléry.

One can imagine the scene on that hot September day : the Loire valley shimmering in the golden light ; its shelving beaches, the islands in mid-stream, the glowing sand ; and the procession winding its way through the flat country, the King's body making its last journey through the meadows and vineyards he loved, entering the sunlit royal nave of Cléry, so high and austere, with but few adornments, only a little moulding, an acanthus flower or a thistle here and there ; the body of King Louis lowered into the sloping grave prepared for it, where his own image awaited him, its face turned towards the Virgin Mother, the patron saint of France. All is brightness and light. The choir chants *Lux perpetua.*

The time of the vintage was drawing near : the finest vintage there had ever been in the memory of man.

INDEX

ACIGNÉ, AMAURY D', Bishop of Nantes, Francis, Duke of Brittany and, 169 ; bishopric seized, 179
Ægidius of Rome, 234
A!bi, Bishop of, 270, 271, 284, 286
Alençon, Jean, Duke of, 37 (and note) ; godfather of Louis, 44 ; and the Praguerie, 70, 71, 72 ; Louis' appeal to, 125 ; liberation of, 145, 155
Alexander (Bourbon Bastard), fate of, 78
Alsace, Louis leaves his freebooters in, 99
Amadeus VIII, 120 (note)
Amboise, the Dauphin at, 290 ; his betrothal at, 299
Amboise, Charles d', Seigneur de Chaumont, 75, 270
Amboise, Louis d', 284
Amelgard (see Basin)
Amiens, Louis' reception at, 83 ; entered by French, 204
Angoulême, Jean of, returns from captivity in England, 105 ; at funeral of King Charles, 140
Anjou, Charles d', 79, 80
Anjou, House of, tradition of, 39
Anjou, Nicolas of, 156
Anjou, Marie of (see Marie)
Anjou, René of (see René)
Anne of France (daughter of Louis), 188
Antoine, Bastard of Burgundy, 127, 131
Archelles, Grâce d', 119
Arcouville, Jean d' (assistant tutor of Louis), 47
Armagnac, Bernard d', Comte de la Marche, 53, 58, 70, 86
Armagnac, Charles d', imprisonment of, 209
Armagnac, Jacques d', Duc de Nemours, imprisoned in the Bastille, 226 ; treachery and execution of, 267
Armagnac, Jean, Count of, 67, 85, 155 ; death of, 209

Armagnac, the Bastard of, 121, 125
Arras, vacillation of townsfolk, 264 ; entered by Louis, 264, 265 ; destruction of, 266, 269
Arras, Treaty of (1435), 54, 82, 83, 102, 160
Avaugour, Guillaume d', 47
Avesnes, funeral service for King Charles at, 146
Aviaries, Louis', 240
Avignon, legation of, conferred on Louis, 171
Avin, Jean, 282
Avranches, Bishop of (see Bochard, Jean)

BAJAZET, Sultan, 301
Bâle, Louis' designs on, 97
Balue, Jean (French Cardinal and minister of Louis), 194, 196, 206 ; arrest and imprisonment of, 15, 16, 170, 202, 232 ; liberated, 172, 284 ; career, 193
Balzac, H. de, 29
Banville, Théodore de, 20, 29-30
Baqueville, Jacqueline de, 109
Barante, M. de, 27
Barbers, royal charter for, 252
Basin, Thomas (" Amelgard "), Bishop of Lisieux and historian, 5 ; career, 6-7 ; surrenders to French army, 6 ; and Joan of Arc, 6 ; his " Apology and History of the Reigns of Charles VII and Louis XI," 8-10 ; treachery of, 122 ; estimate of foreigners in Paris at Louis' state entry, 149 ; allegation against Bourré, 175 ; and nature of Louis' illness, 298
Baudricourt, Captain, 78
Beauchamp, Margaret, 101
Beaujeu, Seigneur de, 286, 287, 293, 299, 303, 304, 305
Beauvais, siege of, 207 ; created a municipality, 207 ; epidemic in, 216
Beauvau, Bertrand de, 101

Bedford, Duke of, 43, 47
Bernes, Gabriel de, 98
Berri, cession of, 186
Bessarion, Cardinal, 171
Bische, Guillaume de, 151-2, 263
Blainville, Lord of (*see* Estouteville)
Blosseville, 108
Bochard, Jean, Bishop of Avranches, 242
Bochetel, Jean (controller of the household and chief secretary), 53, 116
Boisratier, Archbishop de, 43
Boissieu, Antoine de, 116
Boon, John, betrays Count of Armagnac, 209
Bossuet, 23
Bouchage, Seigneur du, 286
Bouchet, Jean, 19
Boulogne, surrenders to Louis, 264
Bourbon, Bastard of (*see* Alexander and Louis)
Bourbon, Cardinal, 282
Bourbon, Duke of, 69, 75, 76, 203; deprived of governorship of Guyenne, 152; agreement with Charolais, 180; raises army against Louis, 182
Bourdeilles, Elie de, Archbishop of Tours, 302
Bourges, Archbishop of, 146, 150
Bourges, Louis' birth at, 43
Bourré, Jean (Louis' secretary and guardian of the Dauphin—known also as M. du Plessis), 116, 175, 201, 204, 244, 251, 290-1, 293
Boutet, Jean (Louis' apothecary), 112
Brachet, Auguste, 40
Branchart, Deniset, 118
Brantôme, 19
Brézé, Pierre de, 89, 91, 111, 113, 158, 233; Louis' hatred of, 144; outlawed, 156; imprisoned and released, 156; and Margaret of Anjou, 159; re-established as Grand Seneschal, 173
Brézé, Robert de, 96
Brienne, Count of, 228
Brittany, Francis II, Duke of, Louis' appeal to, 125; rupture with Louis, 169; refuses to do homage, 178; alliance with Charolais, 178-9; quarrels with Charles of France, 188; letters to Charles of Burgundy intercepted, 209; treaty of alliance with, 224
Brizard, M., 25

Brussels, entered by Louis after his flight, 127
Bueil, Jean de, 93, 114
Burgundian Chroniclers, 10-15
Burgundians, attempt to enter Arras, 264
Burgundy, and loss of Picard towns, 181; end of truce with, 193; Louis' conquest of, 269 *et seq.*
Burgundy, House of, end of, 228-9
Burgundy, Margaret of (*see* Margaret)
Burgundy, Mary of (*see* Mary)
Burgundy, Philip of (*see* Philip)
Bussy, Oudard de, execution of, 264-5

CAGNOLA, 233
Caguin, Robert, 19
Calabria, Duchess of, 90, 104
Calabria, Duke of, 88, 168
Calmette, M. Joseph, 3, 32
Cambrai, Amboise de, 242
Campo Basso, Nicholas de, treachery of, 227
Capefigue, Honoré, 30-1
Cape Verd, Louis sends expedition to for a medicament, 297, 298
Capitouls, meaning of, 66 (note)
Castello, Pierre de (Louis' butler), 248
Cato, Angelo, Archbishop of Vienne, 254; attends Louis after second seizure, 283
Cauchon, Pierre, Bishop of Lisieux, and trial of Joan of Arc, 6 (note)
Cérisay, Guillaume de, 176
Chabannes, Antoine de, Comte de Dammartin, his retort to King Charles, 70; flies for safety, 78; defeated by Swiss Confederates at Prateln, 95; conspires with Louis, 114, 125; King Charles's suspicions of, 138; hatred of Louis for, 144; outlawed, 156; enters Amiens, 204; restored to favour, 251
Chàlon, Jean de, attempt to murder Louis, 276
Châlons, gaieties at, 104; death of Dauphiness at, 112
Chambes, Mme de (wife of Commynes), 287
Champeaux, Guillaume de, Bishop of Laon, baptizes Louis, 44
Chaperons, Mme des (mistress of Charles VII), 137
Charles VII, King, as statesman, 37; and birth of Louis, 43; financial straits, 45, 64; coronation, 46;

Charles VII—*continued*
sends embassy to Scotland, 48-9 ;
and wedding of Louis, 51-2 ;
progress through loyal provinces,
54-6 ; in pursuit of brigands,
56-7 ; at siege of Montereau, 59 ;
state reception in Paris, 60-3 ;
sends Louis to Languedoc and
recalls him, 65, 68-9 ; revolt of
nobles against, 69 *et seq.* ; Louis'
submission and humiliation,75-6 ;
marches against the English, 78
et seq. ; and Louis' victory at
Dieppe, 85 ; reopens negotiations
with English, 87-90 ; amours of,
91, 137 ; marches to aid of René
of Anjou, 100 ; at Nancy, 101 ;
intervenes in negotiations between
Louis and Duchess of Burgundy,
103 ; a pilgrimage with the
Dauphiness, 110 ; court intrigues
against, 113 ; disapproves of
Savoy marriage, 122-4 ; friction
with his son, 124-6 ; takes possession of Dauphiné, 131 ; reported
preparations for war with Burgundy, 137 ; illness, death and
funeral, 137-40 ; service in honour
of at Avesnes, 146 ; constituted
Defender of the Church in France,
166 ; his revenue compared with
that of Louis, 238
Charles VIII, birth of, 251, 256-7 ;
Louis' concern for health and
safety of, 290-1 ; education of,
291 ; his father's visits to, 287,
292-4 ; betrothal of, 299 ; his
father's last instructions to, 304
Charles of Anjou, 71, 104 ; bequeaths
Maine and Provence to Louis, 288
Charles of France (brother), Louis
accused of compassing death of,
19, 206 ; nominal head of conspiracy against Louis, 180-1 ;
wins Normandy, 187, 188 ; submission of, 202 ; accepts appanage
of Guyenne, 202 ; becomes
" premier chevalier " of Order of
St Michael, 202 ; illness and
death, 205
Charles of Orléans, imprisoned in
England, 43 ; liberated, 79, 81,
105 ; receives English ambassadors at Blois, 88 ; at funeral of
Charles VII, 140 ; at Paris after
coronation of Louis, 151 ; mother
of, 157 (note)
Charles the Bold (*see* Charolais)

Charlotte of Savoy, marries Louis,
124 ; children of, 131, 188, 250-1 ;
character and appearance of, 249 ;
her household, 250
Charny, siege of, 58
Charolais, Comte de (afterwards
Charles the Bold), receives Louis
after his flight to Genappe, 127 ;
and his father, 130, 135-6 ;
appearance and character of, 132 ;
at Louis' reception in Paris after
coronation, 149, 151 ; welcomed
by Louis at Tours, 156 ; death at
Nancy, 171, 227 ; alliance with
Francis of Brittany, 178, 179 ;
and loss of Picard towns, 181 ;
reconciliation with his father, 182 ;
marches on Paris, 182 ; wounded
at Montlhéry, 183 ; negotiations
with Louis, 186-8 ; advances
towards Péronne, 193 ; Louis
meets him : he accuses Louis of
treachery, 195-7 ; and Treaty of
Péronne, 197-8 ; and Charles of
France, 201-2 ; conspires against
Louis, 203 ; summoned to appear
before Paris Parlement, 204 ;
three months' truce with, 204 ;
accuses Louis of compassing death
of Charles of France, 206 ; resumes war, 206 ; plight of his
army, 208 ; defection of Commynes, 208, 253 ; truce with, 209,
212 ; siege of Neuss, 212-13 ;
deserts Edward IV, 216 ; stormy
interview with Edward IV, 220 ;
nine years' truce with, 224 ;
identification of his body, 228 :
convicted, after death, of high
treason, 272
Charolais, Mme de, 127
Chartier, Alain, French ambassador
to Scotland, 48
Chartres, Regnault de, Archbishop
of Reims, 50, 52
Chasteaufort, Jean de, 140
Chastel, Pierchon du, execution of,
265
Chastellain, Georges (Burgundian
chronicler), 10-11, 134
Château-Landon, captured by Louis,
58
Chaucer, Alice (Marchioness of Suffolk), 101 (and note)
Chaumont, Seigneur de (*see* Amboise, Charles d')
Chausson, Geoffrey, 122
Chimay, Count of (*see* Croy)

Choisnet, Pierre, " Le Rozier des Guerres " of, 21, 291 ; his history of France, 292

" Chronique Scandaleuse, La," 5

Cléry, Louis as canon of, 171 ; thanksgiving for Dauphin's birth at, 257 ; interment of Louis at, 305

Cœur, Geoffroy, 173, 174

Cœur, Jacques, 121, 173, 174

Coffin, Simon, unremunerative contract with Louis, 247-8

Coitier, Jacques (Louis' doctor), 216, 297, 304

Cologne, Archbishop of, quarrels with his Chapter, 212

Commynes, Philippe de, "Mémoires" of, 4, 5 ; Montaigne's tribute to, 5 ; in service of Duke Charles, 196-7 ; offers his services to Louis, 208 ; as friend and confidant, 176, 211, 213, 215, 217, 219, 221, 222, 223, 225, 234, 252, 254, 278, 284, 286, 288 ; on Louis' scholarship, 233 ; on Louis' observance of a vow, 241 ; his career, 252-3 ; in disgrace, 263 ; restored to favour, 275 ; acts as valet-de-chambre, 283

Conon, peasant of Brabant, 132

Contay, Seigneur de, hears revelation of St Pol's treachery, 219

Copini, Francesco, pronounces papal absolution of Charles VII, 167

Coulon, Admiral, 281

Courcelles, Thomas de, 140

Court of Aids, suppressed and reestablished, 173

Courtebotte, herald of, 57

Cousinot (Louis' ambassador to Rome), 170

Cravant, massacre of, 44

Croy, Antoine de, 160, 162, 182

Croy, Jean de (Count of Chimay), 88, 127, 144, 145, 182, 227

Crussot, Gérard de, Bishop of Valence, 171

Cyvers, Etienne, 118

DAIM, OLIVIER LE (see Le Daim)

D'Albert, Sire, 68

Dambach, Louis wounded at, 99, 236

Danicot, Guillaume, 250

Daniel, Père, 22

Dauphiné, Louis accompanies his father to, 55 ; ten years in, 113 et seq. ; Louis' flight from, 126 ; Italian reinforcements arrive in, 183

Dauvet, Jean, 176

Delavigne, Casimir, stages Louis XI à Péronne, 27

Desmarets, Charles, captures Dieppe, 82 ; and affair of l'Éveillé qui dort, 103

D'Esquerdes, Seigneur, takes oath of allegiance to Louis, 264 ; goes to assistance of Thérouanne, 278 ; and betrothal of the Dauphin, 288, 299

Diderot, 24

Dieppe, taken by Desmarets, 82 ; the English blockade, 82 ; siege and relief of, 84

Dijon, attitude towards Louis, 270 ; entered by Louis, 272

Dogs, Louis' fondness for, 240

Doriole, Pierre (Louis' secretary), 176 ; appointed Chancellor, 205 ; his career, 206, 251 ; reads sentence condemning Nemours to death, 267 ; dismissal of, 301

Doyat, Jean de, 17, 282, 288, 293

Duclercq, Jacques, " Chronicle " of, 15

Duclos, M., 2, 23

Du Flos, Jean, 264

Du Forez, pen-picture of Louis' administration by, 18

Du Fresnoy, Lenglet, 23

Du Lude, Monseigneur, 227

Dumas, Alexandre, 29

Dumbarton, Princess Margaret sails from, 50

Dunois, 158 ; joins malcontents, 180

Du Pont, Marquis, 203

Durand, Guyette, 119

Écorcheurs (see Freebooters)

Edward IV, King, and projected French invasion of England, 158-159 ; truce with, 160 ; defeats Lancastrians, 211 ; plans invasion of France, 211 ; disembarks at Calais, 214 ; letter of defiance to Louis, 215 ; secret mission to, 217-18 ; stormy interview with Duke of Burgundy, 220 ; meeting with Louis at Picquigny, 221-2 ; returns to England, 223 ; reminds Louis of a clause in Treaty of Picquigny, 274 ; double-dealing of, 287

Einsisheim, Treaty of, 99

England, two years' truce with France, 89 ; relations with France (1477-81), 273-4

English, siege of Harfleur, 78 ; disappointments experienced, 214 *et seq.* ; peace negotiations with Louis, 218 ; truce made with France, 220 ; in Amiens after the truce, 221 ; treaty signed, 222 (and note)

Epidemics, Louis' dread of, 251, 259, 281, 290

Esquerdes (*see* D'Esquerdes)

Estissac, Amaury d', 114

Estouteville, Jean d', Lord of Blainville, 108, 109, 228

Eugenius IV, Pope, 8 (note), 38 ; and the Pragmatic Sanction, 166

Eveillé qui dort, affair, of, 102-3

FELIX V, anti-pope, 120 (note), 122

Fénelon, 23

Filleul, Jeanne, a preserved verse by, 107

Flanders laid waste, 266

Florio, Francesco, his admiration of Tours, 261-2

Foix, Jean, Comte de, 67 ; and the dying Charles, 139 ; advances money for funeral of Louis' brother, 205

Foix, Mathieu de, 67

Forges, Louis' first seizure at (1479), 280

Fouquet, Jean, his portrait of Louis, 244

France, two years' truce with, 89 ; relations with England (1477-81), 273-4

Franche Comté, resistance of, 270

Franchise (Arras), 277 (note), 299

Francis of Paolo at Plessis, 302-3, 304

François, Pierre, 118

" Frederic of the Empty Purse," 92 (and note), 94, 98

Freebooters, 92 *et seq.*

Free-bowmen (regiment instituted by Charles VII), unpopularity of, 213 ; disbanded, 284

Fumée, André (doctor of Charles VII), 138 ; attends Louis, 283, 291

GAILLART, MICHEL, 289

Gallican Church, the (*see* Pragmatic Sanction, and Papacy)

Gamaches, Madame de, 51

Gandilhon, A., 32

Gaucourt, Charles of, 71, 140

Genappe, castle of, as residence for Louis, 129, 132

Gerson, Jean, superintends education of Louis, 46

Ghent, treachery and revolt in, 265

Gié, Marshal de, 284

Girard, Regnault, 49, 50

Girolamo, Count, 277

Goethe, 26

Gouge, Martin, Bishop of Clermont, godfather of Louis, 44

Granson, captured by Charles the Bold, 225

Grassay, Gilbert de, 283

Graville, M. de, 50

Grenoble, Louis' state entry into, 116 ; rejoicing at Savoy alliance, 124

Guérin, Olivier, 293

Guinegate, battle of, 278

Guyenne, governorship of, desired by Louis and refused by King Charles, 123, 125 ; Louis' astute dealings with, 172 ; offered as appanage to Charles of France, 202 ; in Louis' possession after his brother's death, 205

HALLWIN, Mme de (lady-in-waiting to Mary of Burgundy), 274

Hardy, Jean, attempted poisoning of Louis, 232

Hare, Christopher, 2

Harenthal, Pierre (Louis' chaplain), 53

Harfleur, besieged by English, 78

Hébert, Jean, Bishop of Coutances, arrest of, 282

Henry VI of England, sends embassy to France, 87 ; betrothal of, 89-90 ; death, 211

Hesdin, Philip of Burgundy's château at, 133 ; conference at, 160-2 ; siege of, 264

History, as breviary of kings, 47 ; Louis' love of, 292

Holy Ampulla brought to Plessis, 303

Howard, John, Lord, 223, 281

Hugo, Victor, 28-9

Hugonet, Guillaume, 263 ; execution of, 266

Humbercourt, Seigneur de, 263 ; beheaded, 266

Iron cages for prisoners, 16, 232, 260
Isabelle, Duchess of Burgundy, negotiations with, 78-9, 102 ; welcomes the Dauphin after his flight, 127 ; and quarrels between husband and son, 135 ; enters a convent, 136
Isabelle de Luxembourg, wedding of, 89
Italian reinforcements for Louis, 183, 185
Italy, relations between King and Pope, 168 ; Louis' admiration of, 233

James I of Scotland, French embassy to, 48, 49 ; assassination of, 77, 107
Jean de Haynin, 15
Jean de Wavrin, chronicler, 14-15
Jean II of Bourbon, 282
Jean IV of Armagnac (see Armagnac, Jean)
Jean-sans-Peur (Duke of Burgundy), assassination of, 103 (and note), 221 (note)
Jeanne (daughter of Louis), marriage of, 191
Joan of Arc, 6 (note), 46, 48, 61, 133, 256
Jouffroy, Jean, Bishop of Arras, 167, 169
Jouvenel des Ursins, Guillaume, Chancellor of France, 206
Jouvenel des Ursins, Jacques, Archbishop of Reims, 47, 145, 146

Kennedy, Hugh, 49

La Beauté, conference between Confederates and Parisians at, 185
La Broquière, Bertrandon de, 72
La Haye, Jean de, 110
Laisné, Jeanne, bravery of, 208
Lalaing, Jacquet de, 104, 109
Lallier, Michel de, 59, 60
La Marche, Olivier de, 10, 11 ; " Mémoires " of, 12 ; taken prisoner, 227
Languedoc, visited by Charles and the Dauphin, 55 ; Louis appointed Lieutenant-General of, 65
La Régente, Mme de (mistress of King Charles), 137
La Rochelle, Princess Margaret arrives at, 50
La Tour, Bertrand de, 101

La Trémoille, Georges de, Lord of Craon, 75, 227, 228, 251 ; appointed Governor of Burgundy, 270 ; defeat of, 271
La Trémoille, Mme de, 45
Laurana, Francesco, his medal of Louis, 244
Laval, Guy de, 45
Lavisse's " History of France," 2
Le Daim, Olivier (barber and confidant of Louis), 17, 130, 228, 252, 282
Legeay, Urbain, 2
Le Gorgias, Pierre, 209
Le Grand, Abbé, 23
Lemaire de Belges, Jean, 10
Leothier, Guillaume (Louis' physician), 53, 55, 65, 110
Les Montils, Louis' hunting lodge at, 257, 262
Liége, revolt of, 195 ; sack of, 199-200
Ligue du Bien Public, 170 ; origin of, 177 ; meeting of Confederates in Paris, 180 ; Charles of France declared Regent, 181 ; Burgundy the soul of the rebellion, 181 ; Louis attacks Bourbonnais, 183 ; battle of Montlhéry, 183-4 ; conference between Confederates and Parisians, 185 ; Louis' negotiations with Charolais, and Treaty of Vincennes, 186-8
Limousin, Louis in, 65
Liskenne, Charles, 28
Loches, castle of, and legends connected with, 17, 232 ; Louis removed for safety to, 45 ; Charles VII refused admittance to, 71
Lock-makers exempted from taxation, 261
Lomagne, Vicomte de, 66, 68
Lorraine, conquest of, by Charles the Bold, 225
Louis XI, contemporary portraits of, 10-24 ; complex character, 21, 34 ; birth, 43 ; baptism, 43-4 ; his godparents, 44, 45 ; nurses, 45 ; education, 46 ; marriage arranged, 48 ; marriage ceremony at Tours, 52 ; household of, 53 ; accompanies his father to Lyons, Dauphiné and Languedoc, 54 ; learns statecraft, 54-6 ; sends gift to his wife, 55 ; pursues Rodrigo de Villandrando, brigand chief, 56-7 ; first command against the English, 58 ; captures Château-

Louis XI—*continued*
Landon, 58 ; in Paris after capture of Montereau, 60-3 ; his command in Languedoc and revolutionary character of his administration, 65-8 ; lieutenant-general in Poitou, Aunis and Saintonge, 70 ; intrigues with discontented nobles, 70 ; conspires with the Duke of Alençon, 70 ; establishes himself in the Auvergne mountains, 72 ; unfilial attitude of, 73-5 ; a prodigal's return, 76 ; becomes governor of Dauphiné, 76 ; as husband, 77 ; in command against the English, 78 ; narrow escape from drowning, 80 ; first meeting with Charles of Orléans, 81 ; relief of Dieppe, 84 ; leads army of Free-lances against Swiss Confederates, 93-5 ; leads free-booters into Alsace, 97 ; offers protection to the Holy Council, 97-8 ; wounded at Dambach, 99 ; claims Rhine frontier for France, 99 ; signs Treaty of Einsisheim, 99 ; moodiness of, 101 ; negotiations with Duchess of Burgundy, 102 ; refuses, but is compelled to ratify, Treaty of Arras, 102, 104 ; further complications with Burgundy, 102-3 ; failure of his marriage and death of the Dauphiness, 106-12 ; plots to overthrow his father and is betrayed, 114 ; banishment to Dauphiné, 115 *et seq.* ; establishes a standing army, 117 ; illegitimate children of, 119 ; treaty with Savoy, 121 ; marriage with Charlotte of Savoy, 124 ; superseded in negotiations with Savoy, 125 ; his terror of his father, 125-6 ; flight from Dauphiné, 126 ; at the Duke of Burgundy's, 127 *et seq.* ; sponsor for daughter of Mme de Charolais, 130 ; as mediator, 130, 136; takes Charlotte of Savoy to wife, 130-1 ; life at Genappe reflected in a contemporary book, 131 ; his father's embassies and remonstrances to, 137 ; impatient for death of King Charles, 138 ; letter from King's Council to, 138-9 ; starts for Reims : his summons to Duke of Burgundy, 139 ; succeeds his father as King, 143 *et seq.* ;

Louis XI—*continued*
moralises on his changed condition, 144-5 ; change of ministers, 145 ; state entry into Reims, 146-7 ; the anointing, 147 ; state banquet, 148 ; state entry into Paris, 149 ; reception at Notre-Dame, 150 ; banquet at the Palace, 151 ; at Les Tournelles, 151 ; returns to Touraine, 153 ; delight in his kingdom, 153 ; attitude towards the middle class and the nobility, 154 ; matrimonial alliances made by, 156 ; reduction of national expenditure, 156 ; narrowly escapes capture, 157 ; relations with England, 157-8 ; and recovery of Somme towns, 160 ; his perpetual pilgrimage, 163 ; daily life, 163-4 ; correspondence, 164-5 ; work as organiser and administrator, 166 ; relations with the papacy, 167 (*post*) ; abolishes Pragmatic Sanction, 167 ; proclaims Gallican ordinances of 1463 and 1464 and restores Pragmatic Sanction, 169, 170; as arbitrator in Italian affairs, 171, 172 ; his secretaries, 175-6 ; coalition against, 177 (*see* Ligue du Bien Public) ; convokes Estates of Tours, 179 ; denounces the rebels, 181 ; Duke of Bourbon raises army against, 182 ; attacks Bourbonnais, 183 ; battle of Montlhéry, 183-4 ; surrenders Picard towns, 187 ; negotiates with Edward IV, 191 ; military measures designed to protect his subjects, 192 ; invades Brittany, 193 ; makes peace with Dukes of Brittany and Normandy, 194 ; negotiates with Burgundy at Péronne, 194-5 ; forced to assist in quelling of revolt of Liégeois, 197-200 ; attempts to win back Somme towns, 203 ; attitude towards the English, 211 ; preparations to resist English invasion, 211 ; orders laying waste of Picardy, 214 ; makes truce with English, 220 ; meets Edward IV at Picquigny, 221-2 ; further conventions, 223-4 ; leaves Charles the Bold to work out his own destruction, 225 ; share of quarry of House of Burgundy, 228-9 ; a character sketch of, 230

Louis XI—*continued*
et seq. ; great object of his life,
231 ; his exceptional cruelty a
legend, 232, 268 ; his consideration for the poor, 232 ; secret of
his power, 233 ; scholarship and
diplomacy of, 233-4, 236-7 ; his
revenue compared with that of
Charles VII, 238 ; care for his
people, 238 ; simplicity in dress,
238-9 ; favourite pastime, 239-40 ;
fondness for animals, 240-1 ; indif-
ference to women, 241 ; his piety,
241-3 ; attitude to the papacy, 243
(*ante, post*) ; orders statue for his
tomb, 244 ; personal appearance,
244 ; household of, 247 *et seq.* ;
ideas on health, 248-9 ; and
birth of the Dauphin, 251, 256-
257 ; collaborators of, 251-4 ;
strengthens fortifications of Orléans and builds palace, 255-6 ;
intrigues with former servants of
Charles the Bold, 263 ; poses as
protector of Mary of Burgundy,
269 ; enters Dijon, 272 ; and
marriage of Mary, 275 ; failing
health, 276 ; another attempt on
his life, 277 ; a year's truce with
Maximilian, 277 ; negotiations
with the papacy, 277 (*ante*) ; receives news of Guinegate, 278 ;
attempts to found *la Franchise* on
ruins of Arras, 279 (note) ; last
years of, 280 *et seq.* ; visits Swiss
mercenaries, 285 ; receives papal
nuncios at Plessis, 285 ; visits his
son at Amboise and instructs him
in his royal duties, 287, 292-4 ;
intrigues for marriage of the
Dauphin, 288, 298 ; inherits
Maine and Provence, 288 ; organises French Navy, 289 ; opens
up trade with the East, 289 ; last
days at Plessis-lez-Tours, 295-6 ;
nature of his illness, 297-8 ;
betrothal of his son, 299 ; receives
delegates at Tours, 300 ; last
appearance in public, 300 ; dis-
misses Doriole, 301 ; complete
success of his foreign policy, 301 ;
sends for Francis of Paola,
302 ; last instructions to the
Dauphin and Beaujeu, 303 ; death,
305
Louis, Bastard of Bourbon, 119
Louis of Luxembourg (*see* Saint-Pol,
Count of)

Louis of Orléans (Louis XII),
marriage of, 251 (note)
Louis of Savoy (*see* Savoy)
Louvain, University of, Louis as
student at, 130
Luçay, Thibaud de, 123
Luillier, Philippe, 226
Lussan, Mlle de, 22
Lyons, fairs inaugurated at, 19 (and
note), 165; Louis' first visit to, 54

MAINE, Comte du, wedding of, 89
Majoris, Jean (tutor), 46, 47, 55 ;
becomes Louis' confessor, 53, 64
Malleta, Alberic, and Louis, 234
Mandrot, Bernard de, 32
Marche, Olivier de la (*see* La Marche)
Margaret of Anjou, betrothal of,
89-90 ; weds Henry VI, 101 ; asks
aid against Edward IV, 158 ;
arrives in France, 159 (and note) ;
reconciliation with Earl of War-
wick, 203 ; taken prisoner, 211 ;
surrendered by Edward IV, 223
Margaret of Burgundy, betrothal of,
299
Margaret of York (*see* York)
Margaret of Scotland (*see* Scotland)
Marie of Anjou, Queen (mother of
Louis), 110 ; confinement of, 43 ;
piety of, 44 ; dire poverty of, 45 ;
and Margaret of Scotland (Dauphiness), 51, 53, 106 ; at Châlons,
102 ; etiquette forbids her visiting
the Dauphiness, 111
Marie of Clèves, 104
Mariette, Guillaume, 121
Martin V, Pope, 44
Mary of Burgundy, disclaims French
suzerainty of Burgundy, 228 ;
question of her marriage, 263,
265, 273 ; suitors of, 273, 274 ;
marries Maximilian, 274-5 ; child-
ren of, 275, 288 ; death of, 288
Masselin, Jean, 18-19
Mathieu, Pierre, 22
Maupoint, Jean, " Journal " of, 5
Maximilian, Archduke of Austria,
marries Mary of Burgundy, 274-5 ;
besieges Thérouanne, 276 ; truce
with, 277 ; and battle of Guine-
gate, 278 ; double-dealing of, 281 ;
intrigues with the Pope, 286
Medici, Lorenzo di, opinion of
Commynes, 254
Mérichon, Olivier, mission to King
Edward, 217-18
Metz, fighting round, 100

Meyer, Jacques, his " Annales de Flandre," 9
Mézéray, Sieur de, 22
Michelet, Jules, his portrait of Louis, 31
Midi, Nicolas, and Joan of Arc, 61
Minims, Order of, founded, 302
Moleyns, Adam, Dean of Chichester, 87
Molinet, Jean, Burgundian chronicler and poet, 10-14, 278
Moneypenny, William, 252
Montaigne, tribute to Commynes, 5
Montereau, siege of, 59 ; assassination of Jean-sans-Peur at, 103 (note), 221 (note)
Montlhéry, battle of, 4, 12, 13, 15, 183 ; both sides claim victory, 184
Morat, battle of, and flight of Charles the Bold, 226
Morillon, Charles, 109
Morvillier, Pierre de, Louis' Chancellor, 176, 179
Munch, Burckard, 96

Nancy, King Charles's winter quarters at, 100 ; surrendered by army of Charles the Bold, 226-7
Narbonne, Archbishop of, 293
Nemours, Duke of (see Armagnac, Jacques)
Neuss, siege of, 12, 13, 212-13
Nominalists, Louis' decree against, 234
Nonchaloir (doctor of Charles VII), 88
Normandy, Louis' activities in, 173 ; recruiting in, 184 ; lost—and recovered, 188, 189
" Notre Dame de Paris," Hugo's, 28 (and note)

Œcumenical councils, 166
Okeghem, Jean, 262
Onzain, Château of, Balue imprisoned in, 202
Orange, Prince of, taken prisoner, 214 ; defeated at Gy, 268 ; foments discontent in Franche Comté, 271
Order of St Michael, foundation of, 202
Orléans, fortifications strengthened, 255-6 ; Louis builds palace at, 256 ; memory of Maid of, honoured in, 256 ; rejoicings at birth of Dauphin in, 256-7

Orléans, Charles of (see Charles)
Orléans, House of, 157 (and note)

Papacy, the, Louis' attitude towards, 167 et seq., 243, 277, 286
Paris, reception of Charles and Louis in, 60-3 ; the Palais de Justice, 62 (and note) ; Louis' state entry, 149 ; meeting of Confederates in, 180 ; loyalty to Louis during Ligue du Bien Public, 183, 185 ; Charolais marches on, 184
Paris Parlement, supremacy established, 37
Paul II, Pope, Louis and, 170 ; death of, 171
Périnelle, G., 32
Péronne, Louis visits Duke of Burgundy at, 195 ; Treaty of, 197-8, 200
Perret, P. M., 32
Petit-Dutaillis, M. Ch., " Histoire de France " by, 2 ; and nature of Louis' illness, 297
Philip, Duke of Burgundy, godfather of Commynes, 4 ; and Louis' army of freebooters, 94, 102 ; sympathy with Louis' opinion of Charles VII, 120 ; first wife of, 126 (note) ; reception of Louis after his flight, 128 et seq. ; quarrels with his son, 130, 135-6 ; character and appearance of, 132-4 ; intention of playing part of protector to King Louis, 143-4 ; congratulates Louis on his accession, 145 ; and coronation of Louis, 147 ; introduces Louis as King at Paris, 149 ; at Hôtel d'Artois, 151 ; popularity in Paris, 151 ; beginning of his disillusionment, 152 ; leaves Paris, 152 ; and proposed invasion of England, 158 ; and Margaret of Anjou, 159 ; negotiates with Edward IV, 159-60 ; and Hesdin conference, 160-2 ; reconciliation with his son, 182 ; death, 190 ; funeral, 191
Pic, Jean, 119
Picardy, war in, 276
Picquigny, meeting of Louis and Edward IV at, 221 ; Treaty of, 222
Piédieu, Guillaume, 65
Pigault-Lebrun, 27
Pillon, Colin, 208

Pius II, Pope, friction with Louis, 167, 169; and abrogation of Pragmatic Sanction, 168; death, 170
Plessis-lez-Tours, Louis' second and fourth seizures at (1481, 1483), 283, 303; papal envoys at, 285; last days at, 295 et seq.
Plessis, M. du (see Bourré)
Poggio, Basin and, 6
Poitevin, Robert, confessor of Dauphiness, 111
Poitiers, Aimar de, 119
Pole, William, Earl of Suffolk, 87, 89, 101
Pontoise, storming of, 79
Pot, Guyot, Governor of Amboise, 305
Pot, Philippe, 136, 148, 159, 269
Pouponne, Jeanne (nurse), 45
Pragmatic Sanction (1438), 8 (and note), 37-8, 166; abolished and restored by Louis, 38, 167, 169, 170
Praguerie, the, 69 et seq.; a second (see Ligue du Bien Public)
Pregénte of Melun, 109
Prie, Seigneur de, 75
Prisoners, committed to care of townsfolk, 259, 260

Quicherat, Jules, 32
Quingey, Simon de, imprisoned in an iron cage, 260; liberation of, 284

Radegonde, Princess, 51; death of, 101
Rathsamhausen, Dietrich von, 96
Ravenstein, Adolphus von, 127
Ravenstein, Mme de, 127, 299
Realist, Louis as, 234
Reims, coronation of Louis at, 147
René of Anjou, King of Sicily, 88, 171, 203; and the Ligue du Bien Public, 180-1; death, 288
René, Comte du Perche, 292
Restout, Guillaume, 274
Reynard, Noble Félise, 119
Richemont, the Constable (afterwards Duke of Brittany), 71, 72, 79, 88, 125, 178
Roche-Guyon, Madame de la, 51
Rochefort, Seigneur de, 140
Rohan, Pierre de, 284
Rothelin, Marquis of, 183
Rouault, Joachim, 53, 55, 102, 145; and siege of Beauvais, 207

Roussillon, annexation of, 162
Rovèra, Cardinal della, arrives in France, 282
Roye, Jean de, diary of Louis' reign, 5
" Rozier des Guerres," Choisnet's, 21, 291

Saignes, Jean de, 57
St Aignan's Church, Orléans, Louis as abbot and canon of, 256
Saint-Jacques, battle of, 95; results of, 96
Saint-Laud, the cross of, 201, 237, 242
Saint-Maard, Jean de, 108
St Martin, legend of, perpetuated at Tours, 260
Saint-Michel, Dame de, 109
Saint-Pol (Louis of Luxembourg), 15, 83, 104, 182; becomes Constable of France, 187, 193; treachery of, 216; his treachery revealed by his own messengers, 219-20; execution of, 224
Saintrailles, 71
Saint-Trond, Liégeois defeated by Charles the Bold at, 193
Sainville, Louis de, reveals treachery of Saint-Pol, 219
Salazar, Jean de, 95, 271
Salignac, Mademoiselle de, 108
Salisbury, Earl of, 101
Saluces, Marquis of, 140
Samaran, M. Charles, 32; and Cape Verd expedition for treatment of Louis, 298
Sarry, Treaty of, 103
Sauval, Henri, 22
Savoy, Louis, Duke of, 120 (note), 121
Scotland, Margaret, Princess of (daughter of James I and wife of Louis), 48; arrives in France, 50; introduction to her boy bridegroom, 51; marriage, 51-2; failure of her marriage, 106; monotony of her life at Court, 106; her love of poetry, 107; jealousy of Louis, 108 et seq.; death of, 112
Scott, Sir Walter, and King Louis, 20, 25-7
Segré, Monseigneur de, 283
Segré, Mme de, 299
Seillons, Charles de, 119
Severac, freebooter, holds Guyenne to ransom, 85
Seyssel, Claude de, 19, 20-1

316

Sforza, Francesco, Duke of Milan, as Louis' hero, 39, 233; alliance with, 157, 174

Sforza, Galeazzo Maria, Duke of Milan, 171; appointed lieutenant in Lyonnais and Dauphiné, 183; forsakes Louis, 213; assassination of, 226

Shrewsbury, Earl of, 101

Sicily, King and Queen of, 88, 89, 90, 100, 171, 180-1, 203, 288

Sillonne, Clémence (Louis' nurse), 45, 238

Sixtus IV, Pope, succeeds Paul II, 171-2; sends envoys to Louis, 285; intrigues of Maximilian and Mary with, 286

Somme towns, recovered, 160; visited by Louis, 174; pass into possession of Charolais, 188

Soreau, Agnes, Charles VII and, 91, 108; Louis tries to curry favour with, 113; death, 121; cause of Louis' hatred of, 241

Stein, H., 32

Stuyers (or Stuyer), William, commander of Louis' Scottish guard, 246

Suffolk, Marchioness of, 101

Suffolk, William Pole, Earl of, 87, 89, 101

Swiss, attack Zurich, 92; Louis leads army of Free-lances against, 93-5; defeat of, 95, 96; pillage camp of Charles the Bold, 225; dealings of Louis with, after his conquest of Burgundy, 275-6

Tanneguy du Châtel, 65

Tartas, capture of, 81

Thérouanne, siege of, 276

Thouars, Louis' manifesto at, 181

Tillay, Jamet de, spies upon the Dauphiness, 108-9, 110, 111

Tonnerre, Countess of (godmother of Louis), 44, 45

Tours, loyalty to Charles and Louis, 45, 46; marriage of Louis at, 52, 257; betrothal of King Henry VI at, 89-90; princes of the blood

Tours—continued summoned to, 179; created a municipality, 258; Louis as virtual mayor of, 258; activities of Louis in, 259; disadvantages of proximity of King's residence, 259; a curious foundation instituted at, 260-1; prosperity of in Louis' reign, 261; Florio's description of, 261-2; Louis' third seizure at (1481), 286; funeral rites of Louis at, 305

Tours, Truce of, 89

Tristan l'Hermite, 22, 251, 268

Vaesen, 32

Valence, foundation of University at, 118, 166

Valentine of Milan, Princess, 157 (note)

Varillas, 22

Vaudémont, Count of, 78, 100

Vaudrey, Guillaume de, defeats La Trémoille, 271

Vaux, Marguerite de, 109

Vendôme, Monseigneur de, 51

Verjus, Simon (treasurer), 53

Vesc, Etienne de, 304

Villandrando, Rodrigo de, pursuit of, 56-7

Villequier, Antoinette de (mistress of Charles VII), 137, 138

Vincennes, Treaty of, 188

Visconti, Valentine, 157 (note)

Visen, Charles de, 196

Voltaire, 23-5

Warwick, Richard Neville, Earl of, fêted by Louis, 191-2; reconciled to Margaret of Anjou, 203; killed at battle of Barnet, 211

Wessel, Jean, 130

Yolande, Queen of Sicily, 89 (cf. Sicily)

Yolande of Savoy, 171

York, Margaret of (widow of Charles the Bold), in London, 281; endeavours to form league against France, 281